The
Struggle
for a
Proletarian
Party

James P. Cannon in 1938

The Struggle for a Proletarian Party

by James P. Cannon

EDITED BY JOHN G. WRIGHT AND WITH A NEW
INTRODUCTION BY GEORGE NOVACK

PATHFINDER PRESS, NEW YORK

Pathfinder Press, Inc.
410 West Street
New York, N. Y. 10014

CONTENTS

CONTENTS

III
DOCUMENTS OF THE STRUGGLE

IV
APPENDIX

INTRODUCTION

The Struggle For a Proletarian Party is an exceptional work. It is both a manual of Leninist party organization and part of the documentary record of a significant political struggle within a Leninist party. It records the development of an internal conflict in the Socialist Workers Party immediately following the Stalin-Hitler pact and the outbreak of the second world war. Under pressure of these great events, a petty-bourgeois section of the party began to reject the theoretical foundations, political principles, and organizational methods upon which the Trotskyist movement had been based since its inception. This grouping, headed by James Burnham, Max Shachtman, and Martin Abern, initiated a seven-month faction fight which led to a deep split within the party.

While the party conflict erupted over the question of the nature of the Soviet Union and the obligation of revolutionists to defend the first workers' state against imperialist attack, many other fundamental problems of Marxism were debated and clarified as the dispute developed. These ranged from the relationship between the dialectical method of thought and political practice to the organizational principles of a revolutionary vanguard party.

The contested issues were critically important to revolutionists not only in the United States but throughout the world. Leon Trotsky, the great revolutionist then living in exile in Mexico, collaborated with James P. Cannon, principal founder of American Trotskyism and National Secretary of the Socialist Workers Party, in leading the successful defense of revolutionary Marxism. The petty-bourgeois assault on the Socialist Workers Party was repulsed, and early in 1940, Burnham, Shachtman, and Abern took their grouping entirely out of the revolutionary Marxist movement.

The full record of this political battle is contained in two companion books — Leon Trotsky's *In Defense of Marxism* and James P. Cannon's *The Struggle For a Proletarian Party.* Trotsky's work centers on the major disputed questions of Marxist theory and political principle, while Cannon concentrates on Leninist organizational principles.

To place Cannon's book in its original context, it is essential to trace the sequence of events in the factional struggle that shook the SWP from August 1939, when the minority leaders started to attack the party's program, to April 1940 when they broke away from the Trotskyist movement.

From their beginning as the Left Opposition in the Russian Communist Party, Trotskyists have unshakeably adhered to the position that the Soviet Union, the product of the October Revolution, remains a workers' state, though terribly degenerated under the Stalinist regime. It has been a fundamental tenet that every revolutionist is duty-bound to rally to the defense of the Soviet Union in the case of imperialist assault or attempted capitalist restoration from within.

After the Stalin-Hitler pact was signed on August 22, 1939, a wave of anti-Soviet propaganda swept through the western "democracies"; a week later, the second world war began. These world-shaking events precipitated a crisis within the Socialist Workers Party.

Unbalanced by the anti-Soviet hysteria, the impact of hostilities in Europe that threatened soon to involve the United States, and the pressure of alien class influences and ideas, a section of the Socialist Workers Party leadership started to question (and some began to disavow) the long-established views of Trotskyism on the character of the Soviet state and the necessity for its defense. The orientation of the opposition grouping was most clearly indicated in the following sentences from the document submitted by James Burnham to the plenum of the National Committee on September 5, 1939: "It is impossible to regard the Soviet Unon as a workers' state in any sense whatever. . . . Soviet intervention (in the war) will be wholly subordinated to the general imperialist character of the conflict as a whole; and will be in no sense a defense of the remains of the Socialist economy."

In a letter to all members of the National Committee, dated

September 8, 1939, Cannon observed that Burnham "proposes to write off the Soviet Union. . . . [and] abandon the defense of the Soviet Union." He declared that this abrupt departure from the party's basic position on the Russian question was not only politically wrong but organizationally unwarranted at a time of grave crisis.

Nevertheless, the opposition persisted in its course, organized into a faction on a national scale, and sought support for its views throughout the Fourth International. Thus the dispute within the Socialist Workers Party became converted into a decisive test of the policy to be pursued during the second world war by the whole of world Trotskyism.

The petty-bourgeois opposition was a heterogeneous combination of three different tendencies. James Burnham, a philosophy professor at New York University, had come into the Trotskyist movement through its merger in 1934 with the American Workers Party headed by A. J. Muste. He was the ideological leader of the opposition and gave the most forceful expression to its anti-Marxist character. Martin Abern, a member of the National Committee of the Communist Party in the 1920s and a cofounder with Cannon and Shachtman of American Trotskyism, headed a clique that said it disagreed with Burnham's views on the Soviet Union, but was most interested in removing the Cannon "regime" from leadership in the party. In the initial period of the dispute on the Russian question, Max Schachtman occupied a provisional ground from which he applied doubts and reservations indiscriminately to both Burnham's innovations and the traditional views of the Trotskyist movement.

These various tendencies formed a common faction, refusing to consider matters of basic principle and demanding that the discussion be confined to immediate "concrete" issues. It was a classic example of an unprincipled combination.

In *The Struggle For a Proletarian Party,* Cannon analyzes the special character of the unprincipled coalition in the light of its development. He noted that each one of the opposition leaders represented a familiar political type. Burnham epitomized the haughty intellectual, still tied to the bourgeois-academic milieu, who refused to commit himself unreservedly to the revolutionary cause and the proletarian party. Abern was the *paterfamilias* of a permanent personal clique subsisting on gossip and organizational grievances. Shachtman was a facile writer and speaker, but a weak and wavering individual who could not withstand powerful external social pressures. In time of stress, he sought to avoid taking firm and clear stands on crucial issues in the class struggle.

The discussion unfolded in a heated atmosphere to the accompaniment of the guns in Europe. There was complete freedom for every viewpoint to express itself. The opposition was given full opportunity to convince a majority and take over leadership in the party. At the convention where the followers of Cannon and Trotsky succeeded in winning a majority of the party to their positions, they did not expel the minority from the party, deprive them of a share in the leadership, or demand that they renounce their beliefs.

On the contrary, representation was offered on all the bodies of the party. Only observance of the principle of democratic centralism was demanded, that the minority abide loyally by the decisions of the majority and confine its opposition activity to further attempts to win the party to its ideas. The majority even agreed to a continuation of the discussion of the controversial issues after the convention in internal bulletins.

The conduct of the majority can serve as a model of correct Bolshevik procedure in carrying on a serious controversy over vital questions and conducting it to a clear settlement.

However, the minority bloc could not comply with the decisions democratically arrived at by the party. After refusing to vote for a Political Committee motion to accept the convention decisions, it set up a separate organization named the Workers Party, issued a newspaper, stole the Socialist Workers Party theoretical organ, *The New International,* and embarked on an independent career along non-Trotskyist lines while half-heartedly pretending (until its dissolution in the 1950s) to be faithful followers of Trotskyism.

The sequel to their break with the methods and principles of Marxism was instructive. Only a month after Burnham and his disciples quit the Trotskyist movement, he disdainfully resigned from Shactman's new organization and openly renounced Marxism. A short time later he expounded his anti-Marxist ideas on world politics in a notorious work published in many languages, *The Managerial Revolution.*

In the years that followed, Burnham kept swinging toward imperialist reaction until he came forward as one of the most vicious anti-Soviet ideologists during the cold war. His calls for a holy crusade by military means against the worldwide "Communist conspiracy" were enunciated in a series of books extending from *The Struggle for World Power* (1947) to *The Suicide of the West* (1964). He is today an editor of *The National Review,* an ultraright organ. In its pages he recently called for a new Bismarck for America, and for a benevolent reevaluation of fascism.

Shachtman's shift to the right has characteristically proceeded at a slower pace, on a reduced scale, and under a "socialist" disguise. Borrowing from Burnham's ideas, he concocted the sociological theory that the USSR embodied a unique and never-before-known kind of socioeconomic formation that was neither capitalist nor socialist but *bureaucratic collectivist.* He became a partisan of the so-called third camp, which sought to find points of support somewhere between the contending forces in the world class struggle. Since he maintained that liberal capitalism was more democratic than Stalinist totalitarianism, Shachtman after the war was led to support the bourgeois nationalist Mickolajczyk against the Moscow-supported Osubka-Morawski government in Poland. In the 1960s he backed the Bay of Pigs invasion of Cuba and U. S. intervention in Vietnam. Thus his search for the nonexistent "third camp" meant in practice alignment with the imperialists against the forces of the colonial revolution and the working class.

In 1958 Shachtman took a remnant of his disintegrating Workers Party into the fold of the Socialist Party of Norman Thomas, which works within the Democratic Party. Today he is a principal ideologue of its extreme right wing, and backs, with certain reservations and pseudo-socialist rationale, the anticommunist moves of the U. S. State Department.

The sole opposition leader who remained by and large faithful to his past, Martin Abern, faded from political activity and died in 1949.

This volume is divided into three sections. The first, *The Struggle For a Proletarian Party,* was originally written at the termination of the internal dispute. It sums up the entire struggle after the main ideas of the contestants had been defined, and each side had fully disclosed its true nature. This article is placed at the beginning to enable the reader to follow and understand the other materials more easily.

The second section consists of letters written by Cannon to various comrades, which record the events of the struggle and the response of the majority to them, day to day, week to week, and month to month. The third section contains documents that register the actions taken by the party at each stage from the beginning of the struggle to the formal expulsion of the petty-bourgeois opposition.

The appendix presents the organizational innovations of the revisionists in their own words, so that the reader can contrast them with the views of the orthodox Trotskyists.

The main value of this book lies in its illumination of the organizational principles and practices of Leninism as they relate to a deep-going theoretical and political conflict and its examination of the problems of building a revolutionary Marxist combat party.

In the school of Bolshevism, the program is the foundation, the decisive factor in the formation and functioning of the revolutionary party. The form of organization is designed to implement the program that guides the working class in its struggle for power.

The specific character of the Leninist theory of party organization is summed up in the words *democratic centralism.* Although that term is well known, there exists a tremendous amount of misunderstanding about its real meaning. The principal source of confusion is the counterfeit of Leninist ideas and the distortion of its practices that Stalinism has introduced into the workers' movement. The Stalinist pattern of the monolithic party, autocratically dominated from above by an uncontrolled and irremovable bureaucracy, is the very antithesis of the genuine Leninist system of organization. It is a regime of bureaucratic centralism and has nothing in common with democratic centralism, under which the leadership and apparatus are responsible to and controlled by the ranks of the party and subject to their democratic decisions.

To some, democratic centralism appears to be a contradiction in terms. How is it possible, spontaneists and anarchists ask, for democracy to be centralized without thereby ceasing to be democratic? Conversely, how is it possible for centralism to be democratized, ask the anti-Leninists of all kinds.

The supreme merit of the Leninist system is that it synthesizes these contrary features, equally indispensable to the effective functioning of a combat party. This form of organization enables the party to maintain its firmness of line and unity of action, while ensuring that the membership determines its policies and exercises control over its functionaries.

The formula of democratic centralism in and of itself can serve only as a general guide in the conduct of the revolutionary party. How it is to be applied, and which one of its polar elements is to be uppermost at a given time, depends upon the circumstances and the needs of the concrete situation, as judged by a competent and authoritative leadership.

This organizational principle provides for democracy within the party in the process of discussing its problems and working out a line. Once its decision has been made, the emphasis shifts to centralism in action. All members and institutions of the party are obliged to conduct themselves in accord with the majority position.

Thus the entire party participates in uninhibited discussion, deliberation, and decision-making. If there are sharp and serious differences of opinion, the majority view becomes that of the party as a whole, and the party operates in the arena of struggle with the majority position. The minority must be subordinate to the majority, as a part is to the whole. That is the meaning of democracy; the majority of the membership has the deciding voice and vote.

The minority also has its rights, which must be scrupulously respected by the official majority. It has the right to constitute itself as a distinct tendency or faction and to solicit support among the members for its position through regular party channels. But once the party has determined its position, the minority must wait for subsequent events to confirm or controvert the position taken and for further opportunities to bring its views before the party.

A combat party that is striving for or has already achieved state power cannot conduct its work with two programs or with two divergent orientations and perspectives without becoming perilously weakened, divided, or paralyzed. It must be disciplined for maximum coordination and striking power in action while being wholly democratic in its inner life.

This book also outlines in great detail the Leninist concept of building a party of professional revolutionaries. Cannon rejects the dilettantism characteristic of petty-bourgeois radicals like Burnham, and calls for a serious, professional approach to revolutionary politics. It is that approach which is characteristic of a proletarian party — in its theory, its political policies, and its organizational methods.

At the time of the struggle, Cannon was already a veteran of the revolutionary movement in the United States. In more than twenty-five years in the movement, he had been an IWW organizer, a member of the left wing of the Socialist Party led by Debs, a top leader of the American Communist Party, and the founder of American Trotskyism. He brought all the knowledge of organizational practices and procedures, accumulated through those experiences, to bear in handling the complicated problems raised by the factional conflict.

Cannon did so as an orthodox Leninist. Like Trotsky after 1917, he undeviatingly adhered to the conceptions of party organization worked out and applied by Lenin in the construction and direction of the Bolshevik Party.

Cannon's book is a manual of party organization that incorporates the lessons of Bolshevik procedure as they have been tested in the difficult task of building the vanguard party of the working class and oppressed nationalities in the citadel of world imperialism. Since its first publication twenty-five years ago, it has proved helpful to many revolutionists here and abroad. They have found in it a viable alternative to the discredited Stalinist and social-democratic types of political organization and a source book for knowledge of what the Leninist norms of party organization really are.

Leon Trotsky, who fought side by side with Cannon in the 1939-1940 struggle to preserve the principles of the proletarian party, valued this contribution of his most highly. He gave the following appraisal of the article that constitutes the first section of this book: "It is the writing of a genuine workers' leader. If the discussion had not produced more than this document, it would be justified."

GEORGE NOVACK
March 1972

THE STRUGGLE FOR A PROLETARIAN PARTY

1—WHAT THE DISCUSSION HAS REVEALED

POLITICAL STRUGGLES in general, including serious factional struggles in a party, do not take place in a vacuum. They are carried on under the pressure of social forces and reflect the class struggle to one degree or another. This law is demonstrated in the most striking manner in the development of the present discussion within our party.

At the present time the pressure of alien class forces upon the proletarian vanguard is exceptionally heavy. We must understand this first of all. Only then can we approach an understanding of the present crisis in the party. It is the most severe and profound crisis our movement has ever known on an international scale. The unprecedented tension in the ranks signalizes a conflict of principled positions which is obviously irreconcilable. Two camps in the party fight for different programs, different methods and different traditions.

What has brought the party to this situation in such a short space of time? Obviously it is not a suddenly discovered personal incompatibility of the individual leaders involved; such trifles are symptoms of the conflict, not causes. Nor can a conflict of this depth and scope be plausibly explained by the flaring up of old differences of opinion on the organization question. In order to understand the real significance of the crisis it is necessary to look for profounder causes.

For those who understand politics as an expression of the class struggle—and that is the way we Marxists understand it—the basic cause of the crisis in the party is not hard to find. The crisis signifies the reaction in our ranks to external social pressure. That is

[1]

the way we have defined it from the outset of the crisis last September, immediately following the signing of the Soviet-Nazi pact and the beginning of the German invasion of Poland. More precisely, we say the crisis is the result of the pressure of bourgeois-democratic public opinion upon a section of the party leadership. That is our class analysis of the unrestrained struggle between the proletarian and the petty-bourgeois tendencies in our party.

We define the contending factions not by such abstract general terms as "conservative" and "progressive." We judge the factions not by the psychologic traits of individuals, but by the programs they defend. The discussion has revealed not a difference of opinion about the application of the program—such differences frequently occur and usually have a transitory significance—but an attempt to counterpose one program to another. This is what has divided the party into two camps. Naturally, these terms, which we have used from the beginning of the discussion to characterize the two tendencies in the party, are meant as definitions and not epithets. It is necessary to repeat this in every debate between Marxists and petty-bourgeois politicians of all types; the one thing they cannot tolerate is to be called by their right name.

The leaders of the opposition consider it outrageous, a malicious faction invention, for us to place this class signboard above their faction, when their only offense consists in the simple fact that they turn their backs on the Soviet Union and deny it defense in the struggle against world imperialism. But our definition and description of such an attitude is not new. Back in the days when Shachtman was paraphrasing Trotsky and not Burnham, he himself wrote:

> At bottom, the ultra-leftists' position on the Soviet Union, which denies it any claim whatsoever to being a workers' state, reflects the vacillations of the petty bourgeois, their inability to make a firm choice between the camps of the proletariat and the bourgeoisie, of revolution and imperialism.

This quotation, from an article written in the *New International* by Shachtman two years ago, can be accepted as a scientific definition of the opposition combination and its present position, with only one small amendment. It is hardly correct to describe their position as "ultra-leftist."

The leaders of the opposition in the past have written and spoken a great deal along the lines of the above quotation. Year in and year out in innumerable articles, documents, theses and speeches the leaders of the opposition have been promising and even threatening to defend the Soviet Union—"In the hour of danger we will be at our posts!"—but when the hour drew near, when the Soviet

Union almost began to need this defense, they welched on their promise.

So with the program in general, with the doctrine, the methods and the tradition of Marxism. When all this ceased to be the subject for literary exercises in times of tranquillity and had to be taken as a guide to action in time of war, they forgot everything that had been said and written and started a frantic search for "new and fresh ideas." In the first half-serious test they revealed themselves as "peace-time Trotskyists."

And this shameful performance, this betrayal of Marxism, has taken place in the American section of the Fourth International even before the formal entry of American imperialism into the war. In the bible of the opposition, their document on "The War and Bureaucratic Conservatism,"* we are assured that the party crisis "was provoked by the war." That is not precisely accurate. America has not yet formally entered into the war, and thus far we have only a faint intimation of the moral and material pressure which will be brought to bear against the proletarian vanguard under war conditions. Not the war, but merely the shadow of the approaching war was enough to send Burnham, Shachtman and Abern on their mad stampede.

Gratuitously attributing to the party their own panic, these philosophers of retreat and capitulation express the opinion that comrades who read their document on the party regime "will draw from it cynical or discouraged or defeatist conclusions." They add: "The future is dark." And Burnham, who bared his petty-bourgeois soul in a special document entitled, "Science and Style,"** proclaims with malicious satisfaction—the wish is father to the thought—the downfall of the Fourth International. The reality is diametrically opposite to these lugubrious observations.

In the proletarian majority of the party there is not a trace of pessimism. On the contrary, there is universal satisfaction that the defection of a section of the party leadership revealed itself in time, *before the war*, and under conditions where it could be combatted openly and in free discussion and beaten down. The virtual unanimity with which the proletarian cadres have rallied to the defense of the party and the Fourth International, the militancy and irreconcilability with which they have met the attack of Burnham, Abern and Shachtman is living proof of the vitality and indestructi-

---

*See the Appendix to this volume.—*Ed.*

**See the Appendix to *In Defense of Marxism*, by Leon Trotsky, p. 187.—*Ed.*

bility of our movement. That is a good omen for the future. It gives us confidence that it will stand up against the real test of war when it comes. It gives grounds for the most optimistic calculation that the Fourth International will not only "survive," but conquer in struggle.

As for the "hard future"—the Bolshevik-Marxists never expected that the period of the death agony of capitalism could produce anything but crises and war with their inevitable repercussions in workers' organizations, including the party of the workers' vanguard. From these "hard" circumstances, the Fourth Internationalists only drew the conclusion that the grandiose social convulsions, which we foresaw and analyzed in advance, create the conditions out of which the oppressed masses, impelled by iron necessity, must carry through the social revolution and the reorganization of the world on a socialist basis. Only one thing is needed: a genuine Bolshevik party of the vanguard. Only Marxism can be the program of such a party. Burnham and his sorry disciples, the ex-Marxists, ex-Trotskyists, offer a program that has nothing in common with Marxism or the proletarian revolution. From this arises the fundamental conflict between the majority and the opposition, a conflict which is manifestly irreconcilable and to which all other questions, however important, are nevertheless subordinate.

In the course of a few months' discussion the differences between the majority and the opposition have reached such depth and scope as to completely overshadow all questions of party regime. If all the alleged faults of the regime were true, and then multiplied ten times over, the whole question would pale into insignificance beside the principled differences which now clearly separate the two contending factions. The struggle of the opposition ostensibly began as a struggle against the "Cannon regime," and as a defense, or at any rate as an anticipation, of the "changing" position of Trotsky. But in a short time it unfolded as a fundamental conflict with the Fourth International over all the questions of our program, our method and our tradition.

Abern, who voted at the plenum [October 1939] for the principled resolution of the majority on the Russian question and accuses us of inventing and exaggerating differences, ended up, by the logic of his unprincipled combination, in the revisionist camp of Burnham. Shachtman, who at the plenum could only be accused of building a bridge to Burnham, became his attorney, writing "open letters" to comrade Trotsky in his behalf, and directing the most venomous attacks against the proletarian majority of the party who remind him of his yesterday. Burnham, in his latest document on "Science and

Style," speaks the language of a hate-inspired enemy of the proletarian revolutionary movement and of all those who remain faithful to it.

This is what has been revealed in a few months of *political* discussion.

2—A NEW STAGE IN THE DEVELOPMENT OF AMERICAN TROTSKYISM

The body of doctrine and methods known as "Trotskyism" is
indubitably the genuine Marxism of our time, the heir and con-
tinuator of the Bolshevism of Lenin and the Russian revolution and
the early Comintern. It is the movement known as Trotskyism and
no other that has developed Bolshevism in analyzing and interpreting
all the great events of the post-Lenin period and in formulating the
program for the proletarian struggle and victory. There is no other
movement, there is no other school that has answered anything.
There is no other school that is worthy of a moment's consideration
by the proletarian revolutionists. Trotskyism, embodied in the Fourth
International, is the only revolutionary movement.

But the road from the elaboration of the program to the organization of firm cadres, and from that to the building of mass parties of the Fourth International, is difficult and complicated. It
proceeds through various stages of evolution and development as
a continuous process of selection, attracting new forces and discard-
ing others who fail to keep step. The American section of the Fourth
International is right now in the midst of a crisis in this evolutionary process. If, as all signs indicate, we are moving toward a radical
solution of the crisis, it is to be accounted for by the speed at which
world events are marching and the immensity of their scope and
the sensitivity of our party to their impact.

The Second World War, no less than the First, strikes all organizations and tendencies in the labor movement with cataclysmic
force. Our own organization is no exception. Like all others, it is
being shaken to its foundations and compelled to reveal its real
nature. Weaknesses which remained undisclosed in time of peace are
rapidly laid bare with the approach of war. Numerous individuals
and whole groupings, whether formally members of the Fourth
International or sympathizers, are being submitted to the same tests.
There will be casualties, which may seem to indicate a weakening
of the movement. But that is rather the appearance of things than
the reality. Trotskyism is the veritable doctrine and method of proletarian revolution; it reveals its true substance most unfailingly in
times of crisis, war and revolutionary struggle. Those who have

assimilated the program, the doctrine, the method and the tradition into their flesh and blood, as the guiding line of struggle, cling all the more firmly to the movement under the pressure of the crisis.

It is only those who took Bolshevism as a set of literary formulas, espousal of which gave one a certain distinction in radical circles without incurring any serious responsibilities; those who adopted Trotskyism as a form of "extreme radicalism" which never went beyond the bounds of sophisticated debate—it is such people who are most inclined to falter and to lose their heads under the pressure of the crisis, and even to blame their panic on that same "Trotskyism" which simply remains true to itself.

Everybody knows the crisis has dealt heavy blows to the imposing movement of Stalinism. With the signing of the Soviet-Nazi pact the flight of the Stalinist fellow-travellers began. They could stomach the Moscow Trials but not the prospect of coming into collision with the democratic government of U.S. imperialism. After the Soviet invasion of Poland and then of Finland, the flight of the fellow-travellers became a rout. This wild migration attracted wide attention and comment. We ourselves contributed our observations and witticisms on this ludicrous spectacle. Up to now, however, we have remained silent on an analogous phenomenon in our own "periphery." The flight of the more sophisticated, but hardly more courageous, intellectual fellow-travellers of American Trotskyism has been scarcely less precipitate and catastrophic.

With the approach of the war Trotskyism as a doctrine and as a movement began to lose its "respectability." Many of the intellectuals, sniffing danger, arranged a somewhat hasty and undignified departure. In truth, there is not much left of that considerable army of drawing room heroes who used to admire Trotsky's literary style and confound the less intelligent periphery of Stalinism with nuggets of wisdom mined from Trotsky's writings. The collapse of the Trotskyist "cultural front" was taken by some people, especially the ex-fronters themselves, to signify a collapse of our movement. In the journals of the class enemy to which they promptly attached themselves some of them have already worked up courage to write about Trotskyism as an "outmoded sectarian tendency." However, it is they who are "outmoded," not the movement of the proletarian vanguard, Trotskyism.

The petty-bourgeois intellectuals are introspective by nature. They mistake their own emotions, their uncertainties, their fears and their own egoistic concern about their personal fate for the sentiments and movements of the great masses. They measure the world's agony by their own inconsequential aches and pains. Insofar as our party membership consists in part of petty-bourgeois elements completely disconnected from the proletarian class struggle, the crisis which overtook the periphery of our movement is transferred, or rather, extended, into the party.

It is noteworthy that the crisis struck the New York organization of the party, thanks to its unfavorable social composition, with exceptional force and virulence, while the proletarian centers of the party remained virtually unaffected. The tendency of the petty-bourgeois elements to flee from our program and to repudiate our tradition is counterposed to a remarkable demonstration of loyalty to the program and to the party on the part of the proletarian membership. One must indeed be blind not to understand the meaning of this differentiation. The more our party revealed itself as a genuine proletarian party, the more it stood firmly by principle and penetrated into the workers' mass movement, the better it has withstood the shock of the crisis. To the extent that our party has sunk its roots in proletarian soil it has gained, not lost, during this recent period. The noise we hear around and about our movement is simply the rustling of the leaves at the top of the tree. The roots are not shaking.

The evolution and development of American Trotskyism did not proceed according to a preconceived plan. It was conditioned by a number of exceptional historical circumstances beyond our control. After the initial cadres had accustomed themselves to withstand the attacks and pressure of the Stalinists, the movement began to take shape as an isolated propaganda society. Of necessity it devoted an inordinate amount of its energy to the literary struggle against Stalinism. World events, one after another, confirmed our criticisms and prognoses. After the collapse of the Comintern in Germany, the failure of the successive 5-year plans to bring "socialism" in Russia, the monstrous excesses of the forced collectivization and the man-made famine, the murderous purges and the trials—after all this, which Trotsky alone had explained and analyzed in advance, Trotskyism became more popular in petty-bourgeois intellectual and half-intellectual circles. For a time it even became the fashion. Party membership conferred a certain distinction and imposed no serious hardships. Internal democracy was exaggerated to the point of looseness. Centralism and discipline existed only in the program, not in practice. The party in New York was more like a sophisticated discussion club than a combat party of the proletariat.

The fusion with the Muste organization, and later the entry into the Socialist Party, were carried out with the deliberate aim of breaking out of propagandistic isolation and stagnation and finding a road to wider circles. These actions brought hundreds of new recruits to the party, and gave us the possibility of expanding our activities. But the successes also brought their own contradictions. The membership of the Socialist Party in New York, including its left wing and its youth organization, was primarily petty-bourgeois in composition, and, despite their good will, were not easy to assimilate. If our party organization in New York had been much larger, and predominantly proletarian in composition, the task would have been much easier. As it was, some of the new forces from the S.P. complicated the problem of proletarianizing the party and contributed fresh recruits to the petty-bourgeois clique of Abern.

At the same time, thanks to our deliberate orientation toward trade union work, the party in other centers of the country was developing in a proletarian direction. Penetration into the trade unions was bringing into the party fresh elements of proletarian fighters; and the contrast between the proletarian centers and the New York organization flared up in numerous skirmishes before it finally exploded in the present party crisis.

The approach of the war, with its forewarning of heavy difficulties and sacrifices for members of the party, brought with it a restlessness and dissatisfaction among many of the petty-bourgeois elements. These sentiments found authentic expression in a section of the leadership. They began to translate their own nervousness into exaggerated criticism of the party and demands upon it which could not be fulfilled in the circumstances. After the signing of the Stalin-Hitler pact, the opposition became more articulate. It began to express itself in the form of a fight against our program and, eventually, in a revolt against the whole doctrine, tradition and method of Marxism and Bolshevism.

It would be utterly absurd, however, to characterize the party crisis as the result merely of political differences of opinion. We would not touch the core of the problem if we confined ourselves to a "political" characterization of the fantastic proposals and flip-flops of the opposition. Serious political struggles, such as these, are an expression of the struggle of classes; that is the only way to understand them. The leaders of the opposition, and a very large percentage of their followers, have shown that they are capable of changing their opinions on all fundamental questions of theory and politics over night. This only demonstrates quite forcibly that their opinions in general are not to be taken too seriously.

The driving impulses behind the opposition as a whole are petty-bourgeois nervousness at the prospect of impending struggles, difficulties and sacrifices, and the unconscious desire to avoid them at all costs. For some, no doubt, the frenzied struggle against our program and our tradition is simply a device to mask a capitulatory desertion of the revolutionary movement in a cloud of dust and controversy. For others, their newly discovered "political position," and their endless talk about it and around it are an unconscious rationalization of the same inner compulsion. In such cases it is not sufficient to stop at a political characterization of the outlandish propositions of the oppositionists. It is necessary to expose their class basis.

The present crisis in the party is no mere episode. It is not to be explained by simple differences of opinion such as have occurred at times in the past, and will always occur in a free and democratic party. The crisis is the direct reflection of alien class pressure upon the party. Under this pressure the bulk of the petty-bourgeois elements, and the petty-bourgeois leaders, lost their heads completely, while the proletarian sections of the party stand firm and rally around the program with a virtual unanimity.

From this we can and must draw certain conclusions:

(1) It is not sufficient for the party to have a proletarian program; it also requires a proletarian composition. Otherwise the program can be turned into a scrap of paper over night.

(2) This crisis cannot be resolved simply by taking a vote at the convention and reaffirming the program by majority vote. The party must proceed from there to a real proletarianization of its ranks. It must become obligatory for the petty-bourgeois members of the party to connect themselves in one way or another with the workers' movement, and to reshape their activities and even their lives accordingly. Those who are incapable of doing this in a definite and limited period of time must be transferred to the rank of sympathizers.

We stand at a decisive stage in the evolution of American Trotskyism from a loosely organized propaganda circle and discussion club to a centralized and disciplined proletarian party rooted in the workers' mass movement. This transformation is being forced rapidly under pressure of the approaching war. This is the real meaning of the present party struggle.

3—THEIR METHOD AND OURS

In the light of these facts, which show the contending factions already drawn up into two camps defending antagonistic and irreconcilable programs and methods, what possible interest can a supporter of the program of the Fourth International and of Marxism in general have in a "regime" of the petty-bourgeois opposition, or vice versa? The whole approach to the question of the "regime" must be fundamentally different in each case, depending on the position taken on the question of the program. The aim of those who stand by our program can be only to correct the shortcomings of the regime, and to improve its functioning, in order to make it a more effective instrument of the program. The critics from the camp of the opposition, on the other hand, insofar as there is any sense or logic in their position, cannot have any real interest in our regime as such. Their fundamental aim is to substitute the present program by another program. For that they require not an improvement of the present regime, but its removal and replacement by another which will realize the revisionist program.

Thus it is clear that the question stands not organizationally in the first place, but politically. The political line is and must be the determining factor. It is and must be placed in the center of discussion. We held to this method in spite of everything, even at the cost of losing the votes of comrades who are interested primarily in secondary questions, because only in that way is it possible to educate the party and consolidate a reliable base of support for the program.

What is the significance of the organization question as such in a political party? Does it have an independent significance of its own on the same plane with political differences, or even standing above them? Very rarely. And then only transiently, for the political line breaks through and dominates the organization question every time. This is one of the first ABC lessons of party politics, confirmed by all experience.

In his notorious document entitled "Science and Style," Burnham writes: "The second central issue is the question of the regime in the Socialist Workers Party." In reality the opposition tried from the beginning of the dispute to make the question of the "regime" the *first* issue; the basic cadres of the opposition were recruited precisely on this issue before the fundamental theoretical and political differences were fully revealed and developed.

This method of struggle is not new. The history of the revolutionary labor movement since the days of the First International is an uninterrupted chronicle of the attempts of petty-bourgeois groupings and tendencies of all kinds to recompense themselves for their theoretical and political weakness by furious attacks against the "organizational methods" of the Marxists. And under the heading of organizational methods, they included everything from the concept of revolutionary centralism up to routine matters of administration; and beyond that to the personal manners and methods of their principled opponents, which they invariably describe as "bad," "harsh," "tyrannical," and—of course, of course, of course—"bureaucratic." To this day any little group of anarchists will explain to you how the "authoritarian" Marx mistreated Bakunin.

The eleven year history of the Trotskyist movement in the United States is extremely rich in such experiences. The internal struggles and faction fights, in which the basic cadres of our movement were consolidated and educated, were, in part, always struggles against attempts to replace principled issues by organizational quarrels. The politically weak opponents resorted to this subterfuge every time.

This was the case from the first days. In the early years of our movement, from 1929 almost uninterruptedly up until 1933, Abern-Shachtman conducted a furious war of words against the "bureaucratic apparatus" of Cannon-Swabeck, which consisted at the time of one typewriter and no stenographer and no regularly paid functionary. The same hue and cry was raised by the faction of Abern-Muste against the Cannon-Shachtman "regime." Then Shachtman, who writes with equal facility on either side of any question, defended the "regime"—the same regime—in an eloquently written and needless to say lengthy document.

In our battle with the centrist faction of Symes-Clement in the Socialist Party of California, the latter controlled the state committee and cheated and persecuted us by every possible bureaucratic trick, resorting finally to our expulsion; this did not stop them from protesting all the time against the "organizational methods" of Cannon. In the dispute over the Russian question, after our expulsion from the Socialist Party and preceding the formal constitution of the S.W.P., Burnham and Carter raised the organization question against us in a special resolution inspired by the conception of Menshevism. Shachtman, who was on the Bolshevik side that season, collaborated with me in the drafting of a counter-resolution on the organization question and defended the "regime."

In the present party conflict, the most fundamental of all, the question of the regime is again represented as a "central issue." This time Shachtman is on the side of Burnham, attacking the regime which he defended yesterday and attacked the day before. The times changed, the attorney changed clients, but the war against "bureaucratism" in the most democratic party in the world is conducted in the same way and for the same ends as before. These "internal problems," says Abern in his letter to Trotsky of February 6th [1940], "have never been resolved satisfactorily." He should

know. He has been conducting the war without cessation for ten years
—in the open when he could find prominent allies, by secret intrigues
and sniping from ambush when he and his group stood alone. But
he never yet got "satisfaction." His numerous organizational combinations, for the sake of which he was always ready to sacrifice any
principle, always collapsed at the critical moment. In each case, a
new stratum of party members who had mistakenly followed him,
learned an instructive if painful lesson in the superiority of principled Marxist politics over organizational combinationism.

All the experience of our rich past has shown that no matter
what temporary successes an organizational combination may have in
the beginning, in recruiting inexperienced comrades by fairy tales
about the regime, the political line always breaks through in the
end and conquers and subordinates the organization question to its
proper place. It is this absolute law of the political struggle that
has frustrated and defeated Abern every time and left him and his
clique isolated and discredited at the end of every struggle.

Abern and his intimate circle of petty-bourgeois gossip-mongers
never learned. But conscientious comrades whose inexperience and
ignorance he exploited, who had no axe to grind, and who took his
expositions of the organization question for good coin, have learned.
That is the great gain from the past struggles. Those comrades of
our younger generation who have had bad experiences with the
attempt, under the tutelage of Abern, to substitute the organization
question for the political line, and even to raise it to first place above
the political line—it is precisely these comrades who are most im-
mune to this kind of factional trickery in the present dispute. From
their unfortunate experiences, and supplementary study, they have
learned to brush aside the clap-trap about the regime at the beginning
of every dispute; they have learned to probe to the bottom of the
political differences, and to take their positions accordingly.

The lengthy document of the opposition on the organization
question was not written for the informed and educated cadres of
the party. It was written for the inexperienced and uninitiated. It
was designed to catch them unawares and disorient them; to poison
them with personal and factional animosity, and thus render them
incapable of making an objective evaluation of the big political
and theoretical disputes that underlie the conflict.

We, from the beginning of the present conflict, steadfastly refused to conduct the battle on this ground. We were determined at
all costs to bring out the political and theoretical essence of the
dispute. Many comrades objected to this strategy. They complained
that inexperienced comrades were being disoriented by this story

and that story, by one alleged grievance and another, and lined up in caucus formation before they had begun to seriously consider the political questions. In spite of that, instructed by the experience of the past, we stuck to our method. The subsequent development of the party discussion confirmed its correctness. The issues are pretty clear now. That is a great gain.

There is no doubt that quite a few comrades have been disoriented and won over to the opposition because, in the early stages of the discussion, we refused to be diverted from the fundamental political and theoretical struggle and allowed most of the gossip and chit-chat about the "regime" to go unanswered. The opposition is welcome to the supporters gained by these means; this must be said in all seriousness and frankness.

We are living in serious times. We stand on the eve of grave events and great tests for our movement. People who can be disoriented and swept off their feet by rumors and gossip and unsupported accusations will not be very reliable soldiers in the hard days coming. The petty bourgeoisie, after all, do everything on a small scale. The gossip and slander campaign of our opposition is not a drop in the bucket compared to the torrents of lies, misinformation and slander that will be poured over the heads of the revolutionary fighters in the coming days of the war crisis through the mighty propaganda mediums of the class enemy. And it is to be expected that for long periods of time we will be gagged and bound hand and foot and have no means of communication with each other. Only those who have thought out their principles and know how to hold to them firmly will be able to sustain themselves in such times. It is not difficult to foresee that those who succumbed already at the feeble anticipation of this campaign inside our own party can be engulfed by the first wave of the real campaign. Such comrades need not simply a reassurance about this or that fairy tale. They need a re-education in the principles and methods of Marxist politics. Only then will it be possible to rely upon them for the future battles.

4—THE ORGANIZATION QUESTION

As long as the real scope of the political and theoretical disputes remained undetermined the talk about the organization question contributed, and could contribute, nothing but confusion. But, now that the fundamental political issues are fully clarified, now that the two camps have taken their position along fundamental lines, it is possible and perhaps feasible to take up the organization question for discussion in its proper setting and in its proper place

—as an important but subordinate issue; as an expression in organizational terms of the political differences, but not as a substitute for them.

The fundamental conflict between the proletarian and the petty-bourgeois tendencies expresses itself at every turn in questions of the party organization. But involved in this secondary conflict are not little incidents, grievances, personal friction and similar small change which are a common feature in the life of every organization. The dispute goes deeper. We are at war with Burnham and the Burnhamites over the fundamental question of the *character of the party*. Burnham, who is completely alien to the program and traditions of Bolshevism, is no less hostile to its "organizational methods." He is much nearer in spirit to Souvarine and all the decadents, skeptics and renegades of Bolshevism than to the spirit of Lenin and his terrible "regime."

Burnham is concerned first of all with "democratic guarantees" against degeneration of the party after the revolution. We are concerned first of all with building a party that will be capable of leading the revolution. Burnham's conception of party democracy is that of a perpetual talking shop in which discussions go on forever and nothing is ever firmly decided. (See the resolution of the Cleveland Conference!)* Consider his "new" invention—a party with two different public organs defending two different and antagonistic programs! Like all the rest of Burnham's independent ideas, that is simply a plagiarism from alien sources. It is not difficult to recognize in this brilliant scheme of party organization a rehabilitation of Norman Thomas' ill-fated "all-inclusive party."

Our conception of the party is radically different. For us the party must be a combat organization which leads a determined struggle for power. The Bolshevik party which leads the struggle for power needs not only internal democracy. It also requires an imperious centralism and an iron discipline in action. It requires a proletarian composition conforming to its proletarian program. The Bolshevik party cannot be led by dilettantes whose real interests and real lives are in another and alien world. It requires an

---

*This refers to a national conference of the minority convoked February 24-25, 1940. This conference resolved that there existed two politically irreconcilable tendencies in the party and that *"the party must extend to whichever group is in the minority at the convention the right to publish a public political journal of its own* defending the general program of the Fourth International [and which] would at the same time present in an objective manner the special position of its tendency on the disputed Russian question." The majority rejected the demands of the minority.—*Ed.*

active professional leadership, composed of individuals democratically selected and democratically controlled, who devote their entire lives to the party, and who find in the party and in its multiform activities in a proletarian environment, complete personal satisfaction.

For the proletarian revolutionist the party is the concentrated expression of his life purpose, and he is bound to it for life and death. He preaches and practices party patriotism, because he knows that his socialist ideal cannot be realized without the party. In his eyes the crime of crimes is disloyalty or irresponsibility toward the party. The proletarian revolutionist is proud of his party. He defends it before the world on all occasions. The proletarian revolutionist is a disciplined man, since the party cannot exist as a combat organization without discipline. When he finds himself in the minority, he loyally submits to the decision of the party and carries out its decisions, while he awaits new events to verify the disputes or new opportunities to discuss them again.

The petty-bourgeois attitude toward the party, which Burnham represents, is the opposite of all this. The petty-bourgeois character of the opposition is shown in their attitude toward the party, their conception of the party, even in their method of complaining and whining about the "grievances," as unfailingly as in their light-minded attitude toward our program, our doctrine and our tradition.

The petty-bourgeois intellectual, who wants to teach and guide the labor movement without participating in it, feels only loose ties to the party and is always full of "grievances" against it. The moment his toes are stepped on, or he is rebuffed, he forgets all about the interests of the movement and remembers only that his feelings have been hurt; the revolution may be important, but the wounded vanity of a petty-bourgeois intellectual is more important. He is all for discipline when he is laying down the law to others, but as soon as he finds himself in a minority, he begins to deliver ultimatums and threats of split to the party majority.

The leaders of the opposition are running true to type. Having recited the whole dolorous catalogue of their petty and inconsequential and mostly imaginary grievances; having been repulsed by the proletarian majority in their attempt to revise the program; having been called in sociological and political terms by their right names—having "suffered" all these indignities—the leaders of the opposition are now attempting to revenge themselves upon the party majority by threats of split. That will not help them. It will not prevent us from characterizing their revisionist improvisations, and showing that their attitude on the organization question is not disconnected from their petty-bourgeois conceptions in general, but simply a secondary expression of them.

Organization questions and organizational methods are not independent of political lines, but subordinate to them. As a rule, the organizational methods flow from the political line. Indeed, the whole significance of organization is to realize a political program. In the final analysis there are no exceptions to this rule. It is not the organization—the party or group—which creates the program; rather it is the program that creates the organization, or conquers and utilizes an existing one. Even those unprincipled groups and cliques which have no program or banner of their own, cannot fail to have a political program imposed upon them in the course of a struggle. We are now witnessing an illustration of the operation of this law in the case of those people in our party who entered into a combination to fight against the "regime" without having any clearly defined political program of differences with it.

In this they are only reproducing the invariable experience of their predecessors who put the cart before the horse, and formed factions to struggle for "power," before they had any clear idea of what they would do with the power after they got it.

In the terminology of the Marxist movement, unprincipled cliques or groups which begin a struggle without a definite program have been characterized as political bandits. A classic example of such a group, from its beginning to its miserable end in the backwaters of American radicalism, is the group known as "Lovestoneites." This group, which took its name from the characterless adventurer who has been its leader, poisoned and corrupted the American Communist movement for many years by its unprincipled and unscrupulous factional struggles, which were carried on to serve personal aims and personal ambitions, or to satisfy personal grievances. The Lovestoneites were able and talented people, but they had no definite principles. They knew only that they wanted to control the party "regime." As with Abern, this question always occupied first place in their calculations; the "political" program of the moment was always adapted to their primary aim of "solving the organization question satisfactorily,"—that is, in their favor.

They were wild-eyed radicals and ultra-leftists when Zinoviev was at the head of the Comintern. With the downfall of Zinoviev and the violent right swing of the Comintern under Bukharin, they became ardent Bukharinites as quickly and calmly as one changes his shirt. Due to an error in calculation, or a delay in information, they were behindhand in making the switch from Bukharin to Stalin and the frenzied leftism of the Third Period. To be sure, they tried to make up for their oversight by proposing the expulsion of Bukharin at the party convention they controlled in 1929. But this last demonstration of political flexibility in the service of rigid organizational aims came too late. Their tardiness cost them their heads.

Their politics was always determined for them by external pressure. At the time of their membership in the Communist Party it was the pressure of Moscow. With their formal expulsion from the Comintern a still weightier pressure began to bear down upon them, and they gradually adapted themselves to it. Today this miserable and isolated clique, petty-bourgeois to the core, is tossed about by bourgeois-democratic public opinion like a feather in the breeze. The Lovestoneites never had any independent program of their own. They were never able to develop one in the years since their separation from the official Communist Party. Today their paper, the *Workers' Age*, is hardly distinguishable from a journal of left liberalism. A horrible example of the end result of unprincipled "organizational" politics.*

The most horrible case of all, with the most immeasurably tragic final consequences, is that of the "Anti-Trotskyist" faction in the Russian Communist Party. It is unquestionable that the Stalin-Zinoviev-Kamenev combination began its factional struggle against Trotsky without any clearly defined programmatic aim. And precisely because it had no program, it became the expression of alien class influences. The ultimate degeneration of the Stalinist faction into a helpless tool of imperialism and a murderous opponent of the true representatives of the Russian revolution is not, as our enemies say, the logical development of Bolshevism. It is rather the ultimate outcome of a departure from the Bolshevik-Marxist method of principled politics.

All proportions guarded, the degeneration of the Abern clique, from formal adherents to the program and doctrine of Marxism into factional supporters of revisionism, has followed the same pattern as the other examples cited. The present ideological and political hegemony of Burnham in the opposition bloc is the most striking proof of the political law that groups and cliques which have no program of their own become the instruments of the program of others. Burnham has a program of a sort. It is the program of

---

*Early in 1941, before the entry of the United States into the war, the Lovestoneite group held a meeting and adopted a resolution to this effect: that the best thing we can do in the interest of socialism is to dissolve.—*Ed.*

struggle against the doctrine, the methods and the tradition of our movement. It was only natural, indeed it was inevitable, that those who combined with Burnham to fight against the "regime" should fall under the sway of his program. The speed with which Abern accomplished this transformation can be explained in part by the fact that he has had previous experience in ideological betrayal in the service of picayune organizational ends, and in part by the fact that the social pressure upon our party is much heavier today than ever before. This pressure accelerates all developments.

5—THE INTELLECTUALS AND THE WORKERS

The outspoken proletarian orientation of the majority is represented by Burnham as an expression of antagonism to "intellectuals" as such, and as an ignorant backwoods prejudice against education in general. In his major document, "The War and Bureaucratic Conservatism," he writes: "Above all, an 'anti-intellectual' and 'anti-intellectuals' attitude is drummed into the minds of party members. The faction associates are taught, quite literally, to despise and scorn 'intellectuals' and 'intellectualism'." For reasons best known to themselves, Shachtman and Abern sign their names to this protest and take sides in a conflict where they have every right to proclaim neutrality.

The *Workers' Age*, organ of the Lovestoneites, which is following our internal discussion with unconcealed sympathy for the opposition, enters the scuffle as an interested partisan. Commenting on a remark in my published speech, to the effect that worker elements engaged in the class struggle understand the Russian question better than the more educated scholastics, the *Workers' Age* of March 9th says: "This is obviously aimed at Burnham, who has the 'misfortune' of being educated. What is this kind of slur but the old Stalinist demagogy contrasting the virtuous, clear-sighted 'proletarian' element to the wicked, confused 'intellectual'? It is the same kind of rotten, unprincipled demagogy, make no mistake about it!"

Let us see. The question at issue is the attitude of proletarian revolutionists to educated members of the petty-bourgeois class who come over to the proletarian movement. This is an important question and deserves clarification. Burnham is indubitably an intellectual, as his academic training, profession and attainments testify. There is nothing wrong in that, as such, and we cannot have the slightest reason to reproach him for it. We are quite well aware, as Marx said, that "ignorance never did anybody any good," and we have nothing in common with vulgar prejudices against "educated people" which are cultivated by rascally demagogues to serve their own ends. Lenin wrote to Gorky on this point: "Of course I was not dreaming of 'persecuting the intelligentsia' as the stupid little Syndicalists do, or deny its necessity for the workers' movement." It is a slander on the Marxist wing of the party to attribute such sentiments to us. On the other hand, we are not unduly impressed by mere "learning" and still less by pretensions to it. We approach this question, as all questions, critically.

Our movement, the movement of scientific socialism, judges things and people from a class point of view. Our aim is the organization of a vanguard party to lead the proletarian struggle for power and the reconstitution of society on socialist foundations. That is our "science." We judge all people coming to us from another class by the extent of their real identification with our class, and the contributions they can make which aid the proletariat in its struggle against the capitalist class. That is the framework within which we objectively consider the problem of the intellectuals in the movement. If at least 99 out of every 100 intellectuals—to speak with the utmost "conservatism"—who approach the revolutionary labor movement turn out to be more of a problem than an asset it is not at all because of our prejudices against them, or because we do not treat them with the proper consideration, but because they do not comply with the requirements which alone can make them useful to us in our struggle.

In the Communist Manifesto, in which the theory and program of scientific socialism was first formally promulgated, it was already pointed out that the disintegration of the ruling capitalist class precipitates sections of that class into the proletariat; and that others—a smaller section to be sure, and mainly individuals— cut themselves adrift from the decaying capitalist class and supply the proletariat with fresh elements of enlightenment and progress. Marx and Engels themselves, the founders of the movement of scientific socialism, came to the proletariat from another class. The same thing is true of all the other great teachers of our movement, without exception.

Lenin, Trotsky, Plekhanov, Luxemburg—none of them were proletarians in their social origin, but they came over to the proletariat and became the greatest of proletarian leaders. In order to do that, however, they had to desert their own class and join "the revolutionary class, the class that holds the future in its hands." They made this transfer of class allegiance unconditionally and without any reservations. Only so could they become genuine representatives of their adopted class, and merge themselves completely with it, and eliminate every shadow of conflict between them and revolutionists of proletarian origin. There was and could be no "problem" in their case.

The conflict between the proletarian revolutionists and the petty-bourgeois intellectuals in our party, as in the labor movement generally in the whole world for generation after generation, does not at all arise from ignorant prejudices of the workers against them. It arises from the fact that they neither "cut themselves adrift" from the alien classes, as the Communist Manifesto specified, nor do they "join the revolutionary class," in the full sense of the word. Unlike the great leaders mentioned above, who came over to the proletariat unconditionally and all the way, they hesitate half-way between the class alternatives. Their intelligence, and to a certain extent also their knowledge, impels them to revolt against the intellectual and spiritual stagnation of the parasitic ruling class whose system reeks with decay. On the other hand, their petty-bourgeois spirit holds them back from completely identifying themselves with the proletarian class and its vanguard party, and reshaping their entire lives in a new proletarian environment. Herein is the source of the "problem" of the intellectuals.

The revolutionary workers' movement, conscious that it "holds the future in its hands," is self-assured, imperious, exacting in the highest degree. It repels all flirtations and half-allegiances. It demands from everyone, especially from leaders, "all or nothing." Not their "education," as the Lovestoneite sympathizers of our party opposition maintain, brings the intellectuals into conflict with the proletarian cadres of the party, but their petty-bourgeois spirit, the miserable halfness, their absurd ambition to lead the revolutionary labor movement in their spare time.

It is not true that the advanced militant workers are hostile to education and prejudiced against educated people. Just the contrary. They have an exaggerated respect for every intellectual who approaches the movement and an exaggerated appreciation of every little service he renders. This was never demonstrated more convincingly than in the reception accorded to Burnham when he formally entered our movement, and in the extraordinary consideration that has been given to him all this time. He became a member of the National Committee without having served any apprenticeship in the class struggle. He was appointed one of the editors of our theoretical journal. All the recognition and the "honors" of a prominent leader of the party were freely accorded to him.

His scandalous attitude toward the responsibilities of leadership; his consistent refusal to devote himself to party work as a profession, not as an avocation; his haughty and contemptuous attitude toward his party co-workers; his disrespect for our tradition, and even for our international organization and its leadership—all this and more was passed over in silence by the worker elements in the party, if by no means with approval. It was not until Burnham came out into the open in an attempt to overthrow our program that the worker elements of the party rose up against him and called him to order. His attempt now to represent this revolutionary action as an expression of ignorant prejudice against him because of his "learning" is only another, and most revealing, exhibition of his own petty-bourgeois spirit and petty-bourgeois contempt for the workers.

A proletarian party that is theoretically schooled in the scientific doctrines of Marxism cannot be intimidated by anybody, nor disoriented by a few unfortunate experiences. The fact that the learned Professor Burnham revealed himself as just another petty bourgeois may possibly engender a little more caution in regard to similar types in the future. But it will not change anything in the fundamental attitude of the workers' vanguard toward the intellectuals from the bourgeois world who approach the movement in the future. Instructed by this experience it is possible that the next one who comes along will have to meet stiffer conditions. It is hardly likely that in the future anyone will be permitted to make pretensions to leadership unless he makes a clean break with his alien class environment and comes over to live in the labor movement. Mere visiting will not be encouraged.

The American movement has had very bad experience with intellectuals. Those who have appeared on its horizon up to date have been a pretty shabby crew. Adventurers, careerists, self-seekers, dilettantes, quitters-under-fire—that is the wretched picture of the parade of intellectuals through the American labor movement as painted by themselves. Daniel De Leon stands out as the great exception. He was not merely an intellectual. He was a man and a fighter, a partisan incapable of any divided allegiance. Once he had decided to come over to the proletarian class, the stale atmosphere of the bourgeois academic world became intolerable for him. He departed from the university, slamming the door behind him, and never once looked back. Thereafter, to the end of his life, he identified himself completely with the socialist movement and the struggle of the workers. Revolutionary workers of the present generation remember him with gratitude for that, without thereby overlooking his political errors. Other, and we hope, greater De Leons, will come to us in the future, and they will receive a whole-hearted welcome from the party of the proletarian vanguard. They will not feel sensitive if we scrutinize their credentials and submit them to a certain apprenticeship. They will not be offended if we insist on an explicit understanding that their task is to interpret and apply the proletarian science of Marxism, not to palm off a bourgeois substitute for it. The new De Leons will readily understand that this preliminary examination is simply a precaution against the infiltration of intellectual phonies and does not signify, in any way whatever, a prejudice against intellectuals who really come to serve the proletarian cause.

The genuine Marxist intellectuals who come to us will understand the cardinal point of our doctrine, that socialism is not simply a "moral ideal," as Burnham tries to instruct us in the year 1940 —92 years after the Communist Manifesto—but the necessary outcome of an irreconcilable class struggle conducted by the proletariat against the bourgeoisie. It is the workers who must make the revolution and it is workers who must compose the proletarian vanguard party. The function of the Marxist intellectual is to aid the workers in their struggle. He can do it constructively only by turning his back on the bourgeois world and joining the proletarian revolutionary camp, that is, by ceasing to be a petty bourgeois. On that basis the worker Bolsheviks and the Marxist intellectuals will get along very well together.

6—THE CASE OF BURNHAM

In the manner of all unreconstructed petty bourgeois, for whom personal considerations, and especially personal grievances, real or imaginary, weigh heavier than the problems of the party and the class, our oppositionists industriously circulate the accusation that we have been "persecuting" Burnham. It is told around that Cannon especially, who is the "embodiment" of all things evil in the party, cannot tolerate any smart people in the leadership and wanted to "drive Burnham out of the party." There is no doubt that this cry gained some sympathy from the humanitarians in the party and netted some votes for the opposition. Others, unappreciated aspirants for leadership, saw in the "persecuted" Burnham a symbol of their own heartbreaking tragedy. All the insulted and injured rallied to his defense with instinctive solidarity.

Nevertheless, this grievance is entirely imaginary. Burnham never encountered any personal hostility from the proletarian wing of the party. On the contrary, as the record amply demonstrates, he has always been handled with silk gloves and given all kinds of liberties that were denied to others. His qualities and abilities were appreciated in the highest degree and every step that he made in our direction, that is, toward Bolshevism and complete integration into the party, was welcomed and encouraged. Far from trying to "drive Burnham out," extraordinary efforts were made to draw him more completely into the party life. At the same time, the more experienced and discerning comrades understood very well that he was standing in an untenable position; that sooner or later he would have to make up his mind to come all the way with us or go back to the bourgeois world. The unavoidable decision, when it finally came, was of his own making.

In looking through my personal files the other day I ran across a letter from comrade Dunne, addressed to me in California, November 21st, 1936. This letter is convincing evidence of good will toward Burnham. Vincent wrote: "I have received from Comrade Burnham quite a long letter of very good criticism about *The Organizer* and the election campaign. I think that Jim does a very good job and it is especially gratifying to know that he follows so closely and is able to speak in terms that indicate he is developing very swiftly. I will send you a copy of his remarks, most of which I believe are quite valid. I think that his estimation of the effects of my candidacy and its relation to the tasks of the union in the election is not very well thought out, but one could not expect this of him, having had little or no experience in the mass movement."

This letter strikingly illustrates the friendly attitude of the proletarian elements toward Burnham and the hopes entertained for his future development. At the same time it puts the finger very deftly on his weak spot—"no experience in the mass movement"—which, unfortunately, Burnham made no effort to remedy and which undoubtedly contributed very heavily toward his failure to assimilate himself into our movement. This letter shows that Dunne was willing to learn from the intellectual. Too bad it never occurred to Burnham that he might learn something from the leader of workers. Had he but known it, there was much he might have learned.

Comrade Dunne might have added another and even equally serious weakness in Burnham's position: his lack of experience in the party. One cannot learn all that needs to be known about a party and its inner life and functioning on weekly visits to the meetings of the Political Committee; and one cannot be a serious leader of the party in his spare time. The pre-war Social Democracy was a sprawling, slow-moving reformist organization which proceeded on the theory that it had unlimited time to advance to socialism at a snail's pace in a completely normal evolutionary process, uninterrupted by wars and revolutions. The leadership in the main corresponded to the character of the party. Lawyers, doctors, teachers, preachers, writers, professors—people of this kind who lived their real lives in another world and gave an evening, or at most two evenings, a week of their time to the socialist movement for the good of their souls—they were the outstanding leaders of the pre-war Socialist Party.

They decided things. They laid down the law. They were the speakers on ceremonial occasions; they posed for their photographs and gave interviews to the newspapers. Between them and the proletarian Jimmy Higginses in the ranks, there was an enormous gulf. As for the party functionaries, the people who devoted all their time to the daily work and routine of the party, they were simply regarded as flunkeys to be loaded with the disagreeable tasks, poorly paid and blamed if anything went wrong. A prejudice was cultivated against the professional party workers. The real honors and the decisive influence went to the leaders who had professional occupations outside the party and who, for the most part, lived typical petty-bourgeois lives which were far removed from the lives of the workers they were presumably "leading."

When we organized the Communist Party in this country in 1919, under the inspiration of the Russian revolution, we put a stop to all this nonsense. We had the opinion that leadership of the revolutionary movement was a serious matter, a profession in itself, and the highest and most honorable of all professions. We deemed it unworthy of the dignity of a revolutionary leader to waste his time on some piddling occupation in the bourgeois world and wrong for the party to permit it. We decreed that no one could be a member of the Central Committee of the party unless he was a full time professional party worker, or willing to become such at the call of the party. I think we had the right idea in 1919. It is all the more right at the present hour of the historic clock when the organization of the proletarian party on the highest possible basis of efficiency is the supreme problem of the revolution.

By and large there is no excuse for any exception to this rule unless the party itself, for reasons of its own, finds it advisable to have a prominent leader in this or that position outside the party to serve party ends. Naturally there are and have been and will be cases where the personal responsibilities of the individual cannot be provided for by the party, and he may have to seek an external occupation for economic reasons. That is the case right now with a great many party comrades who ought by right to be devoting their entire time to the party. But such situations have to be regarded as temporary expedients, to be cut short when the financial resources of the party improve.

It is only natural that a man of the outstanding talents and equipment of Burnham should play a leading role in the party. This was universally recognized. At the same time, it seems to me, it placed upon Burnham the obligation to put himself completely at the service of the party and make party work his profession. In the early days of our acquaintance with him I took it for granted that he had this end in view. Far from barring this road to him, I personally made numerous attempts to open it. I first broached the question to him in the summer of 1935. Even then he was highly critical of the administrative inefficiency of the Trotskyists; he even propounded the theory that this was an inherent weakness of Trotskyism. He was inclined to the opinion that our "regime"—which was then "embodied" by Shachtman and Cannon—was so preoccupied with political ideas and with the conviction that they would prevail in spite of everything, that the organizational and administrative machinery for realizing the ideas was not given sufficient attention. (That was before Burnham discovered that Cannon has no political ideas and no interest in them.)

I proposed to him at that time, in the most friendly spirit, that he help us remedy the undoubted weakness. I proposed concretely that he make an end of the two-for-a-nickel business of instructing college students who have no intention of connecting themselves with the labor movement, and devote his energies and talents entirely to the party. After "thinking it over" for a day or so he rejected the proposal. The reason he gave was somewhat astounding: he said he was not fully convinced of the wisdom of devoting his life entirely to a cause which might not be victorious in his lifetime! Naturally, I could not give him any guarantees. . . .

After my return from California in the summer of 1937, when we were proceeding to form our party again after our expulsion from the S.P., I again raised with Burnham the question of his taking the post of national secretary. Again I received a negative reply. In the pre-convention discussion which preceded our foundation convention in Chicago a little more than two years ago, Burnham began to develop his revisionist theory on the Russian question. In addition he began to raise the "organization question" in a manner that suggested a difference with us that was something far more profound than disagreement over this or that detail of our current work. In reality, his criticisms were directed not so much at the party regime as at the organization conceptions and traditions of Bolshevism.

He began to express a great deal of concern over "democracy" after the revolution, somewhat in the manner of those democrats who identify Stalinism with Bolshevism. We were greatly disturbed by these manifestations. They seemed to indicate quite clearly that Burnham was moving not toward us, but in an opposite direction. Comrade Shachtman and I, who were working very closely together at that time, had jointly elaborated the organizational resolution against the resolution of Burnham. He and I had several personal conversations about these alarming symptoms of Burnham's defection from the line of our movement. We had followed a deliberate course of minimizing personal friction. This was not so easy in view of the haughty and provocative attitude of Burnham, but we did succeed in keeping personal antagonisms down to a minimum. In one conversation which we had with Burnham during this period, he made it quite clear that his apprehensions were directed at our orthodox Bolshevism on the organization question, or at any rate at our interpretation of it. He expressed the opinion that we, as leaders of a future Soviet, would be too ruthless in our suppression of opposition.

However, he was by no means sure of himself on these points. He was obviously going through a difficult period of skepticism and internal conflict which was undoubtedly aggravated, if not inspired, by a hopeless contradiction between his personal life and his position as a party leader. However, it appeared to us that his Souvarinist views about Bolshevism and Stalinism were not by any means fully formed. His revisionist views on the Russian question had not yet led to counter-revolutionary conclusions with regard to defensism or defeatism. We hoped that he would survive his personal crisis and find his way to Bolshevism. To facilitate that, as I said before, we did everything to maintain friendly personal relations, without making any concessions whatever in principle, either on the Russian question or the organization question.

Shachtman and I worked hand in hand in this period, jointly defending the program of the Fourth International on the Russian question and jointly defending the "regime." At that time, with the knowledge and participation of Shachtman, I wrote a letter about the question of Burnham to comrade Crux. I consider it necessary now to publish this letter. I think it will convince any objective comrade of at least two points: 1) that the conflict with Burnham, which has reached the present state of irreconcilability, was clearly foreshadowed more than two years ago; 2) that I personally wanted to do everything possible to maintain good relations with him and to preserve him for the revolutionary movement. Here I quote my letter to comrade Crux in full:

100 Fifth Avenue
Room 1609
New York City

December 16, 1937

Dear Comrade Crux [Trotsky],

The trip to Minneapolis took two weeks out of my schedule at a very awkward time—the eve of the convention. Nevertheless, I think it was worthwhile. From all indications we succeeded, not only in frustrating the frame-up game of the Stalinists, but in dealing them a very heavy blow in the trade union movement, especially. In this case they counterposed themselves, not merely to the "Trotskyites" as a group, but to the organized labor movement of Minneapolis. The results were devastating for them. And I must admit we helped the natural process along.

Our comrades in Minneapolis were on the offensive all along the line. And it appears to me their position in the trade union movement is stronger than ever. Nationally, also, I think we came out of this skirmish victorious. The fact that Professor Dewey, in his radio speech, referred to the Minneapolis frame-up, is somewhat of an indication that our campaign recorded itself in the minds of a fairly wide circle of people who follow the developments in the labor movement.

I now hope to be able to concentrate all my time and attention on the preparations for the convention. I am completely optimistic about it. I know that the active membership throughout the country, especially those engaged in mass work, and they are by no means few in number, are looking to the convention with great expectations and enthusiasm.

We plan to orient the convention along the lines of our general perspectives and tasks, and our concrete work in the trade unions, putting the dispute over the Russian question in its proper proportions. The comrades in the field are up in arms at the perspective, indicated by the internal discussion bulletins, that the convention might resolve itself merely into a discussion of the Russian question.

It has been decided that I should make the trade union report with the objective of raising this question to first place in the convention deliberations. Our comrades engaged in trade union work are securing modest successes in an unexpected number of places. And it is in precisely these places where the party is going forward, drawing in new members, and where the spirit of revolutionary optimism prevails.

The general pessimism and spirit of defeatism, so strong now in the circles of intellectualistic and de-classed radicals, affects our organization primarily in New York. Here, it must be admitted, the social composition is not of the best, and that explains many things. As for the real workers, the harsh exigencies of the daily struggle do not permit them to speculate too much on the sad state of the world, and they have no place whither to retire.

I feel reasonably sure that the convention will be a success from the point of view of organizing and stimulating our mass work, and pointing the whole activity of the party in this direction. At the same time, of course, we will not slur over the principled disputes. I have had several talks with Comrade Shachtman on this matter. We are fully agreed, and firmly resolved, to fight for a clear and unambiguous Bolshevik answer to every question. We hope at the same time to conduct this uncompromising fight in such a manner, and in such a tone, as to avoid any serious disruption of personal comradely relations. We can restrain ourselves in this respect to the utmost because we are assured of the firm support of the overwhelming majority of the party, and in particular of the worker Bolsheviks.

Regarding the suggestion that Comrade B. should be invited to visit you, both Max and I are of the opinion that this is totally excluded before the convention. In truth, I am very doubtful whether it will be feasible after the convention. We must wait and see the outcome of the convention.

I feel it my duty to write you in complete frankness about this matter, and I do so with full confidence that my remarks will remain with you and your immediate co-workers.

We do not want to do or say anything that would tend to sharpen personal relations. Both Max and I are going as far as possible to conciliate and smooth over everything, as long as it is not a matter of blurring principled lines. But that is just the nub of the matter. It appears to us that Comrade B. is undertaking to revolt from fundamental principles in general, and not only on the Russian question.

As the convention approaches, we come more and more into conflict over the conception of the party. The questions of democracy, centralism, irreconcilability, stubborn resistance against the infiltration of alien moods and theories, the necessity of a brutal offensive against the intellectualistic calamity howlers, defeatists, and belly-achers in general—on all these questions, which, in the present situation spell the meaning of Bolshevism, we come more and more into profound, if politely conducted dispute. In such a time as this, when we must take arms against the world of enemies and disintegrating factors, Comrade B. is greatly handicapped by his background, his environment, and his training. He has a strong character, and of his ability, I need not speak, but it seems to me, that the disputes arising from the Russian question, and now from other questions, are not primarily—or, better, not fundamentally—intellectual or theoretical.

Now, I must tell you, dear friend, that I think he is suffering from the intellectual soul sickness. Who can cure that? If he were completely identified with a group of worker Bolsheviks, and could be brought under the influence of their spirit in day to day struggle, one could have more hope. But there's the rub. He does not really feel himself to be one of us. Party work, for him, is not a vocation but an avocation. He is not in a position to travel the country, to take part in the action of our comrades in the field, to live with them, and learn from them, and come under their influence in his personal life. His social environment is entirely different. You know very well that the academic world of the real, as well as the pseudo intellectuals, is weighted down now with the heavy pessimism in general, and with a new skepticism about everything. Without his really comrehending it, Comrade B. himself is affected by this pressure of his daily environment. Combine this with a great tendency on his part to deprecate his party co-workers, and to resist the idea of being influenced or taught anything, even by our international comrades, and you can see the problem doesn't promise any easy solution.

I must say that I sensed for a long time the coming of this personal crisis—that is what it really is—of Comrade B. I know, as we all do, that the Revolutionary Party devours men. Demands everything and repels flirtations. By all rights, now, Comrade B., having established himself as one of the most prominent leaders of the party, and bearing in mind the party's indispensable need of a more active professional staff, should be preparing himself, at least, to become a functionary, with all that it implies. When I returned from California last spring, I had the hope that he would be ready for such a drastic decision. Indirectly, I suggested to him that with our break from the S.P., he should take over the office of national secretary. His failure to react to this suggestion at that time, although there was then no trace of serious differences, filled me with misgivings for the future.

I have written you this extremely frank opinion because I think it is necessary for you to know the nature of the problem, as I see it. Perhaps on that basis you can make suggestions or proposals which will help both us and Comrade B. in finding a common language and a common path.

Comradely,

(signed) J. P. Cannon

From this letter it is evident that my opinion of the petty-bourgeois attitude of Burnham was not suddenly formulated at the outbreak of the present factional struggle. The "intellectual soul sickness"—that is the petty-bourgeois sickness.

But that is not yet the whole story. Shortly prior to the writing of the above letter I had occasion to be in Minneapolis (at the time of the Corcoran murder) as mentioned in the letter to Crux. There I had a discussion with a group of leading comrades about the disputes in the party and about the situation in the leading committee in New York. These comrades, whom the oppositionists now depict as ignorant intellectual-haters, emphasized very strongly to me in this discussion their desire that the dispute with Burnham be conducted in such a way as not to antagonize him unnecessarily, or to weaken unduly his position in the party. They made it clear that they valued his abilities very highly and wished assurances of comradely treatment for him that would facilitate his continued functioning as a party leader after the convention.

I assured them of my readiness to comply with their wishes in this respect. I expressed the opinion, however, that the real trouble with Burnham was not so much his mistaken political position as the more fundamental conflict between his bourgeois personal life and the increasingly exacting demands the party must make upon a leader. In such cases, I told them, I had frequently observed that people unconsciously seek to rationalize their personal difficulties and contradictions in the form of hastily arrived at "political differences" with the party. I said that if we could feel sure that Burnham was really one of us, if he would show some sign of determination on his part to resolve his personal contradictions and come to work in the revolutionary movement in earnest—in that case we could have much more ground to hope that the political differences between us would eventually be overcome in the course of comradely discussion and common work.

Shortly after the convention Burnham requested that Shachtman and I meet him at lunch away from the office to discuss a very important matter. At this meeting he told us that a comrade, who had attended the Minneapolis discussion, had reported my remarks to him. He emphasized, however, that it had been done in good faith and with the best of intentions. I expressed my regret that the question had been put to him in such a point-blank fashion before he might be ready to give an answer. However, the fat was in the fire, and there was nothing to do but face the issue.

Burnham stated frankly that he wasn't sure but that I might be right in my assumption that in his political disputes with us he was simply rationalizing his personal contradictions. He said it was a real contradiction, that he recognized it, and that he was not yet ready to solve it definitively. Instead of plunging deeper into party work, he wanted more time to consider the matter, and wanted to be released for the next period from all party duties except his regular literary work. We discussed the matter in a friendly way; we didn't give him any bureaucratic orders; we acceded to his demands.

The minutes of the Political Committee meeting for January 20, 1938 record the official disposition of the matter as follows:

> Cannon: Reports that Comrade Burnham, in the next period, wants to concentrate his work for the party on writing for the magazine and paper.

Motion by Cannon: For the next period we consider Comrade Burnham's work to be specifically literary and editorial and that he be exempted from routine sub-committee work. *Carried.*

If some worker in the party, who is denied exemption from distasteful duties, reads this extract from the minutes of the Political Committee he may indeed draw certain conclusions about the existence of "second class citizens" in the party. But he will not find any evidence that our foremost party intellectual was placed in this category. (Incidentally, it can be learned from this account that the famous "New Year's meeting" on the auto campaign was not the only occasion when formal decisions of the P.C. were prepared beforehand in informal discussions. There were many such occasions and there will be many more in the future. It is the normal method of any serious "collective leadership.")

What changed since then? What happened to break off all personal and political collaboration and eventually bring us to the present situation? On my part, nothing changed; my course today is the same as it was then. Burnham moved steadily in an opposite direction. And Shachtman, soon after the conversation recorded above, began to shift over into the orbit of Burnham. We drifted apart and now stand in opposite camps. Burnham, as his article "Science and Style" testifies, has broken completely with Marxism and Bolshevism and the proletarian revolution. Shachtman, who yesterday defended Bolshevism against Burnham, today defends Burnham against Bolshevism. Let them try to explain these developments by references to the "bureaucratism" of Cannon and the machinations of a "clique." These are simply excuses invented after the fact. All my efforts, as I believe I have demonstrated, were exerted toward a different end.

7—THE EVIL OF COMBINATIONISM

The opposition is the worst and most disloyal of all types of factional formations in a revolutionary workers' party: an unprincipled combination. Combinationism is the worst offense against the party because it cuts across the lines of political principle; it aims at an organizational decision which leaves the political and principled disputes unclarified and undecided. Thus, insofar as the combinationist struggle is successful, it hampers the education of the party and prevents a solution of the dispute on a principled basis. Unprincipled combinationism is in every case the denotation of petty-bourgeois politics. It is the antithesis to the Marxist method of political struggle.

Marxists always begin with the program. They rally supporters around the program and educate them in its meaning in the process of the struggle. The political victories of the Marxists are always in the first place victories for their program. The organizational phase of the victory in every case, from the election of a definite slate of candidates in a party faction fight up to and including the seizure of power in an armed struggle, always has one and the same significance: to provide the means and the instrument for carrying out the political program. Marxist politics is principled politics. This explains, among other things, the homogeneity of the Marxist formation, regardless of whether it is a faction in a party on a small scale, or a full-fledged and fully developed party directly facing the parties of the class enemy. It is this homogeneity of the Marxist organization which makes possible its firm discipline, its centralization and its striking power.

Petty-bourgeois politics is always a hodge-podge. It never attains to a fully developed and consistent program. Every petty-bourgeois formation, whether faction or independent party, has this characteristic feature. It fights at best for partial aims, and slurs over contradictions and differences within its ranks in order to preserve a formal unity. Petty-bourgeois groupings struggle, not in the name of great principles, but for organizational objectives. To this end, they almost invariably unite people of different views and tendencies, and subordinate the clarification of their differences to success in the organizational struggle. This explains their lack of internal discipline, and their aversion to centralism which is incompatible with a heterogeneous political composition. This determines their tendency to fall apart in the course of a severe struggle, or soon after it, even though they may have gained a momentary organizational victory.

Petty-bourgeois politics is the politics of futility, of the debasement of theory, of the miseducation of the rank and file, of diversion from the primary and decisive questions—the questions of principle—to all sorts of considerations of a secondary order, including the struggle for organizational control. The present struggle between the proletarian and the petty-bourgeois tendencies in our party is a classic illustration of the contrast between principled political methods and unprincipled combinationism.

It was clearly established early in the discussion that the opposition represented a combination of at least three different political tendencies on the Russian question, with only one thing in common upon which they had agreement, namely, opposition to the "party regime." The present factional struggle formally began at the party plenum last October over the Russian question; more

precisely, over two aspects of one and the same question: the nature of the Soviet state and its defense. The "defensist," Abern,
voted for our motion, characterizing the Soviet Union as a degenerated workers' state, and declaring for its unconditional defense
against imperialism. The "defeatist," Burnham, had already introduced a document into the political committee declaring: "It is
impossible to regard the Soviet Union as a workers' state in any
sense whatsoever," and denying it any defense whatever "in the
present war." As for the "doubtist," Shachtman, he "abstained"
from "raising at this time the problem of the class nature of the
Soviet State," and left the question of its defense to future developments.

To the basic theoretical question of the class nature of the Soviet
Union, the criterion by which all Marxists determine their attitude
toward a given state, and to the basic political question of its defense, the three leaders of the opposition each gave a different
answer. That did not prevent them from forming a faction. Their
inability to give a common answer as to the character of the Stalin
regime in the Soviet Union did not prevent them from forming
a common faction to fight against the "regime" in our party. In
their eyes all questions are subordinate to this.

Combinationism violates the Marxist tradition so crudely that
its practitioners always feel obliged to cover their operations by
deceptions and denials. Our present combinationists follow this
familiar routine. They quote the "statement" made by Abern at
the plenum to explain his vote both for our precise motion and
the ambiguous resolution of Shachtman:

> With this basic evaluation I find no contradiction in the reso-
> lution of Shachtman which I accept in its essentials as an inter-
> pretation or analysis of specific current issues therein cited, *not
> invalidating the basic party position*. I am ready to leave to the
> next period the unfoldment or otherwise of the interpretations or
> implications asserted by some comrades here as to *the "bridge"
> character of the Shachtman resolution*, or whether it stands epi-
> sodically by itself; and to make my judgments accordingly on the
> merits of any issue.

Thus they say, they "dispose in passing of the Cannonite contention that the minority is an 'unprincipled bloc'." "In passing," the
statement proves the opposite. The sections of the statement which
I have underlined make this clear. Shachtman's ambiguous resolution was under fire from the majority at the plenum as a *"bridge"*
to the defeatist position of Burnham. Abern's statement was a *reply
to this criticism*, an explanation that he understood Shachtman's
resolution as *"not invalidating the basic party position"* of "un-

conditional defense" for which he had voted, and a declaration that he would "leave to the next period" the "unfoldment or otherwise"—of what? The majority's assertions *"as to the 'bridge' character of the Shachtman resolution"!* It so "unfolded," and not otherwise. Shachtman soon turned up, bag and baggage, in the defeatist camp of Burnham. And Abern—who was going to wait and see if Shachtman's position was a "bridge"? He, the "unconditional defensist" of the October plenum, nonchalantly crossed the "bridge" to "unconditional defeatism." And then he blandly asks, in his open letter to Trotsky, "What is wrong with that?"

To hold one political position and unite organizationally with people who hold a diametrically opposite position against others with whom one has declared fundamental agreement; and then, in a few months' time, to reverse one's original position; and then to maintain that nothing has happened—of course, there is nothing "wrong with that." Nothing wrong, that is, if one is a cynical combinationist who has no respect for the party, and its Marxist tradition, and the intelligence of its members. But in the eyes of a Marxist it is a betrayal of principle—an unpardonable crime against the party.

There was a time when Shachtman knew how to characterize such conduct and to set forth, as he explained, "The established Marxian view on this question." In the *Internal Bulletin* of the Workers Party, No. 3, Feb. 1936, in an article entitled "Marxist Politics or Unprincipled Combinationism?" Shachtman wrote:

> Finally, writing about the case of Mill, who had also made a "little organizational bloc"—just a temporary one!—with a group in the French Left Opposition which he had defined as non-Marxist, against another group which, although he called it Marxist, was charged by him with having bad "organizational methods"; Mill, who logically concluded this political practice by passing over to the Stalinists—Trotsky summarized the situation in a letter written October 13, 1932: "For Mill, principles are in general clearly of no importance; personal considerations, sympathies and antipathies determine his political conduct to a greater degree than principles and ideas. The fact that Mill could propose a bloc with a man whom he had defined as non-Marxist against comrades whom he had held to be Marxists, showed clearly that Mill was politically and morally unreliable and that he was incapable of keeping his loyalty to the flag. If he betrayed on that day on a small scale, he was capable of betraying tomorrow on a larger scale. That was the conclusion which every revolutionist should have drawn then. . . ."

Nothing need be added to that devastating paragraph. The lawyer's arguments Shachtman is now employing to defend the methods he condemned in 1936 do not change the quality of the methods, or the Marxist appraisal of them, in any respect whatever. We will teach the party members to despise such methods and raise a political and moral barricade against them.

8—ABERNISM: THE CASE HISTORY OF A DISEASE

Almost since the beginning of the Trotskyist movement in this country, more than eleven years ago, its normal development and functioning has been impeded by an internal disease which poisoned the blood-stream of the party organism. The name of this disease is Abernism. The characteristics of Abernism, as they have been consistently and uninterruptedly manifested for more than ten years, are: clique politics; ceaseless dissemination of gossip and complaints about the party regime; subordination of principled questions to organizational and personal considerations; unprincipled combinationism in every faction fight; and ideological treachery.

This internal malady has been always present and always harmful. In "normal" times when there were no open factional struggles, it lay dormant, sapping the vitality of the party. At every sharp turn, whenever serious political differences flared up in faction fights, the malady always immediately assumed an extremely virulent form, complicating the ideological struggles in the highest degree and pushing them to the brink of split.

The Abern group is a permanent family clique whose uninterrupted existence and perfidious practices are known to all the older members of the party. For more than ten years it has waged a now open, now concealed, but never interrupted factional struggle against the party leadership. At one time or another in the past, most of the leading comrades have differed and formed temporary factional groupings in the struggle for conflicting political views. Upon the settlement of the disputes, peace was made and good collaboration resumed; the opponents quite often became the best of friends, bearing no grudges. But Abern, without a platform, without once bringing forward any independent political position, never became reconciled, never ceased his inexplicably consistent factional struggle.

In the present dispute Abern is only repeating his time-worn practices. He enters into an organizational combination; he trades off his position on the Russian question for a bloc against the regime; he poisons the atmosphere of the discussion; and now, as always before at every critical stage, he works deliberately in the direction of a split. In his letter to comrade Trotsky, dated January 29th, he announces his intention to "carry on this fight to the end."

And by the end, he obviously means now what he has always meant in similar situations in the past, not a democratic decision by a majority of the party at a convention but a destructive split of the party ranks.

The indefensible record of Abern is written in the history of our party. The young comrades must know this history and not permit it to be slurred over. This knowledge will help them to avoid the treacherous pitfalls of clique politics and combinationism. Shachtman is very busy these days with the attempt to pass off the rich history of our past as a series of quarrels from which no lessons are to be derived. That is not true. We did not fight over trifles. Shachtman objects to references to the record of the past only because it speaks so damningly against his present course. He invents for the present factional struggle the myth of a "Cannon clique" as a super-clever ruse to ward off an examination of the record of a real clique whose indictment he himself wrote in documents which today retain their validity. If some comrades have been shocked and astounded by the nonchalance with which Abern, the "orthodox Marxist," entered into a combination with the revisionist, Burnham, a review of the history of the party will show them that such actions on the part of Abern are nothing new. In his past struggles against the party leadership, Abern did not hesitate to combine with the sectarian, Oehler; with the non-Marxist, Muste; and even with Stalinist agents in the party. Abern in the present fight is only continuing a singularly consistent course.

The attempt of the opposition penmen to revise our history as well as our program is, so to speak, a "concession" to Abern, whose record as a clique-fighter and combinationist taints any faction he supports. But Shachtman and Burnham write too much and forget too soon what they have written. They themselves have characterized the Abern group as an unprincipled and disloyal clique; they have exposed and condemned its unprincipled combinationism; they have recorded its history. They want now to rule out all references to this history, especially to the documents which they themselves wrote, as of no pertinence to the present discussion. That is because they have not yet found anything in the "history" of Abern in our movement which is worthy of their defense.

We say, and we prove, that Abern is resorting in the present critical situation to the same practices and methods that he has always employed in previous party crises. They try to switch the issue by accusing us of raking up out-lived political differences which have no bearing on the present dispute. No, that is not the case. We are not talking about the past political errors of Abern,

although every time he ventured to give his "organizational struggle" against the party regime a political expression he committed
nothing but errors. We are not talking about his opposition to
the entry into the Socialist Party; or, further back, his attempt to
obstruct the fusion with the Musteites; or, still further back, his
ill-fated and hastily-ended ventures on the trade union question.
We are not trying to connect these outlived struggles with the
present life-and-death struggle on the Russian question.

Our specific references are to those features of Abern's past
conduct which have a direct relation to the present—his methods;
his clique politics; his unprincipled combinationism; his betrayals
of principle to serve factional ends. These are the practices he re-
sorts to in the present struggle; these have been his invariable practices in the past. Consequently a review of the past in this respect
is absolutely pertinent to the present struggle. That section of party
membership which has gone through the past experiences knows
this record very well. That is why Abernism is abhorred by the
basic cadres of the party. The newer party members and the youth
need to know this record, they need to understand its indissoluble
connection with the present, in order that they may settle accounts
definitively with this corrupting tendency at the forthcoming convention.

Since the very beginning of the present factional struggle
Shachtman and Burnham have suffered from the most embarrassing
contradiction, as a result of their combination with Abern. They
could not defend the past record of the Abern group. On the other
hand, they could not dispense with Abern since his group is the
organizational backbone of the combination. They tried to solve
the problem by denying the existence of the Abern clique altogether. The "Abern question," says Shachtman, waving his wand—
that is "spurious"—"that does not exist." "Cannon knows what
every informed party leader, and many members, know, namely,
that for the past several years at least there has been no such thing
as an 'Abern group'."

That is good news, only it isn't true, and nobody "knows" it
better than Shachtman and Burnham. We shall prove it out of their
own mouths. The existence of this clique, its nature and method
of functioning, were established and recorded with deadly accuracy
by none other than Burnham, not "several years" ago, but a *bare
three months* before the beginning of the present faction fight. In
a document submitted to the Political Committee of the party on
June 13, 1939, Burnham wrote:

Some years ago Abern built up a following on primarily personal rather than political grounds. This has been kept alive *and still lives*, nourished by extensive personal and correspondence contact, mutual aid and protection in matters of party tasks and posts, by joint distribution of gossip and information *including confidential information*, and by enmity to Cannon. Whatever party posts Abern fills are always ably administered, but at the same time administered in such a way as to help the maintenance of his clique. ("Toward Brass Tacks." My emphasis.)

What prompted Burnham to put in writing in an official document this devastating characterization? What prompted him to establish with such precision the origin, methods, motivations and' *present existence* of the Abern clique? He was simply recording as a matter of course a circumstance which "every informed party leader," including Shachtman, "knows." The fact that he did not look ahead a few months to the time when the opposition bloc would need the collaboration of Abern and find it necessary to deny the existence of his clique, and to denounce the very mention of it as "spurious"—that only testifies to the short-sightedness of Burnham. It does not in any way alter the facts he recorded.

* * *

Shachtman practices deliberate fraud on the party when he tries now to deny these facts which none of us have ever been able to forget. They were always a constant source of irritation and disturbance in the party leadership, even in "normal" times, and a threat to its unity in every serious faction fight. The non-existent clique of Abern was the subject of repeated conversations in the leadership, particularly between this same Shachtman and Burnham —and Cannon. Burnham, more than once, characterized Abern as an incipient "American Stalin," referring thereby to his unceasing intrigues, his disloyalty, his factionalism devoid of principled considerations, and his petty motivations, alien to the spirit of communism, of spite and "revenge."

None of us who really knew Abern placed a very high estimation on his contributions to the leadership of the party. If we agreed to accept him as a member of the Political Committee, it was not for his political contributions; he never made a single one. Assuredly it was not because there was "no such thing" as an Abern group. On the contrary, it was precisely because we knew he represented a group that we accepted him into the Political Committee as a concession to this group, in an attempt to satisfy it and at the same time to disarm it by showing that we did not discriminate against defeated opponents. We accepted him in the Political Committee for another reason, not because we trusted him but because we wanted to have him in a place where we could watch him most carefully. Such are the facts of the matter, and nobody knows them better than Shachtman.

When we had matters of an extremely confidential nature to consider, not once and not twice, but repeatedly, we disposed of these matters informally without taking them before the official P.C. Reason? We did not rely on Abern to respect the confidences of the P.C. On more than one occasion when we slipped up on this precaution we had reason to regret our carelessness. Time and again confidential information was transmitted by Abern to the members of his clique—that is one of the privileges enjoyed by these persecuted "second class citizens"—and then passed on to wider circles, sometimes into the hands of our enemies.

Equally fraudulent is Shachtman's attempt to prove the nonexistence of the Abern group by reference to the fact that the Political Committee elected after the Chicago convention "had on it *four 'ex-Abernites'* out of a total of *seven* members, i.e., a majority!" The four "ex-Abernites" were Abern, Widick, McKinney and Gould. In the first place, there was no design to give them a majority; Widick was elected not as a member of the P.C. but as a candidate, nominated by Shachtman, as the minutes state, "for the reason that he would be able to serve as labor secretary until Farrell Dobbs could take up his duties." Dobbs was elected as the regular member of the P.C. but was not able to serve for other reasons which prevented his coming to the center. Goldman, proposed as first candidate, was likewise unable to come to New York at that time. In the second place, the selections for this P.C. were made on a functional rather than on a political basis. McKinney, at that time District Organizer of New York, was considered necessary on the P.C. because of his functions. As for Gould, his selection was made by the National Committee of the Y.P.S.L. These facts from the record, omitted by Shachtman, are sufficient to show that there was no design to put a majority of ex-Abernites on the committee.

The circumstance that four Abernites eventually found their way onto the committee, because of a selection by function and because of the inability of Dobbs or Goldman to come to the center, and the fact that we raised no objection to this result, does not in any way prove the "non-existence" of the Abern clique. It only proves that they were not deprived of functions because of their past offenses. Moreover, this somewhat accidental composition of the P.C. was deliberately accepted as a test of the individuals concerned; as an effort to break them away from their clique formations and associations by integrating them into the directing body of the party.

For example, in the case of Widick, we felt by assigning him to trade union work, a field completely alien to the petty-bourgeois gossip circles of the Abern clique, the activity in this broader field could operate to cure him of his clique sickness and make a party man out of him.

Gould, as stated, came to the committee as a representative of the National Committee of the Y.P.S.L. But when Gould, during the Chicago convention, inquired as to our attitude toward him as National Secretary of the Y.P.S.L., we gave him certain explicit conditions, *laid down by Shachtman.* At a meeting between the three of us Shachtman told Gould bluntly: "We are willing to support you if you are going to be a party man' in the Y.P.S.L., but not if you are going to be an Abernite. We don't want the Y.P.S.L. to become a plaything of Abernite clique politics. We don't want your work as leader of the Y.P.S.L. to be regulated by the moods and subjective politics of Abern." That is how much Shachtman really believed at the time of the Chicago convention that "there has been no such thing as an 'Abern group'." Shachtman's attempt to give a contrary impression in his "Open Letter to Trotsky" represents simply a deliberate perversion of the facts in order to deceive the party. Shachtman declared the Abern clique "dissolved" only when he needed it in its undissolved reality for purposes of a combination against the party regime.

* * *

Shachtman writes on many subjects he doesn't fully understand, but on the question of the Abern clique, its origin, its methods, its disloyalty and its standing threat to the unity of the party—on this subject he long ago qualified as an authority. And what he wrote yesterday on this subject, when he had no factional necessity to conceal the truth, is fully applicable today, for the Abern group has not changed in any respect whatever.

In February 1936, near the end of the protracted factional struggle over entry into the Socialist Party, when the opposition combination of Muste-Abern was threatening us with a split, Shachtman summed up the history of the struggle, and the history of the Trotskyist movement in America, in a mimeographed document of 70 single-spaced pages which occupied the space of two whole internal bulletins of the party. The burden of its contents is indicated by the title, "Marxist Politics or Unprincipled Combinationism?" From beginning to end it is a sustained polemic against the Abern clique. The purpose of the document, as stated in the introduction, was to educate the youth in the struggle against clique politics and unprincipled combinationism.

It is meant [wrote Shachtman] above all for the militant knowledge-hungry youth of our movement. In a sense it is dedicated to them. . . . The youth must be trained in the spirit of revolutionary Marxism, of principled politics. Through its blood stream must run a powerful resistance to the poison of clique politics, or subjectivism, of personal combinationism, of intrigue, of gossip. It must learn to cut through all the superficialities and reach down to the essence of every problem. It must learn to think politically, to be guided exclusively by political considerations, to argue out problems with themselves and with others on the basis of principles and to act always from motives of principle." (*Internal Bulletin* of the Workers Party, No. 3, Feb. 1936, page 2.)

And when Shachtman wrote about clique politics then he was not referring to an imaginary clique of Cannon. He was fighting shoulder to shoulder with Cannon against a clique that existed in reality then as it exists now. Shachtman has never enlightened us as to the precise origin of the so-called "Cannon clique." On the origin of the Abern clique he gave much more definite information. He promised to prove and did prove that "it was formed in the dark of night without a political platform and without *ever*, in the two whole years of its existence, having drawn up a clear political platform; that its basis of existence is that of an unprincipled personal combination, of a clique that refuses to live down ancient and completely outlived personal and factional animosities; that its principal aim is to 'smash Cannon' (and Shachtman, because of his association with the latter)." (*Idem*, page 22.)

In reality, the clique he is speaking of was "formed in the dark of night" in the first days of the Left Opposition, not "two years," but *seven years* before the above-quoted article of Shachtman was written. Shachtman post-dates the origin of the Abern group to the time of his break with it. The Abern group is always being "broken up" by the defections of people who learn something from an unfortunate experience, and then immediately reconstituted with the basic core intact. Then it begins to draw in new recruits from the ranks of the inexperienced and the uninformed, who mistake gossip, personal grievances, and "organization questions" for revolutionary politics.

What, according to Shachtman, were the recruiting methods of this clique? Then as now: ". . . It has not gained a single partisan by the methods of open honest ideological confrontation of its opponents. Its methods are different: It says one thing in letters, poisonous 'information notes' sent out secretly by Abern but which they never dare put before the party publicly, and says another thing openly. . . ." (Page 61.)

What did the clique represent politically? The ever-dynamic Shachtman, who keeps a straight face while he signs with Abern joint indictments of the "conservatism" of Cannon, had this to say about the politics of the up-and-coming Abern and his group: "It represents political sterility, passivity, negativeness, timidity, fear of bold innovations—a species of *conservative* [Hear! Hear!] *sectarianism*." (Page 61.)

Again: "If we were commanded to give a summary characterization of the Abern-Weber faction, our formula would confine itself to two words that describe its political pre-disposition and its organizational methods: *a conservative clique*." (Page 62.)

What does it represent? "It represents an unhealthy and sinister current in our blood stream—the stream of revolutionary Marxism, which bases itself on principled methods, which detests clique politics and personal combinationism. Its morals, its manners, its customs, its methods, make it an alien system in our movement." (Page 63.)

In the above-cited document and in others issued in the faction fight at the time, Shachtman proved to the hilt that the unprincipled clique of Abern, blind to all goals except to "smash Cannon," combined with the ultra-left Oehlerites, with Muste, and even with thinly disguised Stalinist agents in the party! Each of these combinations had a terrible aftermath. The Oehlerites broke with the party and the Fourth International and became bitter enemies. Undeterred by that, Abern, in combination with Muste, deliberately prepared to torpedo the party with another split. Faced, then as now, with the certain prospect of being in a minority at the convention, Abern steadfastly refused, then as now, to give the party any assurance that he would accept the decisions of the convention under the principle of democratic centralism. On the contrary, he moved forward with a deliberate plan to split our ranks at a most crucial turning point in our history, when we were gathering our forces for a complicated maneuver to break out of our isolation by entering the Socialist Party.

What was the motive of this perfidious program? What was the motive of his drive for split in the old fight of 1933, in the days of our isolation and stagnation, when a split of our meager forces might very well have sounded the death knell of our young movement—a split that was only averted by the intervention of our international organization and the break of Shachtman, Lewit and others away from Abern? What is the motive of the threat of a split in the American section of the Fourth International on the eve of the war and the historic opportunity and test of our movement?

These are the questions which began as unspoken thoughts in the minds of the experienced comrades of our party in the course of this discussion. As the struggle developed, and the perfidious program of Abern became more clearly revealed, the thought became a whisper, and the whisper is today becoming a shout! On guard for the unity of the party! On guard against sinister designs to disrupt our ranks at the most critical moment of our history!

*   *   *

Why did not Abern carry out his plans for a split in 1936? For two very good reasons—both outside his control: 1) The faction was reduced to a small minority; 2) An anti-split tendency paralyzed it from within.

Weber, who had been associated with Abern in the factional struggle, and whose personal influence had been a cover for him, drew back from the prospect of a split. He made a demonstrative break with the split program of Abern and Muste, and came out firmly for the unity of the party. An example for others in the present critical situation! An example of party loyalty which has not yet received its due acknowledgment. Weber was denounced by Abern and his circle as a "traitor." To this day he is "socially ostracized" by the clique, because he demonstrated in the most critical and responsible situation that his highest loyalty was to the party. How shameful and criminal it is to denigrate Weber in order to cover Abern in references to that fight. "Weber did not play the least shabby role in the dispute of those years," says the document of Burnham, Abern, Shachtman and Bern, entitled "The War and Bureaucratic Conservatism." Monstrous perversion of history! Weber played the role of a party-loyal man and helped the party to frustrate the designs of those who would have split it. That action alone far outweighed the errors Weber committed in the faction struggle. Shachtman and Burnham so acknowledged it at that time. Their attempt to pronounce a different judgment now discredits them, not Weber.

How far one can travel on the path of betrayal by substituting combinationism for principled politics is not revealed for the first time by Abern's present bloc with the anti-Marxist, anti-Soviet Burnham against the party and the Fourth International. I have said that in the faction fight of 1935-36 he not only combined with the ultra-leftist Oehlerites and the Christian Socialist Muste against the "Cannon-Shachtman regime," but that he included in his combination some political agents of Stalinism in the ranks of the Workers Party. And these were not hidden provocateurs such as may penetrate into any honest organization or group without disclosing their political identity; there is no reason to doubt that we have such agents in our own ranks. Abern's Stalinist allies in the Workers Party showed their political orientation repeatedly and consistently and over a long period of time. They were consistently fought by the loyal comrades in the Allentown branch and by the Cannon-Shachtman faction in the National Committee, and just as consistently covered and protected by the Abern-Muste caucus. They were kept in the caucus and *even on its leading body*.

The Muste-Abern-Stalinist combination went so far as to combine in the elections to the local Unemployed Leagues in Allentown with official representatives of the Stalinists against the members of their own party! Here is the way the situation was described in Bulletin No. 5 of the Cannon-Shachtman group in the Workers Party, issued under date of January 28, 1936:

> The Musteite, Reich, who has been under criticism for the past year for his pro-Stalinist orientation, finally went so far as to boost a Stalinist meeting at which Mother Bloor and Budenz were to speak. This took place at a meeting of delegates of the Unemployed League of Allentown. The P.C., upon investigation of the matter, came to the conclusion that the Allentown Branch in merely censuring Reich, had taken entirely too mild an attitude toward such a crime. The P.C. ordered his suspension for 3 months, with the proviso that he should retain the right to vote on convention resolutions and convention delegates. . . . They decided to defy the decision of the P.C. . . .
>
> In the elections to the Lehigh County Executive Board of the Unemployed League, [the Muste-Abern] caucus decided to make a clean sweep of their party factional opponents. Three incumbents in office, supporters of our tendency, were taken off the slate for re-election and a slate of six Musteites to fill all 6 places involved in the election was passed by the Musteite majority of the branch, a majority at the meeting of 22 to 21. On appeal of the minority to the P.C., it was decided to correct the slate, to let the three incumbents stand for re-election and to let the Musteite candidates for the other offices stand. This was a fair division corresponding to the actual relation of forces and also to the merits of the individual candidates. This decision was also flatly violated. The Musteites ran in the election against our comrades, and WITH THE AID OF THE STALINIST VOTES, defeated our comrades in the election. . . .

Reich and Hallet, the Stalinist agents at Allentown, together with Arnold Johnson, a member of the national leading group of the Abern-Muste caucus, were closely connected with Budenz, the ex-Musteite who had joined the Stalinist party. Naturally, they were driving with full force to split the party and destroy the possibility of a successful entry into the S.P. The central aim of Stalinist provocateurs in the ranks of the Fourth International in all countries has always been to provoke demoralizing splits at critical turning points. As we drew near the convention of the party, the Abern-Muste faction was reduced to a small minority and balked in its split program by the party-unity stand of Weber and others. Thereupon the Stalinist agents, obviously acting under instructions, decided to show their colors. On the day our party convention opened the Stalinist allies of Abern—Johnson, Reich and Hallet—presented a joint letter of resignation, denouncing us as "counter-revolutionists," and announcing that they were "joining" the Communist Party. This letter was published in the *Daily Worker* the next day.

It is impossible to describe the impression this turn of events made on the convention. What a disastrous outcome of combinationist politics! It is safe to say that never in the history of the revolutionary movement was a faction so discredited and disgraced as the combinationist faction of Abern-Muste at that convention. The catastrophic climax made an unforgettable impression on the minds of young comrades who were getting their first serious lessons in revolutionary politics. Not a few young comrades who had been trapped in the combinationist labyrinth began their re-education at that convention. They learned a profound lesson there. When great principles and political positions are involved in a party dispute nobody will ever catch them again with monkey-chatter about the "regime."

Frustrated and beaten, his faction reduced to a demoralized handful, Abern "submitted" to the decisions of the convention under the principle of democratic centralism, not out of party loyalty but out of helplessness. Even in doing so, he made one final characteristic gesture of venomous spite. Weber, who had been one of the recognized leaders of the opposition, was denied a place on the slate of candidates to represent the minority in the new National Committee. That was designed to "punish" him for putting party loyalty above the interests of the faction and coming out strongly for party unity. It goes without saying that the majority of the convention would not tolerate such a contemptible procedure. The majority withdrew one of its own candidates in Weber's favor. That is the way all of us, Shachtman and Burnham included, appraised the "role" of Weber "in the dispute of those years" when everybody's "role" was clear beyond any misunderstanding.

* * *

That party convention in the early spring of 1936 settled the question of entry into the S.P. The leadership and the great majority of the party turned their attention to the new problems and new tasks. Muste forsook the bloc with Abern against Cannon in order to make a bloc with the Lord against another devil. Abern turned to the task of holding his clique together at all costs by his notorious correspondence-school method of "keeping the comrades informed" of all the most confidential matters of the leading committee.

This sordid business of unceasing intrigue and persistent disloyalty, continued after the convention, was known to all the informed comrades in leading circles and was recorded from time to time in correspondence between them. During an absence from the city a few weeks later on account of illness I received a letter from Burnham stating:

> A letter received last night from Meyers contains the following: "We learned from ——— that you are going to the I.C.L. conference. We learned in the presence of non-members of our tendency that your trip is confidential within the Political Comm. She gives Abern as her authority for that information and some more besides." A letter received at the same time from Kerry contains the following: ". . . Last night in the presence of several comrades and an outsider, Comrade ——— stated that we had ceased to work for the Fourth International. I took exception to the statement and challenged her to produce evidence. . . . She stated that she had received information from a member of the Pol. Comm., that at a recent meeting of the Pol. Comm. this very question was discussed and resulted in a confirmation of her amazing contention. I flatly denied the truth of the contention, and said that I couldn't and wouldn't believe it. Thereupon she proceeded to produce a letter written by Abern and read the part upon which she based her contention. It was to the effect that there was to be a conference of the I.S. and that Jim Cannon was to attend this conference but the entire matter was to be kept very secret and confidential. That Comrade Trotsky was to participate in this conference and it was preparatory to a conference to be called by the I.C.L., etc. . . . She stated that *the fact that our participation in this conference was to be secret, we had ceased to work for the Fourth Intern. Even to the point of affirming allegiance to the Second . . . !*

That is one incident out of dozens that are known to all the leading comrades. Burnham knew what he was talking about when he stated in the document submitted to the Political Committee last June that the Abern clique "has been kept alive and still lives," among other things, "by joint distribution of gossip and information including confidential information." On November 17, 1936, when Burnham was in sharp conflict with me over some questions of policy and procedure in the S.P., but long before the idea of a bloc with Abern had yet dawned in his mind, he wrote to me in California: "We all know Abern's perspective. As usual, he fights for his perspective with his clique methods, stirring up trouble, throwing monkey wrenches when no one is looking, fishing in the stirred up waters. We saw some of it in the first six weeks. The clamping down at our leading committee just before you left, and

Muste's defection slowed him up some. But he continues in his own way; reports come filtering in."

In that same letter, before the clique of Abern had been miraculously dissolved and the "clique" of Cannon just as miraculously invented, he wrote about my methods of fighting for a position with which he disagreed: "Naturally, you do not fight for it nor carry it out as Abern does. You are no cliquist; you favor in your rough Irish fashion 'the Bolshevik fist'." Naturally, Burnham's opinion at that time of my roughness was somewhat exaggerated, as subsequent events showed. Indeed, my methods in those disputes were very mild, even pacifistic. But Burnham was 100 per cent right when he said there was nothing "cliquist" about them. And that evaluation would be 100 per cent correct today, or any other time.

The whole party remembers with gratitude and appreciation the magnificent work that was done by our comrades in the Trotsky Defense Committee in 1936-37. The success of the task required the collaboration not simply of all the members of our tendency, but of the Thomasite Socialists and, also, of a wide circle of unattached liberals and radicals. Tact and discretion and a broad policy were necessary; it would have been fatal to conduct this tremendous enterprise as a narrow "Trotskyist" faction affair. By and large, I think, these dangers were avoided without sacrificing too much in the political content of the Committee's work. But at one stage, during the absence of Novack and the illness of Morrow, Abern was placed temporarily in charge of the office. According to the testimony of all the comrades involved, he immediately converted the office into a factional headquarters, not of the Trotskyist faction as a whole, but of a faction of the Trotskyist faction. Morrow was compelled to return to the office before he had recovered from his illness on the demand of the conscientious office manager, comrade Pearl Kluger.

Abern has always been completely blind to the interests of the party, and even to the larger interest of the general movement, when the interests of his own petty and contemptible clique were involved. It is such occurrences as the one which transpired in the Trotsky Defense Committee that Burnham had in mind when he said the posts that Abern fills are always "administered in such a way as to help in the maintenance of his clique."

In the early summer of 1937 it became evident that our faction struggle in the Socialist Party was coming to a head. A highly confidential meeting of the leading committee of our faction was held to discuss our strategy and make our plans for the unavoidable and necessary split. A few days later Jack Altman had a complete report of this meeting, including its confidential aspects, what this one had said, what the other one had said, and what had finally been decided—all our "military" secrets. Altman published this report broadcast in the ranks of the Socialist Party, and it caused us no little embarrassment and damage. The report of our confidential meeting, which Altman published, consisted of a letter written by Abern to a factional associate in another city who was not even a member of the National Committee and who had no right whatever to the information that was withheld from other comrades for the time being, for obvious reasons. According to Abern, the letter went astray in the mails and fell into Altman's hands.

Needless to say, this betrayal of confidence, on top of all the experience that had gone before, aroused the greatest indignation in the leading circles of our party. Drastic action against Abern was seriously contemplated. Indignation mounted still higher a short time later when it was discovered that a highly confidential letter dealing with our strategy in the split struggle with the S.P. bureaucrats, a letter meant only for the small directing group of our faction, was made known to individual members of the party and discussed throughout the party ranks in New York. We went so far on that occasion as to appoint a control commission (Cannon and Shachtman!) to investigate the leak. The control commission established by the unimpeachable testimony of comrades that Abern had made the contents of this letter known to them. If we did not take drastic disciplinary action against Abern at that time it was only because we were in the very thick of a desperate struggle with the S.P. centrists, and, whether wisely or not, deemed it best to pass over an act of disloyalty once again in order to concentrate all energy and attention on the struggle against the centrist enemy. Besides, our terrible "regime" never punished anybody for anything, and for some incomprehensible soft-headed reason did not want to spoil its record.

* * *

In "The War and Bureaucratic Conservatism" we are presented with a touching picture of a reformed and purified cliquist who, "during the past three years," has not only ceased to make trouble in the party on his own account, but has even played the part of a benevolent policeman settling the disputes instigated by others. "As a matter of fact, Abern, who with Weber led the fight against entry, has during the past three years up to the outbreak of the present dispute, gone to the most extreme lengths to avoid all disputes and to quiet them when they arose."

The truth is simply that the Abern clique was so discredited by its past performances that it did not dare to conduct any struggles *in the open.* The Abern clique has never had a political platform and has never in its ten year history undertaken to conduct an open struggle without influential allies to furnish the political program and the "face." Originally it had Shachtman, then Muste and Spector, and now Burnham—and Shachtman again. Between times the clique keeps under cover, peddles its gossip, mutters grievances and complaints about the regime, disorients young and inexperienced comrades—and lays in wait for the outbreak of a conflict among the influential leaders. Thereupon it seeks to peddle its support for the political program of the opposition—any program—in return for a combination on the "organization question."

When this opportunity is lacking, the Abern group, like a Balkan state, "avoids disputes," not from good will, but from helplessness and fear to stand on its own feet. The entire history of our movement, not merely "the past three years," has shown that the Abern clique, the Balkan state of the party, keeps under cover when there is peace in the party, but is always ready for war the moment it can find a powerful ally to "guarantee its borders" and even open up the prospect of a little extension of "territory."

Clique politics and combinationism and the Abern group which represents and symbolizes these odious practices are indeed, as Shachtman wrote in 1936, "a sinister current in the blood stream of the party." They contribute not to the education but to the corruption of the party. The party must cure itself of this disease in order for it to live and go forward to the accomplishment of its great tasks. The attempt of the opposition combination to slur over the record of the Abern clique has made necessary this extensive account of its real history, compounded from beginning to end of unassailable and irrefutable facts. The Abern clique, like all cliques, thrives in the dark. It was necessary to drag it out into the light of day and show the party what it is and what it has always been. The threat of split in the present situation, to which the perfidious group of Abern has contributed in the highest degree, is a final warning to the party: clique politics and combinationism cannot be tolerated any longer! In order for the party to live, clique politics and combinationism must be destroyed. The forthcoming convention of the party is confronted by this unpostponable task.

9—THE QUESTION OF THE PARTY REGIME

In this section, I intend to discuss the question of the party "regime" and to take up the arguments and accusations contained in that fantastic Winchellized document called "The War and Bureaucratic Conservatism." I should remark at the outset, in justice to Winchell, that he gained his outstanding reputation as a gossip by a more or less careful attitude toward the accuracy of the tidbits he retailed. The gossip column of the opposition lacks this distinction. I picked it up for a critical reading, pencil in hand, with the intention of marking the outstanding points. I soon put the pencil aside, for I found myself marking almost every line of every page.

In the entire document of approximately 25,000 words there is not a single honest paragraph. Those incidents which are reported accurately are only half told. Those which are reported fully and correctly are misunderstood. Suspicions and prejudices are dished up as statements of fact, and spiced by not a few direct falsehoods. Everything that happened over the period they report is tendentiously distorted and misinterpreted. And the most important facts and incidents are passed over in silence. The whole concoction is dishonest from beginning to end—a typical product of that petty-bourgeois politiciandom which counterposes falsifications, petty complaints, personal accusations and morsels of gossip to principled arguments.

Bolshevism has not been the only honest political movement of modern times merely because of the superior moral quality of the Bolsheviks—their moral superiority is incontestable—but because, as the only authentic Marxists of our time, they alone correctly interpret and defend the immediate and historical interests of the workers in their struggle for emancipation. There is no contradiction between the theories and politics of the Bolsheviks and the interests of the workers and of their vanguard party. They can tell the truth—the whole truth. They have no need for the lies and falsifications, the half-truths, distortions and subterfuges which are the stock in trade of petty-bourgeois politicians of all kinds.

Reversing the political method of the Marxists, who always put the political questions first and subordinate the organization questions to them, our petty-bourgeois opposition, like every other petty-bourgeois group, has devoted the main burden of its arguments to a criticism of the party regime, that is, the leadership and its "method" of leading the party. It was this question and not the Russian question which united the leadership of the bloc, and it is indubitable that the bulk of their supporters—who are predominantly petty-bourgeois elements without much political experience —were recruited for the faction by arguments centering around the questions of the regime.

Such questions, in the best case, are secondary in importance to the theoretical and political issues in dispute and had to be subordinated to them in the discussion. It would have been absurd for us, in the early stages of the discussion, to take time out to answer these trivia. However, now that the fundamental questions have been sufficiently clarified, it is timely to take up the secondary questions for consideration and to give to the oppositionist critics the reply they have so insistently demanded. In this field also, there is something to be learned; first, about the facts as against the fiction; second, about the important points of difference as against the trivial incidents that are piled mountain high; and third, about the intimate connection between the disagreements on these points and our conflict with the opposition bloc on the fundamental questions.

If we sift out the great mass of material in the documents of the opposition devoted to the regime, attempt to classify the various complaints and grievances and criticisms and put each in its appropriate pile, we eventually break down the indictment of the party regime into the following main divisions.

1) The regime (the leadership) is conservative in its politics.

2) It is bureaucratic in its methods.

3) The present leading group (the majority of the National Committee) is in reality dominated by a "clique" which stands above the Committee and rules the party in an irregular and unconstitutional manner.

4) The "clique," however, has a "leader cult" and is itself dominated by a single person, the others being merely "hand raisers."

5) The single person who stands above the "clique" and above the Committee, and who exercises a "one-man leadership" in the party, is Cannon.

They place me in mid-air on the apex of a non-existent pyramid. The first necessity is to get down to earth. From that more solid point of vantage it is not difficult to answer all the most important points of the indictment and to explain the situation in the party leadership in terms of reality. If, in doing so, I must undertake the not very pleasant task of speaking a great deal about myself and the part I have played or failed to play in the making of party history, the party comrades must understand that I do so only because the question has been posed in this personal way. I will not evade even the

personal accusations or leave them unanswered. We have no reason
to evade anything because all the truth and all the right is on our
side. Our mistakes and our shortcomings, which are plentiful enough,
are barely touched by the criticisms of the opposition. Their attack
is directed at our merits, not our faults.

The main criticisms cover the whole period since the Chicago
convention, more than two years ago. On the theory or assumption
that all was bad they assign responsibility for everything that was
done or not done to the present majority of the National Committee,
or as they call it, "the Cannon regime." But nobody has been able
to discover any great difference between the methods of the party
regime of the past couple of years or so and all the years that preceded them since the beginning of our movement. The oppositionists
do not attempt to make any such distinction. It is the record as a
whole that is under attack. The question of the regime, says Abern
in his letter to Trotsky, *"has never been resolved satisfactorily* during all these years." And Johnson, the lyrical historian of our movement, who has seen nothing and knows everything, writes: "For ten
years the leadership has been Cannon's." (If Johnson, as it may be
assumed, is referring to the entire history of the Fourth Internationalist movement in America, it should be pointed out that it began
not ten years ago, but eleven and one-half years ago.)

Since I am far from repudiating the record of these past eleven
and one-half years; since I consider it on the whole good, not bad;
since, to speak frankly, I believe that our party, modelled on the
Russian Bolshevik Party, has been built more firmly and stands nearer than any other to the pattern of its great prototype—"it is the
second party in history which has built itself on Bolshevik lines,"
says the ineffable Johnson—since I hold these opinions of our eleven
and one-half years' work and achievements, I have no reason whatever to disclaim any part of the responsibility that can rightfully
be assigned to me. But it is historically inaccurate, and prejudicial
to a real understanding of the present fight in the party leadership,
which has its roots in the past, to assign all the credit, or, if you
please, all the blame, to me. Many people contributed to the building of the party. No party in history was ever more democratic,
more exempt from apparatus compulsion or restrictions of any
kind, than ours. In this free democratic atmosphere our movement
developed as a social organism in which many different forces, tendencies and individuals had the fullest opportunity to reveal their
real qualities, and to make their contributions to the development
of the party and the shaping of its leading cadre.

But our party, no more than any other, could escape the influence and pressure of its hostile class environment. From the beginning of our movement this pressure has been expressed to one degree or another in the struggle of tendencies within the party. Our party has not been a homogeneous Bolshevik party, as the superficial Johnson implies, but an organization struggling to attain to the standard of Bolshevism, and beset all the time by internal contradictions. The present internal struggle is simply the climactic paroxysm of this long internal struggle of antipathetic tendencies.

The leadership of the party (the regime) has never, since the beginning, been monopolized by a single person or even by a single tendency. In times of open factional struggle the majority has always depended upon the minority to one degree or another and been compelled to share responsibilities with it. In times of party peace the central leadership rested not upon a single person but upon a grouping of individuals of different types with points both of agreement and of conflict among them. An equilibrium in this leading group, never too stable, was continuously propped up by the device of mutual compromises and concessions.

The party "regime" since the Chicago convention—more correctly, since 1935—has not been represented by a single harmonious and homogeneous group, but rather by an unstable *coalition*. This coalition held together, despite considerable internal friction, in the absence of fully matured political differences. It fell apart only when the inherent tendencies of its different component parts were compelled to reveal themselves under the pressure of the approaching war crisis. The friction, the instability, and the disagreements and conflicts only occasionally broke out into open struggle, and were far more often adjusted by mutual compromises and concessions. This situation the opposition leaders now try to explain retroactively as the result of the machinations of a secret "clique." In reality, all this simply testifies, on the one hand to the lack of homogeneity in the leading committee; and on the other hand, to the fact that the fundamental differences in general orientation had not yet been definitively established. It required the pressure of the crisis engendered by the approaching war to reveal with full clarity the political physiognomy of the groups and the individuals in the coalition leadership. This is shown in the gradual, long-drawn-out development of the conflict before it exploded in the open in the present faction fight.

It is precisely in times of crisis that the real character of a leader shows itself most clearly. But these inner qualities of the individual are often adumbrated beforehand, and are usually observed by those who are in a position to see things in a close view as they develop from day to day over a long period of time. This has been the case with the representatives of the two camps involved in the present struggle, and it has not taken us by surprise. The leaders of the two camps did not come to their present positions by accident. Neither did the two antagonistic tendencies in the party ranks—the proletarian and the petty-bourgeois—rally around the contending factions in the party leadership without a deep instinctive feeling that this was for them in each case the necessary alignment. The polarization in the leadership produced almost immediately a similar polarization in the party ranks. Each faction in the now divided leadership attracted to itself those elements whose inner tendencies they most truly represent.

The leadership which has now fallen apart into factions can properly be said to have been consolidated in the struggle against the Muste-Abern combination and the sectarian Oehlerites. It took over the direction of the party at the convention in the spring of 1936. During the entire period of our work in the Socialist Party, that is, for a whole year, I was, as is known, absent from the center, in California. The administration and political direction of our faction in the S.P. was in the hands of the present minority, primarily of Burnham and Shachtman. True, I attempted to participate in this direction by correspondence, but without much success. It was during this period that the leaders of the present opposition first showed to me their abominable and intolerable bureaucratic conception of leadership as a function that belongs exclusively to the people in the office at the center. My criticisms and proposals "from the field" got scant consideration.

My stay in California, my personal relations with the comrades there, and my collaboration with them in fruitful political and propagandistic work and in trade union activity, will always remain a happy memory. At the same time, I must say, my futile attempts to participate by correspondence in the work of the New York center; my inability to get from them the slightest sign of understanding, or consideration or comradely aid for the heavy tasks we were undertaking in California; their callous and stupid bureaucratic disregard of our local opportunities, problems and difficulties; their narrow-minded, suspicious, *office-leaders'* hostility to the launching of *Labor Action;* their mean-spirited sabotage of this enterprise, and their attempt even to construe it as a "maneuver" against them—all that stands out as perhaps the most infuriating experience of all my activity in the revolutionary movement. I cannot think of it even to this day without bitter resentment.

"Go fight City Hall!"—says the New York push-cart peddler with ironic despair when he means to say: "It is hopeless; you can't get justice or even a hearing from the office-proud officials there." The people who were running things in the New York center in those days taught me an unforgettable lesson in how not to lead the activities of field workers from the office. I understand how the comrades of our auto fraction felt when they encountered the same attitude from "the office." I know their white-hot anger, because I, myself, have lived it. Down with office leadership! To hell with office leadership! You can never build a proletarian movement from an office!

* * *

The great bulk, though not all, of the concrete criticisms of the opposition are directed at the "regime" which was formally constituted at the Chicago convention [December 1937-January 1938] and which continued in office up till the second convention last July. Very well, whose regime was it?

This not unimportant question must have occurred to the opposition leaders when they finished writing their indictment. After painting in endless pages of denigration a horrific picture of party weakness, sickness and failure, and assigning all the responsibility to the "party regime," and thereby to "Cannon," they suddenly and unexpectedly reminded themselves that the picture must be a bit one-sided. They tacked on a parenthetical remark: "In closing: We do not blame Cannon for all the ills of the party." Naturally, I appreciate this generous gesture "in closing." But the real picture will be still clearer, it will be a more accurate representation of reality, if a few concrete details are added.

The Political Committee which was responsible for the direction of the party during that entire period consisted of six members of the present opposition—plus Cannon. The other members were Burnham, Shachtman, Abern, Widick, McKinney, Gould. Does the history of the international labor movement offer anywhere a more bizarre performance than six out of seven members of a decisive committee—all of them "leaders" by their own admission—complaining about the committee's methods of operation and blaming the seventh member? What were the noble six doing when the seventh member was leading the party astray? Did Cannon have more than one vote? Was anything ever decided, or could anything be decided without their agreement? Were any decisions made, any statements issued, any political directives given, anybody expelled, without their vote? Was anybody, anywhere, at any time, appointed or removed from the terrible "apparatus" without their

sanction? Let them wriggle all they will, they can't get away from
the fact that the P.C., the "regime" about which they are complaining,
was *their* P.C.—plus Cannon.

Moreover, at least a good one-third of the time I was absent
from New York, on trips to the field or abroad. Perhaps during
those intervals, the six Trilbies, free from the influence of any
Svengali, introduced radical improvements in the functioning of
the Committee, substituted "progressive" politics for "conservatism"
and eliminated bureaucratic practices? No, those were just the times
when things really went to hell on a bicycle.

On one of these occasions the emancipated P.C. interpreted our
Labor Party policy in New York to mean that we could support
candidates of the American Labor Party regardless of their endorsement by capitalist parties. The P.C. minutes of September 23, 1938
read: "We give specific critical support to all independent candidates of the A.L.P., irrespective of whether such candidates have
also received endorsement by any other parties or groups. Carried."
This policy, fathered by Burnham, would have obligated us to support LaGuardia, an enrolled member of the American Labor Party,
justified the Thomas-Altman socialists in our big fight and split
with them over precisely this issue, and deflected the party from
the *class line* of supporting the Labor Party only as an expression
of independent class politics. This absolutely untenable position was
changed on my initiative, with the support of Shachtman, after our
return from the World Congress.

On another occasion, during my absence in Europe, they produced the monstrosity of the auto crisis, an incident unique in the
entire history of our movement, insofar as it combined political in-
eptitude with bureaucratic procedure, each in the highest degree
imaginable.

The debacle of the auto crisis sealed the doom of the Committee.
Burnham and Shachtman attempted to compensate themselves for
the wounds inflicted upon their vanity by the auto fraction by working up an intrigue against me; they began to mutter for the first
time about a "Cannon clique" whose members had no "respect"
for the P.C. The Committee as a whole fell into a state of permanent paralysis, lost its authority, and no longer had a justification
or a right to existence. The *coup de grace* administered to it by the
post-convention plenum was indeed a "stroke of mercy."

The record shows that the present majority of the National
Committee was not solely, nor even primarily, responsible for the
party regime from the Chicago convention to the July convention
in New York. That is true also of the interim Political Committee

which existed between the July convention and the October plenum. The majority of the members of this Committee also belonged to the present minority. It was only at the October plenum, when the fundamental dispute over the Russian question was brought to the fore, that the Political Committee was reorganized and the present majority of the National Committee took full responsibility for its composition.

It is established that during the whole period from the Chicago convention to the plenum last October the present minority constituted a majority in the directing body of the party. Surely this little detail must be taken into account in evaluating the criticisms which have been directed against the party regime. To be sure, the members of the majority, and I personally, bear part of the responsibility. To the extent that the present minority, or a part of them, supported our propositions and our methods, or we theirs, we bear the full responsibility and do not in any way disavow it. Nobody led us astray. The individual members of the present minority may disclaim responsibility for their actions and repudiate themselves as much as they please. As for us, we repudiate nothing that was done with our participation and approval.

10—"CONSERVATISM"

The attempt of Burnham, the exponent of "experimental politics," to define the party regime as conservative, and to elevate the question of conservatism to a political principle, contributes only confusion to the party discussion. Different meanings can be given to this word, not all of them derogatory in certain situations. The substitution of such general terms, devoid of class content and class political meaning, for the precise terminology of Marxism in describing groups and tendencies, and their class basis and characteristics, cannot help to clarify the disputes and educate the party. To be conservative, that is, to stand still when there are good opportunities to go forward, is undoubtedly a fault. On the other hand, to stand one's ground when others are retreating is a virtue not to be despised. This kind of "conservatism," which we show in standing firmly on the basic principles of Marxism and the program of the Fourth International, while others are running away from them, has been very aptly characterized as necessary for the preservation of the party.

If conservatism is to be defined as meaning a tendency to routine, sluggishness, slowness in perceiving opportunities to move forward and hesitation in grasping these opportunities—in this sense it cannot be denied that our movement as a whole, and the "regime" along

with it, has been by no means free from sin. Such tendencies are im-
manent in every group which has a "sectarian" origin and is compelled by circumstances to live a long time in isolation. Many sections of the Fourth International fell victim to this sickness to such
a degree as to bring about their disintegration.

The tendency is very strong in all isolated groups to console themselves with the monotonous repetition of adherence to great principles
without seeking ways and means and new opportunities to apply
them. It expressed itself in full flower in our international movement as a whole, and also in the American section, in the resistance
of the sectarian groupings to the famous "French turn" and the
general orientation from a propaganda circle to mass work.

Conservatism, of a sort, expressed itself in the tendency, to which
we all more or less succumbed in the hard years of isolation, to
routine, lackadaisical procedure, over-caution, and an inclination
to be satisfied with extremely modest accomplishments. There is
no doubt that the present majority also is subject to justified criticism on this score. I personally do not believe that we could have
changed anything fundamentally in the position of our party, and
in the relation of forces between it and its rivals, by any amount of
hustling and bustling in this past eleven and one-half years. I do
believe that if we had displayed more energy, more initiative, more
daring, we could be perhaps twice as strong numerically as we are
today and in a better position for further advancement. We must
frankly acknowledge these defects and strive to overcome them. I
doubt, however, that our minority can help us. What we need is
not so much the wisdom of precept as the inspiration of example.
That is always their weak point. They are far better talkers than
doers. Unlike Lenin's Bolsheviks, they do not match the word with
the deed.

I have said that all of us, including the majority, have shown
insufficient energy, initiative, etc. By that we acknowledge that we
are not Bolsheviks in our habits and practices, but only striving
to become such; slovenliness and slackness are Menshevik traits. But
our theory, Marxism, is the only revolutionary theory in the world;
there is nothing conservative about it. Can we be justly indicted
for conservatism in our politics, that is, in the *application* of our
theoretical principles? I do not believe our record justifies such
an indictment. The essence of politics is to understand the realities
of a given situation, to know what is possible and what is excluded;
above all, to know what to do next—and to do it.

In the first period of the Trotskyist movement of America, when
we were an isolated handful against the world, we deliberately re-

stricted ourselves to propaganda work and avoided any kind of pretentious maneuvers or activities beyond our capacity. Our first task, as we saw it, and correctly, was to build a cadre; only then could we go to the masses. The old-timers can well recall how we were pestered in those early days by the bustling windbags of the Weisbord type, who promised us a short-cut to the mass movement if we would only abandon our "conservative" propagandistic routine, substitute a grandiose program of activities for the modest tasks we had set for ourselves, and in general take up "mass work"—as though it were a simple matter for our decision. Some of the hysterical agitation of our present minority is strangely reminiscent of the blather of this revolutionary jitterbug. By sticking to our modest propagandistic tasks we recruited a cadre on the basis of fundamental principles. In the next period, when new opportunities opened up, we were prepared for a decisive turn toward more expansive activity in the mass movement, and made it. As for Weisbord, who had worn himself out with his own agitation in the meantime, he fell by the wayside.

Did we overlook some opportunities for the application of the new orientation toward mass work? Undoubtedly we did. Except in a few localities, we let the great movement of the C.I.O. pass over our heads. But we did grasp some of the main opportunities. The moment the Muste movement began to take shape as a political organization, we approached it for fusion and successfully carried it out. In one operation we cleared a centrist obstacle from the path and enlarged our own forces. When the ferment in the Socialist Party offered favorable opportunities for our intervention, we steered a course directly toward it, smashed the resistance of the sectarians in our own ranks, entered the Socialist Party and effected a fusion with the left wing. We seized opportunities to penetrate the trade union movement in several localities and industries and today have the firmest proletarian bases of the party there.

The main core of the present majority was in the forefront of all these progressive enterprises. This record cannot properly be described as conservative. Just the contrary. We must admit that by far not enough was done with the most basic task of all, the penetration of the trade union movement. But what was done in this field was done almost entirely by us. That speaks not only for our dynamically progressive political line but for what is still more important, our *proletarian orientation*. It is precisely the petty-bourgeois elements in the party, above all the clique of Abern, now shouting at the top of their voices against our "conservatism," who have displayed from beginning to end the most conservative tendencies and the greatest aversion to any real participation in the turbulent mass movement of the workers.

The opposition, following Burnham, began to designate us as conservative only when we refused to accept a revision of the program of the Fourth International on the Russian question after the signing of the Soviet-Nazi pact, and instead, reaffirmed our fundamental position. Their whole case rests on this. From it they construe a conservative tendency in our whole past record. They also rail at our stick-in-the-mud attitude toward the fundamental concepts of Marxism—the class theory of the state, the class criterion in the appraisal of all political questions, the conception of politics, including war, as the expression of class interests, and so forth and so on. From all of this they conclude that we are "conservative" by nature, and extend that epithet to cover everything we have done in the past.

Such "conservatism," which they consider a fault, we hold to be a virtue. We aim to "hold on" firmly to these principles which have been verified in the test of the greatest historic events, and which in our view constitute the only program of proletarian liberation. We have carefully examined the substitutes offered to us by Burnham. They are not the products of his own manufacture. He is not the inventor or originator of anything. The offerings of Burnham are shoddy stuff, and if you inspect them closely you will see on every item the trade mark of another class. Burnham is merely the broker of shop-worn merchandise that has been palmed off on the workers time and again by bourgeois idéologists and always to the detriment of their struggle. We will have none of it. We stick to our own program. We accept no substitutes. If this be conservatism, make the most of it.

11—"BUREAUCRATISM"

In all the documents and speeches of the opposition, the party leadership is represented as bureaucratic in the most invidious sense of the term. More precisely, the party regime is depicted, sometimes by insinuation, sometimes openly and directly, as Stalinist in character. Burnham, who denies the inevitability of socialism, is nevertheless convinced that Stalinism develops "inevitably" out of Bolshevism. From that viewpoint he indicts us in the name of supra-class morality as "a cynical group of small-time bureaucrats" who constitute "the rotten clique of Cannon." ("Science and Style.") And Johnson, who learned all about Bolshevism and Stalinism from Souvarine, assures the party that, "He [Cannon] is showing more nakedly the Stalinist conceptions of party struggle and party discipline which he brought with him from the Third International into the

Fourth." The lengthy document on "The War and Bureaucratic Conservatism" was written to sustain this fundamental thesis of the opposition: The party regime is Stalinist in character.

The argument is not a new one. Every opposition in our movement, since its inception more than a decade ago, has sung the same song and has always attracted supporters on that basis, as the present opposition attracts them. Why? The explanation is simple.

Stalinism has not only disoriented its own supporters, but, to a considerable degree, also its opponents. Many of them see in Stalinism only bad methods. They overlook the privileged social grouping and the anti-proletarian policy which these bad methods are designed to serve. Victims of this superficial view of Stalinism never lack, at least up till now they have never lacked, unscrupulous demagogues to exploit their prejudices and to cry "Stalinism" when they run out of political or theoretical arguments. Shachtman, together with Abern, played this demagogue's role in the early years of the Left Opposition in this country, before our tiny movement had yet attained an "apparatus," to say nothing of a privileged stratum controlling the apparatus. By 1935, however, Shachtman found himself on the side of "Stalin-Cannon" in the struggle for entry into the Socialist Party; and the "anti-Stalinist" folderol was being directed against *him*, as a leading representative of the party "regime." Thereupon in self-defense, Shachtman—always acutely sensitive to anything that touches him personally—thought better of the matter and submitted the charge of "Stalinism" to an analysis. This analysis is worth quoting here. Neither the regime nor the old arguments launched against it have changed in any fundamental respect since he argued on the other side of the question.

In an article entitled "The Question of 'Organizational Methods'," signed by Shachtman under the date of July 30, 1935, and published in the Workers Party *Internal Bulletin*, No. 1, he answers the argument about "Stalinism" as follows:

> But then (it is now argued by some), didn't Lenin launch a struggle against Stalin purely because of the latter's organizational methods, his rudeness and disloyalty, and propose on those grounds to remove him from his post? To this reference is added the broad insinuation that we here constitute a similar bureaucracy, with similar methods, who must be fought as mercilessly as Lenin and Trotsky fought Stalin.
>
> The analogy does not even limp because it hasn't a leg to stand on. It is of the most superficial nature and betrays a failure to understand the problem of the Stalinist bureaucracy and Lenin's attitude towards its central figure. (1) It is not true that Lenin opposed Stalin solely on organizational grounds. The famous testament is prefaced by the significant observation that the rule of the

proletariat is based upon a collaboration of two classes. This creates the whole environment for the growth of a Soviet Bureaucracy. This bureaucracy, in the period of its degeneration, in the midst of a constantly self-reproducing capitalism, represents the pressure of alien classes. Because of this fact, *the bureaucracy tends more and more to bear down upon the proletarian kernel of the country; it shows an increasing contempt for it and a growing inclination to lean upon enemy classes.* Stalin was the personification of this bureaucratic tendency. If the testament is read in connection with the noted articles and letters Lenin wrote shortly before his death, the political and class connection will become apparent. If nothing is learned from the testament except that "Stalin is rude—remove him!"—then, indeed, nothing has been learned. (2) *The bureaucracy in the Soviet Union is a social phenomenon.* It has deep roots in Russia's past and present historical development. It has close class connections. It has tremendous material and intellectual power at its disposal—power to corrupt, to degenerate, to undermine the proletarian base of the Union. To speak of our pitiful little "bureaucracy" in the Workers' Party—or any section of it—in the same breath with the Stalinist bureaucracy, can be excused only on the grounds of political infantilism.

That quotation deserves study by the comrades in the party who want to probe to the bottom of this light-minded talk about "Stalinism" in connection with the regime in our party. The whole paragraph deserves study line by line and word by word. I have underlined a couple of especially important sentences. "The bureaucracy tends more and more to bear down upon the proletarian kernel of the country." That is the universal characteristic of every privileged bureaucracy. It is precisely in order to serve their own special privileged interests, as against the interests of the proletarian mass, that every labor bureaucracy ties itself up in one way or another with "enemy classes." As Shachtman aptly says, it "leans upon" enemy classes and "bears down" upon the proletariat. It is in order to carry through this policy, against the interests and against the will of the proletarian mass, that bureaucratic formations of the privileged groups and bureaucratic methods become necessary. That is true not only of the Stalinist bureaucracy; it is true also of the trade union bureaucracy, the bureaucracy of the parties of the Second International and of all reformist labor organizations.

Now I want to put two questions to the leaders of the opposition:

1. Where and when did the regime in our party "bear down" on the proletarian kernel? Name me one branch, or one trade union fraction, that has complained in the discussion of bureaucratic mistreatment by the party leadership. The whole discussion, with its voluminous documentation, and its innumerable speeches, has not

brought to light a single such case *insofar as the present majority of the National Committee is concerned!*

The air has been shattered with the shrieks of the individual leaders of the petty-bourgeois faction—God, how they suffered! But not a word of complaint has come in from "the proletarian kernel" of the party. From all parts of the country, during the discussion, I received letters from rank and file comrades asking "information" about the bureaucratism in the party, but nobody among them volunteered to give any information. A very strange animal, this bureaucratism, like the purple cow; everybody hears about it, but nobody knows about it. Nobody, that is, except a coterie of thin-skinned petty-bourgeois intellectuals, half-intellectuals and would-be intellectuals who magnify a few pin-pricks suffered by their individual persons into a murderous bayonet charge against the rank and file of the party.

I say that bureaucratism in the real sense of the word is not known in our party! Some of our best friends, hearing this stupid and venomous charge repeated over and over again, and reasoning that "where there is so much smoke there must be some fire," may be thinking: "Perhaps a little self-criticism would be in order here." *Not on this point!* The proletarian majority of the National Committee has plenty of political faults and sins to account for; it has to admit a great deal of inefficiency, neglected opportunities, slackness in discipline, etc. But bureaucratic mishandling of the party units or the trade union fractions—*none whatsoever!*

Practically every proletarian branch of the party supports the majority! Every trade union fraction in the party from coast to coast, with the sole exception of a couple of white collar fractions in New York City, supports the majority unanimously, or almost unanimously! This is not by accident. Bureaucratism strikes, first and last, at the proletarian sections of every organization; bureaucratism "bears down upon the proletarian kernel." If the proletarian sections of the party were instinctively drawn to the majority and repelled by the opposition from the first day of the discussion, it is because, among other reasons, they are most sensitive to every concrete manifestation of bureaucratism. It is because they judge the "organization question" not by what they read in ponderous documents, and still less by what somebody buzzes in their ear, but by what they see and know from their own experiences with the party leadership and its different sections.

2. You call the apparatus of the party a bureaucracy, Messrs. Abern, Burnham and Shachtman? You go further and describe it as "Stalinist" in character? Very well, gentlemen. Tell us, please, what

is the social basis of this "Stalinist" bureaucracy in the American section of the Fourth International? What are its privileges? Where is manifested its "inclination to lean upon enemy classes"—What classes? What special interests does it have to serve which compel it to "bear down upon the proletarian kernel?" Shachtman, in 1935, in the document cited above, informed Oehler-Abern-Muste that "the bureaucracy in the Soviet Union is a social phenomenon." What kind of a "social phenomenon" is our "pitiful little bureaucracy"?

After all, what is the "apparatus" of our party? What is this selection of people whom the self-sacrificing Burnham disdainfully calls "a cynical group of small-time bureaucrats" and a "rotten clique"? Let's take up this question, once and for all, and have it out. The "apparatus," that is, the National Committee and the functioning full-time staff of party workers, is not an economically privileged group and has no special interests of its own that are different from the interests of the party members as a whole. The reality is quite different. The full-time functionaries of the party are those comrades who are distinguished either by exceptional ability, which propels them into professional party work by the universal consent and approval of the party membership, or by the capacity for self-sacrifice, or both—those comrades who are willing to undertake functions as party workers for less compensation than even the most poorly paid worker as a rule can secure in private employment.

The rank and file of the party knows this very well and doesn't want to hear any more denigration of the professional party workers, especially from people who shrink from the sacrifices and duties of professional party work. Our party is not a party like the social democracy. We will not permit our movement to be led by spare-time heroes while the coolie work is done by the professional functionaries, who in addition have to stand the abuse of the "lords" who come around to visit the party once a week. The party honors and respects its professional staff. It considers the occupation of a professional revolutionist to be the most honorable of all occupations. The highest aspiration and ambition of every young party member should be to qualify himself for such a profession in life.

Our party "apparatus" is neither a bureaucracy, nor a faction, nor a clique. It is a selection of people who fulfill different functions according to their merits and capacities and experience and their readiness to serve the party at the cost of severe economic penalties. There has been no element of "patronage" in their selection; the very suggestion of such a thing is an intolerable insult, especially when it comes, as it usually does, from well situated dilettantes who never missed a dinner appointment for the revolution. Neither can it be justly maintained that there has been any factional discrimination or favoritism in the selection of party functionaries. The opposition has been represented, and well represented, especially in the editorial and office positions in the center.

The oppositionists themselves testify to this: "It is true that the members of the minority occupy many posts. . . . Cannon has not the least objection to everyone in the party doing as much work, even in prominent posts, as he is capable of handling." Then what are they complaining about? What kind of a bureaucracy is it that "has not the least objection" to anybody having any function he can "handle" even in "prominent posts"? Try to discover such a situation in a real bureaucracy—the Stalinist or Lewis-Green bureaucracies, for example. Their "posts" are almost invariably assigned to supporters of the "regime," and by no means to "anybody." If the party field workers are, almost without exception, supporters of the majority, it is not in repayment for "favors." It is rather because the petty-bourgeois minded type of secondary leaders, who gravitate naturally to the opposition, tend to shy away from field work, with its arduous duties and economic uncertainties. They prepare for civil war by first preparing for the civil service. A candidate for leadership in the camp of the majority, on the other hand, isn't taken very seriously until he has done a good stretch of field work, and shown what he can do and what he can learn in direct contact with workers in the class struggle.

As for the prominent trade unionists, they have attained positions of prominence in their field, not by "appointments" from New York, but by their own activities and merits which have been recognized by the workers. If the field workers and the trade unionists of the party tended from the outset of the fight to "take sides" against the office leaders of the opposition, it is not because they are addicts of some preposterous fascistic "leader cult" but, rather, from considerations of an opposite nature. The nature of their work, which is directly and immediately affected from day to day by the actions and decisions of the central party leadership, gives them a more intimate understanding of its real qualities. This determines a more critical attitude on their part than is the case of those party members, remote from the class struggle, who judge the leaders solely by their articles and their speeches. The party trade unionists know all the party leaders too well—they know people too well—to be "slavish idolators" of anybody, or to expect perfection from anybody. If the performance of the leaders of the majority at the center is by no means satisfactory to them—and that is no doubt the case—

they are in no hurry to exchange them for others whose performance has been worse. They are practical people; if they have to choose between evils, they take the lesser evil.

The fact that our party has no socially privileged bureaucracy, that its internal life is dominated by democracy rather than bureaucratism, does not of course obviate the possibility of bureaucratic practices and bureaucratic tendencies on the part of individuals and even of groups. But it is just these very critics of the opposition who have manifested such tendencies most crassly, and more times than once. Indeed, the tendency of the petty-bourgeois leaders is toward bureaucratic practices. From the nature of the faction it could hardly be otherwise. There are glaring instances which show how they manifested this tendency when they had a free hand and were able to act without the counteracting influence of the majority. Their conduct in the auto crisis is a classic example of intolerable bureaucratic procedure from beginning to end. And the end is not yet, for they have not yet acknowledged or corrected their indefensible procedure; they still refer to the auto crisis only in an attempt to explain away their own actions, to justify themselves at the expense of their critics, and to switch the issue and turn the attack against their critics.

In "The War and Bureaucratic Conservatism" they have space in a document of approximately 25,000 words for only one paragraph on the auto crisis. And this single paragraph is devoted, not to a discussion of the crisis and their conduct in it, but to a completely extraneous matter so as to make it appear that "Cannon," who was three thousand miles away at the time of the auto crisis, was nevertheless responsible for their debacle in this situation, as for everything else. In a remarkable article that belongs now to party history, "The Truth About the Auto Crisis," comrade Clarke has written the full account of the auto crisis, an account which is verified and documented at every point. That article will speak for itself, and will be source material for every discussion in the future over the concrete meaning of bureaucratic practices on the part of an office leadership.

Here I wish to make only a few general observations on this unsavory affair. The present minority were in full charge of the Political Committee; the seventh member, who had been responsible for all of their troubles, was across the wide ocean, and in no position to hamper or restrict their operations in any way. The auto crisis was a real test of the regime—their regime. It was a real test of their capacity to lead the party and to lead workers in a difficult and complicated situation. What did they do? They began by bungling the policy. This policy, cooked up in Burnham's study, pre-scribed a course of action for our fraction which was contrary to the movement of the workers in the industry, and which, if it had been followed out, would have swept our comrades out of the auto union in the space of a few weeks' time. When the whole auto frac-tion, which included the ablest trade unionists in the party and *four members of the N.C.*, rose up against them they "reaffirmed" their former position by a vote of *three to two, with one abstaining*, called that the decision of the party, and appealed to discipline and formal authority!

When they finally yielded to the pressure of the auto fraction, supplemented by the pressure of all N.C. members who had oppor-tunity to express themselves, they did it in a contemptible fashion. They washed their hands of the affair, and placed upon the auto fraction the full responsibility for carrying out the new policy. Then they made a spiteful attack on the auto fraction in a statement sent to the branches which also "warned" that the auto comrades would have bad luck with their policy and that the "line of the party"—that is, the line of Burnham, Widick and Abern—would be proved to be correct. Then, in typical Lovestoneite fashion, the typical fashion of any group of arrogant petty-bourgeois intellectuals, they turned the attack against the field workers who had corrected the false policy and shown their independence in protesting against it, announcing the discovery that they were mere "hand raisers" who belonged to a "rotten clique" of "small-time bureaucrats." It would be hard to find in the history of our movement a comparable exam-ple of haughty, ungracious and spiteful bureaucratism in a concrete situation. Bureaucratism indeed "bears down" upon the "proletarian kernel" of the party. But this proletarian kernel proved to be hardy and resistant and capable of asserting itself. That is its real crime in the eyes of the offended petty-bourgeois leaders-from-an-office.

Another example of unadulterated bureaucratism of the same type was shown in the proposals of Burnham and Shachtman in re-gard to the election policy of the Minneapolis branch last spring. Incalculable damage might have been done to the party and to the relations between the central leadership and the Minneapolis branch if these proposals had not been frustrated. The branch had originally nominated its own independent candidate for mayor. When a con-ference of trade unions nominated a labor candidate, the branch de-cided to withdraw its candidate and support the labor candidate. I was directed by the P.C. to investigate the matter while on a visit to the Minneapolis branch at that time. On my visit, I inquired about the conference which had nominated the labor candidate. I was told that it had been a well-attended conference of important unions and that the labor candidate was sponsored by them. I expressed the opinion that the action of the comrades in withdrawing their own candidate in this case, and supporting the labor candidate, was fully in accord with party policy and so reported to the P.C. at its meeting on May 2nd. Burnham promptly made a set of motions against the action. I quote the minutes of the Political Committee of May 2, 1939:

> Motions by Burnham: (1) That the P.C. considers the action of the Minneapolis local in withdrawing its own candidate from the mayoralty primaries and going over to support of Eide as (a) an opportunist concession to the conservative trade union bureaucrats, and (b) with respect to the support of Eide, a practice in conflict with the party's position in favor of genuinely independent working class political action.
>
> (2) The secretary is instructed to communicate with the Minneapolis local and present a thorough analysis of the action in the light of the above motion.
>
> (3) A carefully worded explanatory article on this situation and the point of view of the P.C. with reference to it shall be published in the *Appeal.*

A truly astounding proposal! Without further parley with Minneapolis, Burnham wanted to repudiate their policy publicly in the columns of our official organ in the midst of an election campaign. Shachtman expressed himself as ready to vote right then for Burnham's motion. (It was obvious that these two people, who are ostensibly opposed to all informal consultations between committee meetings, had discussed the matter between themselves and "convicted" Minneapolis in advance.) In this incident they showed the same traits as in the auto crisis a few months earlier, and demonstrated that they had learned nothing from that experience. The political line of Burnham's motion was absolutely incorrect; the Minneapolis comrades were right; and the proposed procedure—an out-of-hand repudiation in the public press of the party—was abominably bureaucratic.

Fortunately, on this occasion there were restraining influences in the Political Committee. Goldman, present as an N.C. member, moved: "That we instruct the secretary to write the Minneapolis local, asking for a full explanation of their action in withdrawing Comrade Hudson as candidate for Mayor and in supporting Eide." His motion was accepted and action deferred until more detailed information could be sent by the Minneapolis comrades. The P.C. minutes of May 16th, two weeks later, record further developments:

> Letter received from Minneapolis giving details as to the Minneapolis election situation.

Question raised by Burnham of need for information on several points.

Motion by Burnham: To ask the Minneapolis party for further information and that we lay over the document until that information is received. Carried.

The Minneapolis question was again on the agenda briefly and is recorded in the P.C. minutes of May 31st.

Letter from Minneapolis read, answering the last questions addressed to them on the election policy.

Motion: That the matter be laid over to the next committee meeting when Comrade Burnham will be present, since he made the original motion on this point. Carried.

The matter was finally disposed of at the P.C. meeting of June 6th. The minutes of this date cover the matter as follows:

Summary by Cannon of further information received from Minneapolis regarding the election situation.

General discussion.

Withdrawal by Burnham of his motion presented in the meeting of May 2nd, 1939, with following statement: "The further information that we have received indicates that the opinion which I formerly held and formulated in motions to the effect that support of Eide in the Minneapolis elections is incompatible with our labor party policy is incorrect and I, therefore, wish to withdraw the motion."

Motion by Cannon: That the P.C. considers that the action of the Minneapolis branch in withdrawing their candidate and supporting the candidacy of Eide was politically correct under the circumstances. Carried unanimously.

A truly illuminating chronicle of political irresponsibility and bureaucratism. Let every local organization of the party that is sensitive to the slightest danger of bureaucratic practices ponder over this incident. If Burnham-Shachtman had prevailed, the action of the Minneapolis comrades would have been repudiated in the *Socialist Appeal*, and they would have been publicly discredited. They would have had no alternative but to withdraw their support of Eide, the labor candidate, and re-enter their own independent candidate. Then, five weeks later, and about one week before the election, they would have been blandly informed that, after more thorough investigation, the P.C. motions were "withdrawn" and the Minneapolis branch free to make another flip-flop in public and support the candidacy of Eide after all. Perhaps the P.C. might even have been generous enough to repudiate its repudiation of the policy of the Minneapolis comrades. However, that is quite a speculative assumption. Even after Burnham had been compelled to withdraw his motion of censure he didn't have the decency, as the record shows, to make a positive motion of approval.

The leaders of the petty-bourgeois faction complain a good deal about the way their "prestige" has been undermined in the proletarian sections of the party. But the most malevolent enemy could not deal heavier blows to their influence and authority than they dealt themselves by such practices and methods as they employed in the auto crisis and in the case of the Minneapolis local elections.

12—THE "CLIQUE" AND THE "LEADER CULT"

The opposition has made no effort to establish the existence of a party bureaucracy as a privileged group whose interests are antagonistic to the interests of the rank and file, and whose policy, designed to serve these interests, must be imposed upon the party by bureaucratic means. Neither have they attempted to find any social basis for a ruling "clique" with its "leader cult." Yet, the Marxists analyze every labor bureaucracy or clique and explain its methods by first uncovering its social basis. It was by this method that Trotsky and the Bolshevik-Leninists disclosed the real nature of the Stalinist bureaucracy in the first instance, not as an accidental formation created by the arbitrary will or personal traits of an individual, but as a *social phenomenon*, which did not *begin* with a "leader cult" but *came to it* from necessity.

The Stalinist bureaucracy represents privileged social groupings which have appeared for the first time in history on the basis of a workers' state. The Marxists alone—that is, the Trotskyists—found the key to the real mystery of Stalinism. They first revealed its social base. Then they demonstrated that its privileges and special interests collide irreconcilably with the interests of the masses in their march toward socialism. In order to serve their special interests the Stalinist bureaucracy was compelled to introduce a line of policy which contradicted the program and tradition of the party. In order to impose such policy upon the party and upon the country, they were compelled to suppress party democracy, to force their line through by means of bureaucratic violence, and to concentrate all power in the party apparatus.

But the conflicts of class interests in the country, and the numerous rivalries and conflicts of interest between the various privileged groups, found a distorted expression in factional struggles within the apparatus itself. This unsettled the regime and created possibilities for the intervention of the party rank and file, and of the working mass in general. The Left Opposition for a time made its way through just such fissures in the apparatus and threatened its overthrow. This demonstrated to the bureaucracy the iron necessity of a still narrower concentration of power. The conflicting privileged groups required a means for the arbitration and regulation of their conflicts without the intervention of the masses, and in such a way as to unite them all against the masses. Out of this necessity, after the revolutionary wing of the party had been annihilated, emerged the single, all-powerful leader, the arbitrator, the Soviet Bonaparte, Stalin.

Stalin thus appears as a "leader" of an entirely different type from Lenin, who also enjoyed exceptional authority, and one who arrived at his position by an entirely different practice. Lenin, the Marxist, the revolutionist, truly expressed the interests of the masses and maintained his position by the consent and even the love of the most conscious section of the proletariat. Lenin consequently *leaned upon* the masses and required party democracy to mobilize their support against the privileged elements within the country and in the party. Stalin, the revisionist, the betrayer of the revolution, came to his position not by the voluntary will of the masses but in a struggle of the privileged groups against them. Stalin is not the "leader" because the people "love" him; it is obligatory to "love" him because he is the dictatorial power, the Soviet Bonaparte, whose prestige must be artificially inflated and promoted in order to strengthen his position as the arbitrator, defender and best representative of the privileged elements in the population. If anyone disagrees, there is the G.P.U. to convince him.

All the "methods" of Stalinism grew from the necessities of an unstable and highly privileged bureaucracy which cannot maintain itself by other methods, and dares not permit democratic procedures that would permit the masses to intervene. As for the Stalinist bureaucracies in the parties of the Comintern, they are simply the extensions of the Russian social phenomenon, its foreign agents. The main social base of the bureaucratic gang in the American Communist Party is in the Soviet Union. That explains the peculiarities which distinguish it from the bureaucracies of the trade union movement, the reformist political parties, etc.

When the light-minded oppositionist leaders attempt to establish an identity, or even an analogy, between our party staff and the Stalinist bureaucracy, they are constructing a house of cards which falls to pieces at the first touch. Turning their backs on the sociological analysis from which Marxism construes its politics, these self-styled "independent thinkers" reveal themselves, on this question also, as nothing but slavish imitators of the philistine journalists and petty-bourgeois moralists who have judged Stalinism by its methods and techniques, without understanding the social basis and role of Stalinism which dictate the employment of these techniques.

Many superficial anti-Stalinist journalists, noticing the political similarities of Stalinism and fascism—bureaucratic violence, one-man dictatorship, "totalitarian" suppression of all opposition—easily arrive at the conclusion that Stalinism and fascism are identical. The same people, mostly social democrats and radicals disillusioned in the proletarian revolution, observing that the Fourth International also has a leader of outstanding influence and authority, and without bothering to inquire whether this personal authority has a different source and significance, hasten to equate the defenders and betrayers of the Russian revolution and to announce: "Stalinism and Trotskyism—the same thing."

The theory that the distinguishing feature of Stalinism is its "leader cult" was the brilliant contribution of Brandler-Lovestone at the time when they were defending the domestic policies of the Stalinist party in the Soviet Union, denouncing the Fourth International's advocacy of a political revolution there as counter-revolutionary, and explaining that all the trouble was simply the result of a "bad regime" in the Stalinist party. It was their contention that if a reasonable amount of democracy was introduced into the Stalinist party, and the "cult of the leader" replaced by a situation in which Stalin could be "first among equals," everything would be all right, including the mass-murder of the Trotskyists.

It was these same profound and original thinkers—Brandler-Lovestone and the leaders of the Brandlerist off-shoot, the German S.A.P.* (Walcher and Co.)—who first put in circulation the theory that the movement of the Fourth International is afflicted with the "cult of the leader." The fact that Trotsky had at his disposal neither an army nor a G.P.U. nor control of employment to terrorize, nor money to corrupt people into "loving" him and acknowledging him as the supreme leader—these trifling details of difference were left entirely out of consideration. When one leaves the ground of Marxism he invariably overlooks precisely those details which are primary and fundamental and decisive. The centrists who had broken with Stalinism only after Stalinism had rejected their advances for the thousand and first time, were determined at all costs not to fall under the control of another "leader." They were hell-bent for "independence"—from Trotsky, that is, from Trotsky's ideas which they could not successfully combat or refute. And they demonstrated

---

*The S.A.P.—the Socialist Labor Party of Germany, a centrist organization. Among its leaders were Walcher, Froelich, and others. —*Ed.*

their independence by uniting with the Norwegian Labor Party and the London Bureau on the road to the People's Front and the social-patriotic betrayal in the "war of democracy against fascism."

The petty-bourgeois opposition in our party did not invent the theory that we have a "leader cult" and a "one-man regime" in the American party and in the Fourth International; they borrowed that, as they borrowed everything else, from alien sources. In the first days of the present discussion in our party the Lovestoneites, searching for kindred spirits, issued "An Appeal to Members and Followers of the Socialist Workers Party." The "Appeal" invited any waifs and strays we might have to join the Lovestoneite organization. The inducement? "There you will find an organization that works out its own policies, independently and democratically, to meet the needs and interest of the workers and not to follow a 'party line' laid down by the 'leader' in Moscow or in Mexico City." (*Workers' Age*, Oct. 21, 1939.) I reprint this quotation here as a free advertisement, so that those who are really interested in the commodity of "independence" from the "leader cult" will know where they can get the original article.

Offering grist to the mill of these shysters, Shachtman published a venomously falsified account of our October plenum for the purpose of showing that the majority of our party leaders, who have been sifted out and selected by the democratic action of the membership after more than ten years of common political work, are nothing but a collection of religious holy-rollers who take things on faith. In *Internal Bulletin* No. 3, Shachtman wrote:

> At the plenum the majority presented for a vote the document of comrade Trotsky which had arrived only a few hours earlier. There could not have been an opportunity for any comrade to reflect on this document. Some of them had not even had a chance to read it. Moreover, it was physically impossible for anybody to have read it in full for the simple reason that one page of the manuscript was accidentally lost in transit. Nevertheless, read or unread, studied or unstudied, complete or incomplete, the document was presented for a vote and finally adopted by the majority on the grounds, as one comrade expressed it, of faith in the correctness of comrade Trotsky's position.

Shachtman's account is false both in fact and in interpretation. (1) A synopsis of Comrade Trotsky's document, "The U.S.S.R. in War," was known to all members of the National Committee plenum not "a few hours earlier" but *two weeks* earlier. The plenum voting took place October 1. Under date of September 12 Trotsky wrote us: "I am writing now a study of the social character of the U.S.S.R. in connection with the war question. . . . The *fundamental*

ideas are as follows: . . ."* He then stated his ideas in outline form
—nobody could misunderstand them. This outline was mimeographed and sent to all members of the N.C. on September 14, more
than two weeks before the plenum, under the heading: "Plenum
Material." Thus, all concerned knew, well in advance of the plenum,
the main line of the thesis elaborated in the finished document.

(2) The document was not "presented for a vote and finally
adopted by the majority," as Shachtman says. The adopted motion
reads as follows: "The Plenum *endorses the political conclusions*
of the document of Trotsky on 'The U.S.S.R. in War' and instructs
the Political Committee to publish it as an evaluation and elucidation of the new events *on the basis of our fundamental position.*"
An earlier motion "to endorse the document" as a whole was
changed, and restricted to an endorsement of "the political conclusions," precisely because some comrades, who fully agreed with
the conclusions, wanted to study the document more thoroughly before voting to endorse it in its entirety. The procedure of the plenum
majority in this matter was directly opposite to Shachtman's slanderous report.

(3) "A page was missing"—and therefore the line of the document could not be accepted without a resort to "faith." This contemptible piece of petty fakery is designed for those who think one
inspects a political document like a proof reader and accepts it
only if every word and every comma is in place. The *line* of the
document was clear to all, the *political conclusions*, which were endorsed, were succinctly stated. *That is enough* for a serious revolutionist to determine his attitude toward any political document.
Shachtman knows this as well as we do. He quibbles about a "missing page" only to support the alien thesis that the leaders of the
party are not thinking revolutionists but weak-minded addicts of
religious "faith."

I have taken the space to cite the record in this instance and
to expose Shachtman's falsifications at some length because it is
out of such flimsy material that our enemies, the Lovestoneites and
their like, construct their thesis of a "leader cult" in the Fourth
International. They did not fail to seize upon Shachtman's tidbit.
It was gleefully reprinted by the same *Workers' Age*—it was written
for their benefit—with the sarcastic remark that they were doing
so "merely for the purpose of illustrating how widely the atmosphere in that party [the S.W.P.] differs from the uncritical, totalitarian, leader worshipping spirit of Stalinism."

---

*Cf. *In Defense of Marxism*, p. 1.

But, it may be objected, the opposition complains of a "leader cult" only in the Socialist Workers Party, not in the Fourth International. No, no, no, that is not what they mean. It is the Fourth International, and its "leader cult," and its "leader," that Burnham is shooting at. "Cannon," after all, is only a faith-stricken "leader cultist" himself, who "upon all occasions without exception, accepts the *politics* of Trotsky, accepts them immediately and without question." Cannon at best, you see, qualifies only as a "Gauleiter," not as the one and only "Fuehrer."

Burnham brought this conception of the Fourth International from the American Workers Party. Here is what he wrote in the days when the fusion negotiations with the Muste organization were in progress in 1934:

> The A.W.P. also distrusts the dependence of the Communist League and the Fourth International on a single individual. No organization except perhaps a fascist organization should have a single individual occupying the position that Trotsky does in fact occupy in the Communist League. And it is worth noting from history that Trotsky, though an incomparably brilliant political analyst, has never been a person able to function effectively in a party. After all, Trotsky has failed. (Memorandum of James Burnham issued by the National Office of the American Workers Party.)

* * *

Burnham, according to his highly moral custom, "withdrew" this thesis, that is, he kept it in reserve until such time as he would find the courage to proclaim it openly in our ranks. Shachtman and Abern, by their support, have given him this courage. But they have not added any merit to the thesis, nor cleansed it of its dirty trademark as the invention of the enemies of the Fourth International.

As for the "clique" and the "leader cult" in our party, the theory is just as shallow as the Brandler-Lovestone theory applied to our international organization, and the evidence just as flimsy. When we speak about a real clique in our movement—the Abern clique—we give a detailed and documented account of its operations over a long period of time and prove that it left a trail as wide as a cross-country highway. Our accusers are much more sparing in their evidence. "Do you doubt the existence of the Cannon clique?" they ask—"It can be confirmed by a single incident." Let us take this "single incident" apart and see what it really proves.

As we came to the end of the concluding session of the July convention and reached the last point on the agenda, the election of the new National Committee, Shachtman arose to present a slate. It was very late, the delegates were tired and restless, and many of them

wanted to get a few hours' sleep in preparation for their departure
the following day. Naturally, this could not deter Shachtman from
making a speech. Naturally, also, the speech was detailed and lengthy
and full of pious homilies, pronounced on the assumption that the
delegates didn't know what they wanted with regard to the composition of the new N.C. and had to be told. Stripped of pretentious
and hypocritical verbiage, Shachtman's slate amounted to a proposal
to shift the center of gravity in the National Committee by the addition of a number of New York professional "youth" whose experience has been confined pretty largely to the class room and the
office of the Y.P.S.L.

Without making a speech—the delegates had openly manifested
their impatience by frequently interrupting Shachtman—comrade
Dunne then presented another slate weighted on the other side.
Dunne's slate corresponded in its general tendency more to the desires of the majority of the delegates. They knew the leading people,
they had listened to endless hours of debate on the organization
report, and it is sheer impudence to assume that they had given no
thought to the composition of the new National Committee in the
light of the debate. An adjournment for consultation was requested,
and then—horror of horrors!—"As at a signal, 30 or 35 delegates
then proceeded like a man to the back of the hall, where they held
a caucus meeting." What is wrong or abnormal about that procedure?
The "30 or 35 delegates," that is, *a majority of the convention,* obviously wanted to make some amendments to the Dunne slate.
How else could they do it except by an open consultation?

The opposition tries to isolate the elections to the N.C. from
everything that had preceded and led up to it in the convention.
These proceedings, especially the debate on the organization report,
clearly intimate a brewing struggle between the proletarian and the
petty-bourgeois tendencies, the struggle which broke out with such
violence a few months later. These intimations did not pass unno-
ticed by the delegates from the proletarian centers. They didn't know
everything, but they sensed the direction in which the conflict was
moving and began to align themselves accordingly. So also did
the minority of the delegates who automatically rallied around the
Shachtman slate without the formality of a caucus consultation.
Dunne and Shachtman each signify certain things in the party. Any
speeches they may make at the eleventh hour of a convention change
nothing. Shachtman will never know it, but speeches are judged
not only by what is said but also by who says it.

I personally took no part in the caucus on the slate, as the opposition's document testifies, and for definite reasons. I was anxious

to avoid a struggle in the party as long as the differences had not been clearly defined in specific resolutions. At the beginning of the convention I proposed that a nominating commission, consisting of representatives from the main delegations, be set up to sift out the nominees and present a slate to the convention on the basis of the qualifications of the individual candidates and their support in the ranks. I consider it best for the central leaders of the party not to interfere too much in the selection of the personnel of the N.C. Members of the N.C., in order to have real authority, should be pushed up from below, not lifted from the top.

I know that comrade Dunne would not have presented a slate to the convention if Shachtman had not taken the initiative. Dunne's original slate, drawn up during Shachtman's speech, was not entirely satisfactory to some of the delegates as a definitive list. Consequently, they promptly moved for an adjournment in order to permit a consultation between the delegations which supported the general tendency of the Dunne slate. The fact that they openly asked for this consultation, and that they held it in the back of the convention hall in the sight of everybody, only demonstrated that they knew what they wanted in general and that they were not hiding anything from anybody. If there were any secret maneuvers or clique operations at the convention it was not on the side of the majority. On their part everything was regular, proper, and open and above-board. This "single incident," which was to "prove" the existence of a secret clique, in fact indicated the direct opposite. All the other "incidents" are on the same order.

Cliques and cliquism and permanent factions are abhorrent to proletarian revolutionists who seek the realization of their socialist aims through a workers' mass movement led by a mass party. The only permanent formation that can claim our allegiance is the party. Factions are for us only temporary groupings, to be dissolved in the party when the immediate issues in dispute are settled. To speak of cliques, that is, groupings of chums and friends without a principled basis—we did not wage an educational struggle against such abominations since the inception of our movement to wind up with a clique of our own. The accusation is sheer slander without a trace of justification in fact.

13—THE PROLETARIAN ORIENTATION

One of the capital crimes charged against the party majority was the famous "New Year's meeting," at which the plans for the auto campaign were worked out. Comrade Clarke has dealt with this incident at length in his admirable article on the auto crisis. "Cannon," says the document of the minority, "never repudiated it [the meeting] or what it symbolized." That is correct. I go further and say that this meeting, initiated by us and later "repudiated" by Burnham and Shachtman, does indeed "symbolize" the difference between their orientation and their methods and ours. We established new trade union connections; we conceived a plan to utilize these connections for an intensification of our work in the auto union; we invited the two political leaders of the present opposition to an informal discussion of the plan and the assignment of personnel before taking the proposals in finished form before the Political Committee for official action. Their role in the whole affair, including their criticism, was a negative one.

The leaders of the opposition confine their remarks to only one aspect of the meeting, and, in my opinion, to the least important aspect—the procedure. The meeting is cited as one of their big "proofs" of the existence of a secret clique which decides things and substitutes itself for the official leading body of the party. If it was a clique operation, why then were Burnham and Shachtman invited to participate in it? A more reasonable interpretation would be that the informal meeting with them was designed to secure their collaboration in the working out of the plans before they took finished form. That interpretation would be entirely correct, as far as our motivations were concerned. Burnham and Shachtman raised no objection to participation in the meeting; their discovery that it was a bad business was made long after the fact. Such informal meetings, prior to official meetings of the P.C., have been held dozens and scores, if not hundreds, of times in the past; it is the normal method of collaboration in a genuinely functioning "collective leadership." Only long afterward did Burnham and Shachtman discover that there was something wrong in the procedure and ask, with an air of violated virtue: "By what authority did this body sit as the *deciding* body, usurping the functions of both P.C. and N.C.?" The New Year's meeting committed no usurpations whatever, either "by authority" or otherwise. The plans formulated at the meeting were fully reported to the regular meeting of the P.C. on January 3 and formally *decided* by that body, and by that body alone. The informal meeting *prepared* the plans—the official meeting of the P.C. *decided* on their adoption. That is the way we have handled important matters hundreds of times in the past; that is the way we will handle them hundreds of times in the future. There was nothing wrong or irregular about the procedure.

But this simple and straight-forward explanation of a common method of operation among the members of any serious leading body will not do for our mystery writers. There was something sinister afoot; nobody is going to delude our perspicacious Hawkshaws with the cock and bull story that Dobbs and Dunne had travelled 1,300 miles simply to give our trade union work an impetus in the auto field. They remind their readers that Cannon, forgetful about the interests of his "clique," "was about to leave for Europe." And here they pluck out the heart of the mystery: "This meeting was designed to sterilize the P.C. during his absence." That was undoubtedly a very devilish "design." But why was the whole meeting confined to the auto situation? The P.C. and the party as a whole were already pretty well "sterilized" in this field; the plan was to fertilize its work and provide the means for it to expand and grow. The only other question discussed at the meeting was the assignment of Shachtman to full-time editorship of the *Socialist Appeal.* To be sure, that was a certain imposition upon him, as his stubborn resistance testified, but it did not infringe in the least upon the powers and prerogatives of the P.C. in all fields where it had been operating with unsterilized "authority" before Cannon "was about to leave for Europe." The meeting discussed, and the P.C. later ratified, not questions of policy but plans of organizing our trade union work in the auto field and the personnel of the field staff. And since four members of the N.C. were to be in the field, it placed the direction of the organizing campaign in their hands. Is that an abnormal procedure infringing upon the rights of the P.C.? Not at all. Trade union campaigns, if they are to be lifted from the pages of our press and realized in life, *must* be directed by those who specialize in trade union work and concentrate their attention and energy upon it.

If our critics are not satisfied with this explanation, and still consider that in some Machiavellian way or other they were hornswoggled, and the P.C. "sterilized," when the "clique" dispatched one of its members to France and others to the auto field—if they still feel this way about it, I offer them a simple proposal to even the score. Let them establish some contacts with workers or trade unionists in some trade or industry; let them work out a plan to utilize these contacts to extend and develop our trade union work in this field; let them come to the P.C., with or without prior consultation with us, and propose that the plan be approved and that they be put in charge of the campaign. I will promise in advance to vote with both hands to adopt their plans and place the whole campaign under their direction. They can hold me to this promise regardless of whether their plan contemplates the organization of steel workers, sailors, hod-carriers or the janitors of City College or New York University.

This fair offer is not likely to be accepted. Their orientation toward trade union work is literary; ours is more real. That is the meaning of the much discussed "New Year's meeting." We regarded, and still regard, the New Year's meeting as a stage in the development of an ambitious plan to expand our trade union work. They see it in retrospect only as a "maneuver" against them. They don't even understand that our maneuver was aimed exclusively at the auto bosses and their labor agents.

The conflict between the proletarian and petty-bourgeois tendencies in the party was expressed for a long time primarily in this difference of orientation. In the present discussion it has taken programmatic form. We have been compelled to reinforce our fight for a proletarian party, proletarian in composition and rooted in the workers' mass movement, by an irreconcilable struggle for a proletarian program. It was this revelation of programmatic differences which caused the muffled struggle, already evident at the last convention, to break out in the open on a wider front. At the last convention both sides undoubtedly sensed the coming storm. But we on our side hardly expected it to break out so soon, and with such force and irreconcilability, on what we have always considered the fundamental questions of our program and doctrine. From this point of view, the articles* which I wrote in the *Socialist Appeal* before the last party convention, in behalf of a proletarian orientation, require supplementation and emphasis on the programmatic side.

The document of the opposition refers to these articles as "articles on 'organization'." That is a superficial and incorrect appraisal of their content. They further state that "many of the ideas . . . were a collective product even though they were printed as a personal contribution." That is not correct either. If the ideas I expounded in those articles had really been common ideas, I could have been well content, as in so many other cases, to leave the actual writing to those whose hands were free from administrative and other duties which occupied me quite fully at the time. The contention that the articles "were written essentially for the purpose of *warding off* the necessary criticism of the party leadership between the two conventions," is wholly without foundation. I agreed

---

*These articles appeared in six consecutive issues of the *Socialist Appeal*, June 13, 16, 20, 23, 27 and 30, 1939.—*Ed.*

with most of the criticisms and the articles represented my personal opinion of the way to improve the situation.

I still think those articles point the road to the future for our party. Our basic problem still remains, as stated there, to "turn our faces in the right direction. That means, first of all, to turn our backs on the pessimists and calamity howlers, the soul-sick intellectuals and tired radicals who whine and dawdle around the fringes of the movement and even, to a certain extent, infest our ranks." I still think that "most contemptible of all are those who seek to cover their desertion and retreat by hurling newly invented 'ideological' disagreements with Marxism over their shoulders. Taken altogether they are an unattractive and uninspiring aggregation. It is nothing less than a monstrous travesty to consider them as in any way reflecting the movement of workers' emancipation which, by its very nature, is alien to all pessimism and defeatist tendencies. It is criminal folly to waste time or even to argue the question with these runaway boys and heralds of defeat before the battle."

I wrote before the last party convention: "Our convention must let the dead bury the dead and turn the face of the party to the workers who are the real source of power and inspiration and well-grounded optimism. We have said this before. More than once we have incorporated it in resolutions. But we have not made the turn in forthright fashion. That is why we are lagging behind. That is the main reason we are suffering a certain stagnation. That is why we are even flirting with the danger of a degeneration of the party along the lines of conservative passivity, introspection and futility."

I wrote: "The proletariat of the United States is the source of unlimited power, it can lift the whole world on its shoulders—that is the unshakable premise of all our calculations and all our work . . . the workers of America have power enough to topple over the structure of capitalism at home and to lift the whole world with them when they rise!"

Those words—the theme of all my pre-convention articles last year—hold good today. In retrospect, they read more prophetically than I knew at that time. I did not know how deep, how great, was the "danger of degeneration" implicit in the bad composition of the party in New York and its inadequate contact with the mass movement of the workers.

I said in that article: "Our program has withstood all the tests of theory and experience and stands unassailable." I must admit that I wrote these words on the assumption that I was stating a truism to which we all subscribed, and that the differences between us concerned only matters of orientation, emphasis and application.

I could not know that within a few months the ambitious plan of expansion adopted by the convention on my motion would be disrupted and crowded off the agenda by a factional civil war in the party.

I, along with other comrades, expected future trouble from the intellectualist wing of our leadership. But we did not foresee that they would undertake to lead an insurrection against our fundamental program, our doctrine, our tradition and our organizational methods. This demonstration compelled us to put aside— to postpone—the execution of our ambitious plans for external work until the hegemony of Marxism in the party had again been established by struggle. That struggle is now drawing to a close. The victory of Marxism, and thereby of the proletarian tendency, is already assured. On that basis the party convention can and will again decide to implement the proletarian orientation by measures no different in basic content than those adopted at the convention last July.

The convention will meet and conduct its work under the sign of *the proletarian orientation*. That is the way to meet the coming war. Preparation for war means, for us, not some esoteric special task. It means turning the face of the party to the workers, penetrating deeper into the trade unions. It means taking drastic measures to proletarianize the composition of the party membership. And, in the light of the experience of the faction struggle, the proletarian orientation means above all—and in order to make all possible—a firm decision to continue on all fronts the implacable war against any and all opposition to the doctrine and program of proletarian revolution—Marxism, i.e., Trotskyism.

New York, April 1, 1940.

LETTERS TO COMRADES

EDITOR'S NOTE:

The "Letters to Comrades" which constitute the second section of this book cover the period of the struggle against the petty-bourgeois opposition within the S.W.P. from its inception to its consummation. They were written in the heat of the struggle itself; cover virtually every phase; are almost a day-to-day chronicle and form in fact, an integral part of the struggle. Therein is their primary interest and value.

While the definitive history of this stage of the development of American Trotskyism belongs to the historians of the future, these letters provide the indispensable material both for such a history and for a correct understanding of the struggle itself. At the same time they supply an unexampled schooling for the Trotskyist youth, and the vanguard parties still in process of formation throughout the world. In their own way, these letters, along with the other documents in this volume, serve as a model in conducting a proletarian fight for the program of the revolution.

Many of these letters were circulated among the entire party membership; others, exclusively among members adhering to the Trotskyist majority; still others are here made public for the first time.

They are reproduced without changes except for a few deletions which are noted in the text.

LETTERS TO COMRADES

A LETTER TO ALL MEMBERS OF THE
NATIONAL COMMITTEE

New York, September 8, 1939

Dear Comrade,

In a letter dated September 5th you received the motions made in the last meeting of the Resident Political Committee relating to the preparation of our plenum.

For your information I will state that these are motions made by myself as opposed to other proposals to call an immediate plenum without documentary preparation and without adequate time to supply the non-resident comrades with the necessary material for study and consideration beforehand. The gist of my position as represented by the motions which were received by you was this:

(1) That for practical affairs of organization the Resident Committee can proceed. In any event it will have to execute the plans, which are more or less obviously indicated.

(2) The proposal to reopen the Russian question must be considered separately from the organizational question. And the Russian question should not be projected at a hastily summoned plenum until the different positions have been formulated and communicated to the non-resident members for their study and consideration beforehand.

* * *

Comrade Burnham has submitted a document which comes to you in the same envelope with this letter. I confine my remarks here to the second section of the document entitled, "The Nature of the Russian State in the Light of the War."

At the meeting of the Political Committee where these opinions of Comrade Burnham were advanced orally, I took the position that nothing particularly new in the policy of the Stalin bureau-cracy has taken place since our party convention two months ago except the signing of the Stalin-Hitler pact. Those who propose now to reopen the Russian question in our ranks can logically do so only on the basis of the signing of the Stalin-Hitler pact.

This pact, however, is new only in the sense that an old policy of Stalin on the field of foreign policy, of which we have spoken more than once, has reached diplomatic realization through the agreement of Hitler. The position of the party and of the Fourth International which was taken after such extensive and all-sided discussion, and with almost complete unanimity as far as our party is concerned, did not at all depend on the oscillations of Stalin's foreign policy between the fascist and democratic imperialist camps. We arrived at our position from the economic structure of the Soviet Union and from the Marxist principle of evaluating each and every state, without exception, from the point of view of its basic class character.

Has the economic structure of the Soviet Union undergone a profound change since our party convention two months ago? As far as my knowledge of the situation goes, it has not changed funda-mentally. For my part, I am not willing to revise the well-considered decisions of our party convention unless someone can demonstrate that the considerations which motivated the decisions have undergone a profound change in the meantime.

I believe this will also be the opinion of the majority of the plenum. How can it be otherwise? The position of the party and of the International was not the result of snap judgment. The question was discussed amply—and more than amply—beforehand. Volumi-nous documents on all sides of the question were written and studied and debated. I do not consider it necessary to repeat all that was said before; it is sufficient to mention and refer to the existing documents.

Comrade Burnham proposes to write off the Soviet Union. As far as I can judge his reasoning, it is approximately the same as that employed in arriving at his old position. Only now he proposes to add one new detail: to abandon the defense of the Soviet Union. I cannot follow him there and I cannot offer that advice to the Russian workers. If the idea of the defense of the Soviet Union had meaning in practical application precisely in the event of war, I do not propose to drop the idea just at the moment the war knocks on the door.

*   *   *

The question raised by Comrade Burnham, however, has another

aspect, namely, the attitude towards party decisions taken by convention after adequate discussion. To me this is no less important
than the other side of the question. I say this because I firmly believe that the right conception of the party, the proper functioning
of the party, and the subordination of every individual to the collective will of the party are the conditions for the successful leadership of the revolutionary proletarian struggle.

Naturally, everybody has a right to his opinion. But the party,
as a party, also has the right to its opinion. And the collective opinion of the party, especially at moments of crisis, *must have the right
of way*.

Consider for a moment the fact that we concluded our second
convention only two months ago. This followed by a year and a half
the previous convention which took a position on the Russian question
by a vote which closely approached unanimity. At the convention of
last July—after all that had intervened—not a single comrade could
be found to make a motion or demand a reconsideration of the party
position on the Russian question. Now, two months later, simply because Stalin has signed the pact which he sought for more than five
years, a pact, moreover, which was contemplated and even predicted
long ago in our ranks, we are abruptly confronted with the demand
to change our policy on the Russian question fundamentally.

Permit me to ask you a small question. Isn't this just a little bit
like making fun of the party? Isn't this something like assuming
that the party has no sense and didn't know what it was doing when
it took its Russian position so firmly and so categorically, and
after such thoroughgoing and all-sided discussion?

Add to this the scandalous fact that the editors of the *New International* went so far as to set forth, by oblique writing, a new position on the Russian question, in contradiction to the established party
position, in the editorial on the Stalin-Hitler pact in the September
issue.

The party position, with the most extreme meticulousness in
the choice of words, has described the Soviet bureaucracy as a
parasitic caste, and not a class. The September *New International*,
not in a signed discussion article but in an editorial which presumably sets forth party policy, suddenly announces that the bureaucrats are *exploiters*, i.e., a ruling *class*. Isn't this something like an
insult to the party? That is the way it appears to me.

There is one more point. It is needless, I hope, to point out that
decisions taken by party convention cannot be changed by the
plenum, to say nothing of being changed by individual editors at
their whim. The party membership, which is sufficiently patient

and long-suffering, will rise up against any such pretensions. Of that we can be sure.

The positions cannot be changed without a discussion and a new convention. Can we afford ourselves the luxury of a new discussion at this time, in the face of the difficult practical tasks, and so soon after a party convention? I doubt it.

Of course circumstances can arise which compel abrupt changes at any cost. It would be foolish to bar ourselves off from the possibility of correcting an error in policy or of adapting an old policy to new circumstances. But in the present case, it seems to me that those who propose now a change which they did not propose in the convention and pre-convention discussion so recently concluded, are obliged to motivate their demand for a new discussion on new conditions of a fundamental character which were not known to us at the time of the party convention, and which, up to the present, have not been revealed to us.

J. P. CANNON

A LETTER TO JOSEPH HANSEN

[In October 1939, Joseph Hansen went to Mexico City to work in Trotsky's secretariat. The following and other letters addressed to him during his stay there were also written for the information of Trotsky.—*Ed.*]

New York, October 24, 1939

Dear Joe,

I received the second article on the nature of the Soviet State* yesterday and am turning it over to the Committee for publication. It answers many of the concrete questions which have been troubling some comrades and will aid materially in the clarification of the whole problem, insofar as clarity is really sought.

Since your departure the internal situation has taken a very sharp turn. Two membership meetings on the disputed questions here in New York have been very heated. It is obvious now that a good deal of factional work has been going on in the party. It is now coming out into the open in a quite violent form.

We have a rainbow-colored bloc against us which includes those who want to revise the Marxian theory of the state and those who maintain an orthodox line on this not unimportant point; it includes frank defeatists on the question of the Soviet Union and unconditional defensists; those who deny the identity of Bolshevism and Stalinism and those who imagine that Stalinism somehow or other is the logical outcome of Bolshevism in the sphere of organization. The latter question has already asserted itself as a great motor force generating the factional antagonisms to the party "regime." With only half an eye one can easily discern a considerable volume of disguised and not so well disguised Souvarinism in the New York section of the party.

Moreover, it is an actual fact that a good fifty percent of the supporters of the rainbow bloc are completely defeatist on the question of the USSR in their sentiments. The speeches from the floor in the membership meetings have clearly indicated this. However, that does not deter our friends Shachtman and Abern from proclaiming a firm solidarity of the combined opposition and directing all fire against the "conservative" majority. In New York, as I have said, the dispute has taken an extremely violent turn from the outset. As to the situation in the rest of the country, I have not yet heard anything.

Above I give you only an outline of the situation in New York,

---

*See *In Defense of Marxism*, p. 24.—*Ed.*

with my customary moderation and restraint. Perhaps it is not surprising that the devastating impact of the world crisis on the intellectuals should call forth some Souvarinistic reactions in a section of the party with the social composition of New York. It is a bit awkward, however, not to be able to combat this pitiful sickness by means of a united leadership.

I must admit that we have taken too superficial and complacent a view of the dangers that can arise in a moment of crisis from the social composition of the New York section of the party. It comes now like a sharp fillip on the nose, if not a blow over the head. It is a payment, so to speak, for our failure to put the O'Brien* letter on the social composition of the party before the convention for forthright consideration. The Old Man can say now with full justification, "I told you so."

Can we again buy ourselves off from a sharp struggle in the party by conciliation and compromise at the top, at the cost of obscuring deep and basic conflicts which lurk in the whole situation like unexploded mines—the course we have followed more or less consistently for a long time now—or is it necessary to bring some

---

*On the eve of the July 1939 convention of the S.W.P., Leon Trotsky sent a personal letter to James P. Cannon. In this letter of May 27, 1939, Trotsky—in connection with discussions in the Political Committee over the *Socialist Appeal*—sounded a warning concerning the danger latent in the then existing social composition of the party, with a preponderance of petty-bourgeois elements in large cities, especially New York.

The concluding section of this letter follows:

"A radical and courageous change is necessary as a condition of success. The paper is too wise, too scholarly, too aristocratic for the American workers and tends to reflect the party more as it is than to prepare it for its future.

"Of course it is not only a question of the paper, but of the whole course of policy. I continue to be of the opinion that you have too many petty-bourgeois boys and girls who are very good and devoted to the party, but who do not fully realize that their duty is not to discuss among themselves, but to penetrate into the fresh milieu of workers. I repeat my proposition: Every petty-bourgeois member of the party who, during a certain time, let us say three or six months, does not win a worker for the party should be demoted to the rank of candidate and after another three months expelled from the party. In some cases it might be unjust, but the party as a whole would receive a salutary shock which it needs very much. A very radical change is necessary.

"Comradely,
"V. T. O'BRIEN [Leon Trotsky]"

As comrade Cannon stresses in his letter, neither Trotsky's warning nor his proposal was given proper heed or consideration at the time.—*Ed.*

clarity into the situation by means of a frank and unambiguous political struggle and draw sharp lines of demarcation?

I would like to have your opinion and your advice in this respect. In this situation it seems to me that a lazy and pacifistic approach could at best only buy for us a short term ticket to a fool's paradise. What do you think?

Fraternally yours,
J. P. CANNON

A LETTER TO VINCENT R. DUNNE

New York, October 25, 1939

Dear Vincent,

I judge that you have received a copy of a letter addressed to Joe Hansen, which was mailed to you yesterday. Since dictating it we received a copy of Crux's [Trotsky's] reply to a letter from Comrade Stanley on the internal party situation.* This reply of Crux was enclosed with the copy of my letter to Comrade Hansen.

You are perfectly at liberty to show my letter to interested comrades so they will know my point of view. The same applies to the letter of Crux, as it will very likely be published in the internal bulletin.

From all indications we are in for a serious struggle. The struggle for the Fourth International is concentrated right now in the struggle for programmatic intransigence within the American section. Only in this way will we be able to preserve a firm unity and really prepare our ranks to meet the war and go through the war without encountering explosive crises at every difficult moment.

In such a moment each man must stand at the post where he can best serve the cause. In the opinion of comrades here this signifies that for the next period I must be relieved to the greatest extent possible of administrative routine and freed for political work, externally as well as internally. For my part I am ready to accept such a rearrangement of duties and to carry my full share of the responsibility in the struggle.

This raises in the sharpest form the future work of Comrade Dobbs. In a recent letter he states that the big work which occupied his attention in the recent months is completed through the signing of the union contract with the employers. He adds: "I am in the midst of the mopping up operations. I expect to be able to discuss with you soon the question of future work." It would greatly facilitate matters if we could now carry through our original program of bringing him to the Center for party administrative and organizational work.

I know that the new difficulties of the Minneapolis comrades in connection with the prosecutions makes this a somewhat risky shift. As I see it, the difficult situation in Minneapolis precludes for the time being the demonstrative transfer of Comrade Dobbs from trade union to party work. That might bring unfavorable repercussions

---

*See *In Defense of Marxism*, pp. 34-36.—*Ed.*

for you. At the same time, the party in its present struggle—which if we want to call it by its right name is nothing less than a struggle to vindicate eleven solid years of programmatic preparation to stand up under a crisis—has the right and the duty to summon every individual to the post where he can be most useful.

I think we can reach a transitional solution of the question of Dobbs' work without infringing too deeply on the requirements of the Minneapolis sector, in the following way: Dobbs should arrange, in the shortest time possible, for a leave of absence from his trade union post without any announcement of his intentions with regard to the party and without cutting himself off from the possibility of reentering the trade union situation, insofar as Minneapolis is concerned, at a critical moment. The party purposes can be very well served in the transition period by his activity under a suitable party name without any public fanfare.

Naturally, we cannot very easily carry through such a decisive step without the agreement of the Minneapolis comrades. But we have reason to believe that when the party necessities are placed before us in such categoric form as at present, you will be ready on your part to make the necessary local sacrifices.

Aside from the immediate requirements of the party there is another aspect to this question which deserves consideration. I refer to the preparation of Comrade Dobbs for all-sided political work in the future, as distinct from the limited field of trade unionism. By entering the direct service of the party now, at a difficult moment of internal crisis, in an unobtrusive and even anonymous manner, he will be put sharply before a salutary experience in the vicissitudes of revolutionary political activity. He will face a point-blank test of his ability to adjust himself promptly to a radical transformation in the nature of his activity and the conditions under which it is conducted.

To be the leader of a workers' mass movement and show an ability to meet and solve the comparatively simple and broadly-outlined problems of an ascending trade union—that is one thing. I don't need to tell you that I fully appreciate the personal qualities of a militant who is capable of distinguishing himself in this field. But to be able to lead the organization work of a small political party which is still further restricted in its activities by a paralyzing internal crisis, and at the same time to take a resolute part in the struggle for a programmatic solution of that crisis—that is another thing.

A leader of the proletarian revolution must be able to shift his activity from one field to the other as the circumstances require it.

It should be added that experience is indispensable for the efficient execution of each of these assignments. We have often had occasion to say that one can't learn how to lead a trade union out of a book. From books he can learn the history and theory of the trade union movement, but its actual leadership he must learn in practice. The same thing holds true in regard to the party. One cannot learn how to lead a party out of a book either. If that were so there would not be such a poverty of political-party leadership everywhere.

The test of experience is decisive in this field above all others. By coming to the party service now, at a moment of acute crisis in a chauvinistic encirclement, the experience of Comrade Dobbs will be one hundred times more concentrated and will advance his political education one hundred times faster than if he came in normal times. His merits or demerits as a political-party leader will be established far more precisely and in an incomparably shorter time by this test.

Needless to say we all share the same optimistic opinions in regard to Comrade Dobbs' potentialities as a party leader. But six months after he begins party work under these conditions, we, as well as he, will know more about it and know more definitely.

*   *   *

The internal crisis of the party, which at bottom reflects the pressure of its encirclement, is already beginning to have a crippling effect on the working out of the ambitious program of expansion elaborated at the party convention. The financial difficulties which are besetting us are a barometer.

We must strive by all means to see that the internal struggle does not drive the party in upon itself to the neglect of its external agitation and organization work. That would only prolong the crisis which can find a real solution only on the road of an expansive public activity and a recruitment of new proletarian elements of stabilization.

We will most likely have to call on the Minnesota comrades for unexampled financial support to sustain our program of public activity during the internal struggle. I think the party is entitled to turn to the Twin Cities comrades once again with this demand.

To no small extent our trade unionist wing in Minnesota has floated in recent years on the stream of success made possible by the heroic struggles of 1934, which were in turn inspired—it should not be forgotten—by the patient and stubborn theoretical and political work carried out in isolation by the leading cadre in the six years which preceded the 1934 strikes. This fairly comfortable situation could exert negative influences on the mentality of our trade unionist comrades if they do not keep in mind the instability of their present situation; if they begin to imagine that their improved circumstances and standards of living are permanently assured and begin, unknown to themselves, to develop petty-bourgeois habits of life and illusions of security in a world situation which is exploding at every seam.

It will not be bad for them to begin even now to shake themselves loose from these possible illusions. The whole trade union upper stratum of the Second International could remain secure and grow fat and complacent and satisfied with things as they were only in the period of the stabilization and ascending progress of the capitalist world order. Such possibilities do not exist in these days. The sooner all our comrades face this question to the end and adjust themselves to the prospect of new and violent shocks and displacements the better.

A modest beginning in preparation to swim once more against the stream can be made by the voluntary agreement of the affected comrades to double their assessments for the material support of the party in its present critical test. The same holds good for all serious comrades in the party.

Fraternally yours,
J. P. CANNON

A LETTER TO JOSEPH HANSEN

New York, October 26, 1939

Dear Joe,

The answer of Crux to Stanley was received. It will not add to the popularity of Crux in some circles. But I long ago came to the sad conclusion that it is impossible to take a firm stand on political questions and please everybody at the same time.

We intend to utilize the intervention of Crux with the greatest discretion and responsibility. This is doubly necessary now because there are some ugly nuances in some of the sentiments of sections of the opposition.

There is a good deal of talk here against the "one man party," but trailing closely behind it like an afternoon shadow behind a Kansas jackrabbit is the objection to a "one man international." This is most outspoken on the part of Burnham who really sets the course for the rainbow combination, precisely because he has definite conceptions not only on the Russian question, but on the question of Bolshevism in general and particularly the Bolshevik system of party organization.

I remember very well the objections raised in their time by the heroes of the S.A.P.* against the preponderant influence of Trotsky in the Fourth International. For my part I have always been ready to agree that a predominant influence of two men with good ideas is better than the predominance of one. In fact, I am ready even now to go further and to say that ten leaders who lead by means of ideas and not with a club of corruption and persecution are better than two; but that, I think, is the maximum concession one could make to this S.A.P.ist theory which does not improve with age.

However, you can be sure in any case that we will take all the exceptional circumstances of the personal situation of Crux into consideration and take upon our shoulders the responsibility of the struggle which is from start to finish a struggle over ideas, and not of personalities.

There is one little favor I wish you would do for me, Joe. About two years ago, more or less—I think it was in January 1938 after our first convention—I had occasion to write a letter to the Old Man in regard to Burnham. In my shifting about from one house to another and packing and unpacking my stuff I have not been able to find the copy of this letter in my files. I wish you would see if it

---

*See page 72 of this volume.—*Ed.*

can be located in the files at Coyoacan and send me a copy along with a copy of the Old Man's answer.

This matter has a certain importance for me in connection with attempts which are being made to interpret my objections to Burnham's sorties and sallies on the programmatic front as a personal opposition and a refusal to recognize his positive qualities. I want to refresh my memory of the development of the antagonism between us.

I reported to the last meeting of the P.C. the indications that the services of yourself and Chris might be necessary there for a few weeks in preparation for the Austin affair.* It was unanimously agreed that there is no objection here to your accepting this assignment.

All things considered, everything is going along O.K. Isn't it a real piece of American luck to have the opportunity at this hour of the clock to thrash out the question of the program of the Fourth International under conditions of free democratic discussion. The time between the outbreak of the war in Europe and the entry of the United States is indeed a precious interlude in this respect.

I take a completely optimistic view of the ultimate results. . . .

As ever,

J. P. CANNON

---

*The reference is to the Dies Committee which had scheduled a special session at Austin, Texas, inviting Leon Trotsky to appear as a witness. Trotsky accepted and then Dies reneged. See *In Defense of Marxism*, pp. 85-86, 91 ff.—*Ed.*

A LETTER TO LEON TROTSKY

New York, November 2, 1939

Dear Comrade Hansen [Trotsky]:*

I received your letter of October 28th.**

Several comrades to whom I have shown the letter express no objections to the suggestions and proposals you made. I personally will support them.

The situation is very sharp and it is possible that action on our part along the lines of your proposals can add in moderating the atmosphere or, failing that, in clarifying the issue.

Even if I didn't agree with the steps you propose I wouldn't hesitate at all to make such a concession to a co-fighter for programmatic intransigence.

I send you this brief note to reassure you that we will do every-

---

*Because of the conditions of Trotsky's residence in the various countries in which he lived after his exile, letters were frequently forwarded to him in the name of his English secretaries.—*Ed.*

**This letter was inadvertently omitted from the volume *In Defense of Marxism,* and is printed here for the first time.—*Ed.*

October 28, 1939

Dear Jim:

Two things are clear to me from your letter of October 24: (1) that a very serious ideological fight has become inevitable and politically necessary; (2) that it would be extremely prejudicial if not fatal to connect this ideological fight with the perspective of a split, of a purge, or expulsions, and so on and so forth.

I heard for example that Comrade Gould proclaimed in a membership meeting: "You wish to expel us." But I don't know what reaction came from the other side to this. I for my part would immediately protest with the greatest vehemence such suspicions. I would propose the creation of a special control commission in order to check such affirmations and rumors. If it happens that someone of the majority launches such threats I for my part would vote for a censure or severe warning.

You have many new members and uneducated youth. They need a serious educational discussion in the light of the great events. If their thoughts at the beginning are obsessed by the perspective of personal *degradation,* i.e., demotions, loss of prestige, disqualifications, eliminations from Central Committee, etc., and so, the whole discussion would become envenomed and the authority of the leadership would be compromised.

If the leadership on the contrary opens a ruthless fight against petty-bourgeois idealistic conceptions and organizational prejudices but at the same time assures all the necessary guarantees for the discussion itself and for the minority, the result would be not only an

thing we can along the lines of your suggestions to keep the main political issues in the foreground and to eliminate or compromise the secondary organizational questions.

Fraternally,
J. P. CANNON

---

ideological victory but an important growth in the authority of the leadership.

"A conciliation and compromise at the top" on the questions which form the matter of divergences would of course be a crime. But I for my part would propose to the minority at the top an agreement, if you wish, a compromise on the methods of the discussion and parallelly on the political collaboration. For example, (a) both sides eliminate from the discussion any threats, personal denigration, and so on, (b) both sides take the obligation of loyal collaboration during the discussion, (c) every false move (threats, or rumors of threats, or a rumor of alleged threats, resignations, and so on) should be investigated by the National Committee or a special commission as a particular fact and not thrown into the discussion and so on.

If the minority accepts such an agreement you will have the possibility of disciplining the discussion and also the advantage of having taken a good initiative. If they reject it you can at every party membership meeting present your written proposition to the minority as the best refutation of their complaints and as a good example of "our regime."

It seems to me that the last convention failed at a very bad moment (the time was not ripe) and became a kind of abortion. The genuine discussion comes some time after the convention. This signifies that you can't avoid a new convention at Christmas or so. The idea of a referendum is absurd. It could only facilitate a split on local lines. But I believe that the majority in the above-mentioned agreement can propose to the minority a new convention on the basis of two platforms with all the organizational guarantees for the minority.

The convention is expensive but I don't see any other means of concluding the present discussion and the party crisis it produces.

J. HANSEN [Leon Trotsky]

P.S. Every serious and sharp discussion can of course lead to some desertions, departures, or even expulsions, but the whole party should be convinced from the logic of the facts that they are inevitable results occurred in spite of the best will of the leadership, and not an objective or aim of the leadership, and not the point of departure of the whole discussion. This is in my mind the decisive point of the whole matter.

J.H. [Leon Trotsky]

A LETTER TO LEON TROTSKY

New York, November 4, 1939

Dear Comrade Hansen [Trotsky],

I received the copies of the old letters of December 1937,* regarding Comrade B. [Burnham] and thank you very much for sending them to me. They are very useful to me personally as a self-assurance that the present difficulties in this respect were foreseen, along with their basic causes, and have not been provoked by obtuseness and tactlessness on my part.

The situation here is developing very rapidly. I hope you will follow the course of developments very attentively from week to week, and even, insofar as information at your disposal permits, from day to day, and participate further in the discussion.

I could very well be satisfied with an attitude of aloofness or a very restrained and limited intervention on your part in an ordinary dispute. But it is becoming clearer every day that we are concerned now with a fundamental struggle for the program and the general ideology of our movement; not simply for the victory of the Bolshevik doctrine on this or that point, but for the supremacy of the system and method of Bolshevik politics and organization.

In your letter to Stanley of October 22d, you castigate the attempts to muddle up the discussion of the Russian question with arguments about the "regime." You touched only in passing—reserving for later comment, I hope—on the positively infuriating nonchalance with which comrades holding different positions on the political question in dispute (the Russian question) have combined in a bloc for the purpose of changing the "regime."

We have subjected this downright unprincipledness to a pretty militant attack in the New York membership meetings. In my speech last Sunday I quoted from the records of the plenum the three different positions of Abern, Burnham and Shachtman on the nature of the Soviet state. Abern voted for our resolution, which characterizes it as a degenerated workers' state. Burnham denies that it is a workers' state "in any sense whatever." Shachtman declares he does not raise the question at the present time.

Without questioning the right of each comrade to his separate opinion, I simply put to the audience and to the leaders of the minority this question: What will be the position of the *party* on this question if the minority becomes the majority at the conven-

*See pp. 27-29 of this volume.—*Ed.*

tion? Similarly, I showed from the documentary record that the three named comrades each give a different answer to the question of the defense of the Soviet Union. I repeated then the same question: What will the *party* say about the defense of the Soviet Union if the bloc gains the majority?

You can imagine the devastating effect on the minority bloc of such questions. A political observer might say very confidently that such a political attack, conducted with the necessary persistence and militancy, is bound to break the bloc. To a certain extent this impression is already being realized. We are witnessing now a very noticeable shift of rank and file comrades from the untenable position of the bloc over to the support of the majority.

But what about the leaders? From numerous indications, they are attempting to extricate themselves from their impossible position, not by each defending his own standpoint and letting the bloc go to the Devil, but by readjusting their principles to the exigencies of bloc politics. That is, they appear from all signs to be working out a common position by making mutual concessions, in order to arrive at uniform answers to the questions in dispute.

I understand that the ambiguous resolution of Shachtman, which served up to now as the platform of the bloc, interpreted by each of its three divisions as it saw fit, is to be replaced by a new resolution to which all will subscribe.

By this, they evidently hope to escape the accusation of combinationism and to present themselves as a single group with one platform. To us this will only signify another demonstration of the game of playing with ideas, which can only promote political cynicism among the youth. It can never educate them in the spirit expressed so cogently by De Leon: "Be serious about principles and be honest about them."

* * *

We have decided to make a general codification of the various arguments and answers on the Russian question in the form of a resolution which will be submitted as our platform for the convention. Along with this, we plan also a resolution on the character of the party and the question of the internal regime. It is somewhat ironic to recall that contrasting resolutions on these two questions defined the issues between the majority and the Carter-Burnham minority before and at the convention two years ago. Nothing has since changed in the essence of the disputes except that Burnham has taken further steps away from us while Shachtman and Abern, who stood at that time on our side, have simply crossed over to the other side.

In view of the fact that under the conditions of the war our discussion on the Russian question becomes in essence the discussion of the Fourth International, we think international participation in the drafting of the Russian resolution is decidedly in order. The question for us is not the authorship of the resolution but of having the most precise and instructive formulation on each and every point as a guiding line for the whole International.

We are working on a resolution here, but we would also be very glad if time permits you to submit a draft. At the same time it is our plan to forward to you the draft of our resolution for criticism and amendment.

*   *   *

As I remarked in the early part of this letter, I consider your intervention not only on the Russian question but also on the other problems of ideology and political method as absolutely in order and imperative. It would be simply absurd to run the risk of leaving one question unclarified or a single serious comrade in doubt, for party tactical or diplomatic reasons.

From all indications, the proletarian centers of the party are standing absolutely firm on all the basic questions. . . .

Fraternally,
J. P. CANNON

A LETTER TO LEON TROTSKY

New York, November 8, 1939

Dear Comrade Hansen [Trotsky],

(1) At last night's meeting of the Political Committee, I introduced the enclosed statement on the regulation of the discussion.* It was accepted by the minority and adopted unanimously. It was decided also to send this statement to all party branches. I think it will help somewhat to provide a more favorable atmosphere for political discussion, and consequently for clarification of the great questions. At the same time, it will put a serious obstacle in the road of anyone who may want to play with the adventure of split.

(2) Politically, the minority draws further away from us and the political hegemony of Burnham in the combination is becoming more manifest. At last night's meeting of the Political Committee we discussed the new manifesto of the Comintern and our line in regard to it. On this point, also, it appears we are no longer able to find a common language, because we no longer agree on the role of Stalinism.

It appears that revisionism in our ranks is becoming somewhat "imperialistic"; it wants to conquer in all fields, one by one. Perhaps another way of explaining the new divergence would be to say that the Russian question, because of its fundamental nature, dominates a political orientation in general, now as in the past.

We began the discussion in the P.C. without motions, as an exchange of views and information about the new Stalinist turn, particularly from the point of view as to how we should combat it in the American labor movement. In the course of the discussion, however, it became evident that Burnham's estimate of the aims of the Soviet bureaucracy is somewhat different from ours.

We explain the "peace" offensive of Stalin and the threats of revolution as simply a repetition of the whole Stalinist game of using the Comintern and its parties in the capitalist countries to serve the current needs of Soviet foreign policy. The left turn is designed, as was the People's Front ballyhoo, not for fundamental struggle against the imperialist powers, but as a means of pressure upon one camp or the other. Fundamentally, Stalin doesn't want to fight any of the big powers; he wants them to let him alone.

This view of the role and tactics of Stalinism on the world arena

---

*See "Resolution on Party Unity" in the next section of this volume entitled *Documents of the Struggle.—Ed.*

used to be taken for granted amongst us, and didn't need to be repeated in every discussion. In fact, during the discussion I began to formulate some practical motions in regard to the tactics of our comrades in the trade unions, without bothering to put this accepted analysis as a preface to the motions. Thereupon, Burnham introduced a motion from a decidedly different standpoint. The gist of his theory is contained in point "b" of his motion which I am sending along in this letter, together with the other motions presented by me.

The discussion then took a new turn and we spent quite a long time on the question of the *aims* of the new line of Stalinism. We explained at some length, as has so often been explained in the past, that the Stalinist bureaucracy is an excrescence on the Soviet state and is in radical conflict with its own economy. Hence, its extraordinary instability and its fears of any social shocks or disturbances such as wars and revolutions. Its subsidized parties in the capitalist countries create activities in support of the current zig-zag of the Soviet foreign policy. These activities are designed, not to overthrow or conquer this or that group of imperialists, but as blackmail to buy them off or scare them off.

Burnham, and Shachtman following him, elucidated more frankly and fully than before their new theory that everything is changed, and that the Stalin gang is stepping out on a sort of Napoleonic path of world aggression. Burnham's point "b" says "the Soviet bureaucracy aims to capture control of potential popular uprisings against the war in order to serve and expand its own power and privilege." In the discussion that followed this was explained in the most fantastic manner, especially by Shachtman. He drew a picture of Stalin spending millions of dollars to buy up the nationalist leaders in India and of setting on foot a great uprising against Britain, which would be controlled bureaucratically from Moscow.

We explained that in our opinion Stalin could take the path of Napoleonic conquest not merely against small border states, but against the greatest imperialist powers, only on one condition: that the Soviet bureaucracy in reality represents a new triumphant class which is in harmony with its economic system and secure in its position at home, etc. That if such is really the case, we certainly must revise everything we have said on the subject of the bureaucracy up to now, and admit at the same time that the regenerating revolution in the Soviet Union, along with the proletarian revolution in the West, must be crossed off for a long time to come.

The debate ended by the decision to draft resolutions for consideration at the next meeting. My motions are taken as the basis for the resolution of the majority and Burnham's for the resolution of the minority.

It must be borne in mind that both motions were formulated on the spot and, therefore, lack a finished and rounded-out shape. Nevertheless, they give the gist of the two conflicting opinions.

I should mention that Abern sat silent throughout the discussion, as he almost invariably does when important questions are on the agenda. He almost always sits silent and waits and adjusts his position to the exigencies of the internal faction struggle, not vice versa.

On the vote, all four members of the minority voted for Burnham's formulation. The eight members of the majority voted for mine.

I will forward to you the copies of the conflicting resolutions as soon as they are prepared. I am sure that you will want to comment at length on this new attempt to throw overboard all that has been thought and said and done on the subject of the role of Stalinism, and start all over again on the eve of the war.

It is clearer than ever that we are in for a fundamental struggle over the programmatic basis of our movement. But I, for my part, face it without a trace of pessimism or discouragement. That also is the attitude of all my closest co-workers here. We are only profoundly gratified that this hidden weakness is brought out into the open before the entry of the United States into the war, and under conditions which permit a solution and a reeducation of the cadres of the Fourth International in free discussion.

Fraternally,
J. P. CANNON

A LETTER TO ALL MAJORITY GROUPS

New York, November 20, 1939

Dear Comrades,

In a previous letter I informed you about the dispute between us and the minority over the meaning of the new turn of Stalinism.

Their theory of an imperialistic Stalin, launching on a Napoleonic path of conquest throughout the world, stems directly from Burnham's thesis that the Soviet bureaucracy has, to all intents and purposes, emerged as a new victorious class.

It is remarkable how the other people in the combination, Shachtman, Abern, etc., more and more adapt themselves in the political conclusions they draw to this basic theoretical premise of Burnham which has been ostensibly "withdrawn."

Anyone with half an eye can see that Burnham has simply made a shrewd bargain. In return for the formal withdrawal of his document, he succeeds in smuggling it in piece-meal into the practical political conclusions of the whole minority.

Joe Hansen sent me the enclosed copy of a prospectus the Old Man drew up for an article for *Liberty* magazine. You should study it very attentively in the light of our new dispute over the role of Stalin. It seems to us to confirm entirely our analysis as communicated to you in a previous letter.

All comrades should acknowledge the receipt of each letter as it arrives, and also give us information about the local party situation.

Fraternally,

J. P. CANNON

A LETTER TO C. CHARLES

New York, December 1, 1939

C. Charles
Los Angeles, Cal.
Dear Comrade,

I received your letter today. Also received letters from David Stevens and Mark Knight. Please take this as an acknowledgment of all three and show it to the others.

Naturally we are all gratified to hear that all three of you take a firm position on the Russian question. I can state, however, that I personally never expected anything different. I could not assume that comrades who have participated most actively in the theoretical and political disputes and discussions out of which our program has been crystallized really learned nothing from the experience. In general, I can state that your reactions are similar to those of the basic cadres of the party throughout the country.

We are in for a thoroughgoing programmatic fight. It is incorrect to delay organization of our forces. On the contrary you should proceed immediately with the organization of a firm political caucus strictly confined in membership to those who take a clear and unambiguous position in support of the program of the Fourth International. We want no blocs or combinations with half-way people, but a straight-out fight for the program, the whole program and nothing but the program. This caucus should map out a campaign of struggle to win a firm majority for the forthcoming convention. You should also designate some comrade as secretary to receive communications from us and to send us information and reports.

We are having the regular semi-annual city convention in New York tomorrow. According to the results of the branch elections the opposition will have a majority of approximately two to one. This is to be explained in part by the unfavorable social composition of the party in New York and the frightful demoralization of petty-bourgeois elements in general before the assault of bourgeois democratic public opinion. We have not a few people who react to every headline and editorial against the Soviet Union in the bourgeois press as a seismograph reacts to tremors in the earth.

In part, the momentary victory of the minority here is to be attributed to the fact that we are confronted with a *combination* of people of all kinds of differing and contradictory views on political questions, who are united in their opposition to the "regime," i.e., a firm political line and a corresponding organizational system.

In part, the immediate advantage of the combination in New York can be attributed to the fact that they began the factional struggle secretly long in advance. We had the preliminary rumblings of this at the national convention, when a two-thirds majority of the New York delegates suddenly turned up as opponents of the national leadership without any advance notice to anybody.

Of interest to you will be the fact that Abern is being put forward as the candidate of the combination to replace Frank as City Organizer. This—so to speak—is to be Abern's *organizational reward* for capitulation to Burnham on the Russian question.

The line-up of well known leading people presents no surprises. The attempts at revisionism (Burnham), the pitiful vacillations (Shachtman), and the crass subordination of political and even programmatic questions to "organizational" considerations (Abern)—all this is confined pretty much to individuals who have exhibited these tendencies time after time in the past. In the present circumstances, under the pressure of the war crisis, they are only running true to form.

Their supporters at the beginning—and as has always been the case, such oppositions are far stronger at the beginning than at the end of a discussion—consist mainly of the inexperienced comrades who have not had the advantage of the previous educational discussions, plus the incurable cliquists who lie in wait from year to year for somebody else to lead a political struggle, in the course of which they hope to present their "organizational" claims.

The line-up of the party on a national scale (including New York) from the point of view of personnel is simply devastating for the combination. All the outstanding proletarian and trade union leaders of the party, with perhaps an incidental exception here and there which is not yet known to us, firmly support the party program. The same is true of the experienced party activists whom we have relied upon at every decisive turn in the past.

We suffer at the moment, once again, from an ironic twist of the dialectic contradiction involved in fusions with centrists and entries into reformist organizations. You recall that we had to force through the fusion of the Trotskyists with the centrists of the Muste organization against the opposition of the Oehlerites and in part, also, against the Abernites. Nevertheless, at the next stage after the fusion had been consolidated in a formal sense, both Oehler and Abern found new points of support for a new struggle against us precisely among the unassimilated centrists. It required a new internal struggle to complete the fusion in a political and ideological sense and isolate the sectarians on the one hand and the sterile cliquists on the other. Nevertheless, the political dregs of the old Musteite organization remained with the Abern clique and helped to nourish its subterranean existence throughout these years.

We are having an analogous experience now as a deferred payment on the overhead charges of the entry into the S.P. The left social-democratic elements who were not made over in the process of fusing with us, who didn't succeed in assimilating the ideas and methods of Bolshevism into their blood—and not few of whom haven't yet got them straight in their heads—these comrades are today the chief base of support for the opposition combination. We "entrists" of 1935 have to take upon ourselves now the task of completing our work of re-educating and assimilating the ex-socialists in the course of a very sharp and concentrated ideological and political fight.

The center of this fight naturally is in New York. We have every reason to be confident that we will succeed even here. But we require the overwhelming support of the rest of the country, and particularly of the proletarian sections, in order to discourage any further attempts to tamper with the program of the Fourth International after the forthcoming national convention.

In the course of the political fight which has been going on here for some time now, we are having the most gratifying successes in the ranks of the youth. The young comrades who were stampeded in the beginning on all kinds of extraneous and inconsequential issues and gossip are beginning now to review the question in the light of fundamental considerations. The "solid block" of the youth, with which the opposition combination expected to intimidate the National Committee, is falling apart. A considerable number of the most able comrades among the youth in New York have completely changed their position and are now leading a struggle for the program and for principled methods of struggle. We gain in this field not only from week to week but even from day to day. After this struggle is concluded and its experiences are fully assimilated I think we can be confident that never again will anyone be able to count on "lining up" the youth as a body to support an assault on the program of the party.

The discussion preceding the New York District Convention has taken place ostensibly around organization questions of a local character without reference to any of the national political resolutions. In reality, however, the combination mobilized solidly to take revenge on the local Executive Committee and the local organizer, Comrade E. R. Frank, for their support of the party program on the Russian question. By their announcements in the discussion they have given a clear indication of what they mean by a change in the "regime." The present local leadership is to be thrown out of office, and the organizer removed from his post in favor of a new committee standing on the political platform of the combination, with Abern as the organizer.

This also foreshadows their national plans in the event of victory. I doubt very much whether this kind of a regime will prove very attractive to the serious and experienced and informed cadres of the party throughout the country, including those (like myself) who can point out more than one flaw in the "regime" we have at present.

I hope you will not take these references to the prospect of an Abern "regime" as "scare propaganda" designed to terrorize everybody into line for the present "regime." I simply give you the facts of the New York plans of the combination and their projection nationally and leave you to draw your own conclusions, with only one pertinent quotation from the cautious Hamlet of Shakespeare: "Rather bear the ills we have than fly to others that we know not of."

As a matter of fact, the campaign against the New York local leadership, and against Frank as the organizer, is a positive outrage. On the merits of their work during the past six months they deserve not censure but congratulation and approval. The one place where we made a real stir in the struggle against the Coughlinites and in general activity since the party convention was precisely here in New York under this leadership. All the records and facts show, not simply a modest improvement in the work in New York during the past six months, in comparison with the preceding six months, or with the same period a year ago, but a multiplication of activity in practically all fields.

Since I am somewhat familiar with the activity of the party in other parts of the country, I can testify that the same comparison to the advantage of the New York organization during the recent period holds good there also. When we come to discuss the organization question at the national convention, I am quite sure that on the basis of the record the report of Frank as the leader of the New York work during the past six months will stand out above all others.

The attempt to remove and disgrace Frank and to replace him by Abern should have an interest for all comrades in the party who take seriously the orientation towards trade union work and proletarianization in general. In the person of Frank we have a comrade who, despite his youth, distinguished himself in the trade union field and became one of the outstanding party trade union leaders.

He brought to his work as party organizer a rich experience in the mass movement and a proven capacity to deal with workers, to organize them, and to understand their language. Such comrades are rare enough in our ranks.

But if we mean seriously to change the character and the composition of the party by turning its face towards the workers, shouldn't we deliberately aim to strengthen the composition of our professional party staff by the inclusion of more organizers of this type? Moreover, although he always talks and acts like a man, from the point of view of age Frank is still a youth—26 years old. In years he is younger than several of these professional and eternal Yipsels who are almost old enough to have children in the Yipsels but who are nevertheless everlastingly whining that a sharp word addressed to them is unfair to the "youth"—the youth, who, it is maintained, are as yet too fragile to be exposed to the realities and brutalities of our manners, which, God forgive me, I must confess are not always the manners of the salon or the college class room.

Abern, on the other hand, with his merits and defects which are known to each and every one of the experienced people in our party, is and always has been a strictly internal party man. His experience has been confined exclusively to inner party work and activity, with the exception of the brief period when he assisted me in the work of the International Labor Defense years ago. To be sure, this does not disqualify him from holding one or another party post where his administrative talent can have free play. But as the organizer of the most important political district of the party, at a time when we are constrained to make heroic efforts to turn the activities of the party outward towards the workers and not inward upon ourselves, he can only be the symbol of a step backward. The replacement of Frank by Abern will be a miscarriage of the line of our last convention dictated by shortsighted factional considerations.

One more point—and not a small one either. You have seen the resolution unanimously adopted by the P.C. in favor of party unity and the settlement of the dispute within the framework of the party and the Fourth International, without expulsions on the one hand or splits and withdrawals on the other. The whole party was waiting for this reassurance and welcomed it. But how does the violent campaign for the replacement of Frank by Abern reenforce this assurance? In the past we have known of two attempts by Abern to organize a split in the party. If he did not succeed it was perhaps, on the one hand, because he is not as good an "organizer" as he is cracked up to be and, on the other hand, because we placed a few obstacles in his path. To be more precise, we pounded his program so mercilessly that his splitting caucus fell apart and was reduced to such a small circle of diehard personal adherents as to be incapable of making a split that anybody would notice.

The party has not yet made proper acknowledgment of the party-loyal action of Comrade Weber in separating from Abern and paralyzing the split program at the decisive moment, just before the convention preceding our entry into the S.P. (Needless to say, the Abern clique has neither forgotten nor forgiven the "treachery" of Weber. They ostracize him socially up to this day and even at the last convention they made a surreptitious attempt to remove him from the National Committee. The sentiment of revenge, apparently, has a longer memory than the sentiment of gratitude.)

It is time now to recall also that in the old Cannon-Shachtman struggle in the C.L.A.,* which, as we all remember, brought us to the very brink of a split which was only prevented by international intervention—it was precisely Abern who resisted the peace agreement and the dissolution of the contending factional organizations. Shachtman has testified to this in a party document. It was only the revolt of Shachtman, Lewit and others which paralyzed a split at that time.

It should be noted, also, that Abern, who took the post of local organizer in New York at the time when split was on the order of the day, and in that capacity sharpened and accentuated the struggle with the National Office in every possible way, immediately resigned his post as local organizer when the peace agreement was made.

I would be the last one to rake up past errors of anyone in a new situation if there is reason to believe there is no connection between the past and the present. But we have now a very grave crisis in the party over the most fundamental questions that have ever created divisions in our ranks. The atmosphere in New York is extremely sharp. Our experience teaches us to see in every factional dispute the possibility and the danger of a split. In my own personal experience of twenty years of American communism, to leave aside the previous experience of the war and pre-war movement, I have observed that faction struggles have led more often to splits than to reunifications on a higher basis.

From this experience we must all conclude that it is necessary to take every possible measure at the outset of a dispute to safeguard

---

*Communist League of America (C.L.A.) was the original name of the Trotskyist movement in this country, after the expulsions of the American Trotskyists from the Communist Party of the United States of America, fifteen years ago.—*Ed.*

the party unity. This attitude dictated our proposals for the joint adoption of the unity statement; for the setting up of the parity commission to examine grievances; for the joint editorship of the internal bulletin to guarantee the minority against discrimination; the removal of organization complaints to the point where there is not a single grievance at the present time before the parity commission and has not been since it was constituted.

But I think we can also testify from experience that unity is safeguarded not merely by pacifistic gestures and concessions toward those elements of a minority who want in good faith to preserve party unity. There must also be the dialectic complement of militant struggle and exposure of all elements who venture even to play with the idea of a split, in order to separate the conscientious comrades from them, to isolate them, and thereby paralyze any split adventure.

Abern was never interested in the post of city organizer in New York at any time during the past two years of more or less normal party peace. At every city convention—in New York they take place every six months—there has been a suggestion from someone or other of Abern's personal clique that Abern take the post of organizer. Each time he refused entirely to consider the proposition. Now, at the height of a faction fight, the sharpest and bitterest we have ever known, Abern proposes to take the post of New York organizer and, in the process, to remove and disgrace a young comrade who has done a good job.

It is proposed, in addition, to set up a New York local committee which would aim in effect to be a rival political center to the National Committee which alone has authority in political matters under our constitution. Whatever the design of the minority combination may be in this procedure, the whole proposition, especially the designation of Abern as organizer in the present situation, has for us a sinister implication.

You can depend upon it that we will be on guard, for we have set for ourselves as revolutionary task—or more precisely, double task—number 1 the realization of the following two slogans: Maintain the program of the Fourth International, and maintain the unity of the party on the basis of the program.

Fraternally,
J. P. CANNON

A LETTER TO JOSEPH HANSEN

New York, December 14, 1939

Dear Joe,

Wright told me that you inquired about the article on the workers' guard. He translated that for us but we have only one copy. From the content of the article it is unclear to us whether it is designed for publication in the press, the internal bulletin or in a circular to branches. Will you please check this right away and let us know what disposition is desired? Then we will take care of it right away.

I am now having some concrete figures compiled on the social composition of the party in New York City. As you perhaps remember, a registration was taken sometime recently. According to the statement of Sam Gordon, who checked the registration in connection with his trade union work, only about one-sixth of the membership of the party and YPSL in New York is composed of industrial workers. This figure seemed to me so astounding that I have asked the City Office to give me an exact report. I will forward a copy to you as soon as I get it.

The big preponderance of the minority in New York gives us quite a handicap in the national contest. I had been proceeding on the theory that the strong majority in the more proletarian districts would easily overbalance the New York handicap. However, a rather careful check which I made yesterday on the basis of the last convention figures of representation doesn't present too optimistic a picture. On the face of things now we appear to be assured of a small majority at the convention. A few shifts or surprises could change the situation in the other direction.

You mustn't forget for a moment that we are up against a general combination of all elements opposed to us on every conceivable ground. The opposition as represented by its political leader (Burnham) is indubitably a right-wing opposition, not simply on the Russian question, but also on the organization question. This does not prevent the remnants of ultra-left opposition who remained in the party from rallying around the combination. And, needless to say, the combination leaders in no way repel support from this direction also. In addition, they count on the votes of all the insulted and injured, regardless of who insulted or injured them. Many of our New York youth, for example, who were justifiably offended by McKinney's rudeness and brusqueness, are lined up against the "regime"—along with McKinney.

On the other hand, we have the overwhelming majority of the proletarian activists on our side. This applies in New York as elsewhere. Among the statistical data being compiled by Comrade Edwards some figures on this are also to be included.

We are making steady headway in the youth. But here we had to begin from nothing. The youth had all been lined up before the fight started on the basis of gossip or small grievances of one kind and another. A great many of them were so poisoned and disoriented that a serious political discussion has had difficulty in making its way among them.

Together with our leading youth comrades I am arranging to devote from now on one night a week for political discussions with the youth. A long series of lectures has been mapped out, beginning with explanations of what principled politics really means. This has to be explained to our youth who have been cruelly miseducated and disoriented by the clique politicians of the Abern school on the one side, and the ex-Socialists in the youth leadership who haven't yet completely shed their skins. The latter are better material than the former. There is reason to hope that in time most of them can learn. The others, however, don't want to learn.

In my elucidation of the principled method of politics I intend to sketch out for our young comrades a history of the American Communist movement in the light of its internal struggles. I will also draw heavily on the experience of our international organization for the past ten years. Together with Wright, I have been compiling all the necessary material from the old internal and international bulletins. If you want to spend a few profitable hours you should dig this material out of the files and read it over. The things that were written by the Old Man years ago in the conflicts with Landau, Naville, Nin, etc., appear startling in their freshness and timeliness and their pertinence to the struggle that has broken out in our party under pressure of the war crisis. We have remarked about several of these articles that, with a very slight editing and change of names, they could be printed in our internal bulletin today as contributions to the present discussion.

I am very glad indeed to hear that Crux is writing another article on the most fundamental aspects of the present dispute. A really positive intervention on his part, which will present things as they really are, is perhaps the one thing now that can save for the Fourth International those who are worth saving.

Fraternally,

J. P. CANNON

A LETTER TO BILL MORGAN

New York, December 15, 1939

Bill Morgan
San Francisco, Cal.
Dear Bill,

The results of the New York City convention must put all comrades throughout the country on guard and convince them of the necessity of making the most thorough preparations for the forthcoming National Convention of the party on the organizational as well as on the political field.

As I wrote in a previous letter, the opposition combination won the elections by approximately two to one. Their representation in the City Convention was somewhat even better than this as a result of certain maladjustments in the proportional representation and the addition of the YPSL delegation. This relation of forces, in view of the large number of New York delegates, means that we will come to the National Convention under a very heavy handicap. Unless we make a real effort to see that the majority sentiment in the branches throughout the country is fully represented, the results of the convention can represent a catastrophe for the Fourth International.

I am enclosing herewith a blank form which you are requested to fill out without delay in order that we may have the necessary statistical information to get a fairly clear picture of the convention prospects. In addition, exceptional efforts must be concentrated now on seeing to it that all membership lists are carefully checked, that dues of members are paid up, and that each branch is represented at the convention by the exact number of delegates to which it is legitimately entitled under the convention rules—no more and no less.

I write on this subject for the first time in the eleven years' history of our movement because we have reasons, as a result of the experience in New York, to be apprehensive of attempts at manipulation. We have already uncovered one case of an outright election fraud and we are conducting a rigorous investigation into some other suspicious incidents. You will be given concrete information about this a little later. In the meantime, *begin now* to devote serious and concentrated attention to the organization side of the convention preparations. Study the convention rules and see to it that they are strictly adhered to.

The right-wing combination gave us a real dose of Tammany

Hall politics in the campaign preceding the New York City convention. They mobilized all their political supporters without presenting any political resolutions. On the other hand, they appealed for the support of those in political agreement with the majority who had organizational grievances or criticisms of one kind or another. They were as busy on the technical side of convention preparations—figuring the proportional percentages, wangling a vote here and there, shifting people from one branch to another in such a way as to exploit the most favorable factional percentages, paying back dues of supporters, etc.—as any set of precinct captains. In addition, they hit us over the head with a considerable bloc of "graveyard votes"—people who hadn't been seen or heard from for a long time, and from some carelessness remained on the books of the branches, suddenly turned up to pay back dues and vote on election night. Some of these "election workers" didn't learn much from us in the Socialist Party, but they learned plenty from Jack Altman. We can expect a transference of these methods to other parts of the country.

The bourgeois political method manifested itself in another characteristic way. Every bourgeois politician always promises to reduce taxes and increase efficiency at the same time. This campaign demagogy and bombast, hitherto absent from our discussions, came out in full bloom in the New York pre-convention period without the slightest relation to reality and without discrimination between the different departments of city work. Everything done during the past six months was condemned as wrong and inefficient, and unfulfillable promises were made that everything would be done better under the new administration. They promised everything but Socialism; that naturally has to wait until the main enemy —which apparently is not "in our own country" but in the National Committee of our own party—is overthrown. One can easily admit that one result of this bourgeois campaign—the replacement of one set of local officials by another—can eventually be rectified. But the other and more important result—the miseducation of the party, the promotion of cynicism, the spirit of electioneering, etc. —that will not be so easily overcome.

The new City Committee, which was installed at the convention, consists of twenty-one members including the alternates, who attend all meetings without vote. You will perhaps say that a committee of such fantastic size is not properly adapted to the efficient organization of local work even in normal times, and that a serious preparation for war conditions in any case must dictate the construction of smaller committees all along the line, for greater safety and mobility. But such objections leave out of account the necessity of the combination to provide representation for each of its various tendencies, as well as to "take care" of various individuals who were against the old committee precisely because they were not members of it.

The first session of the new committee gave us a dose of spoils politics and at the same time gave those comrades throughout the country, who are worried about the "regime," an advance picture of a different one. Frank was replaced by Abern as City Organizer. The director of unemployed work was replaced by one of theirs. Then the director of the party educational department, Comrade Wright, was also summarily removed and replaced by Carter. This removal has aroused a particular antagonism and resentment. Everybody knows the conscientiousness with which Comrade Wright undertakes and carries out every task assigned to him. And nobody could have reason to doubt that a party school under his direction would teach *Marxism*. From all reports I have heard, the work of Comrade Wright as educational director was highly regarded by the party generally. No serious attempt was made to justify his removal, except to maintain that the majority had a right to remove and appoint whomever it saw fit to any post. This "right" is unassailable. But if we take the New York performance as precedent for general application, the party will undoubtedly experience something new in the way of an internal "regime."

In order to present an absolutely fair and complete picture I must admit that one post was left to the defenders of the Soviet Union, that of trade union director. Frank, removed from his post as party organizer on the ostensible ground that he is no good for organizing, was entrusted with the task of organizing and directing the trade union work. Was this a concession to the minority of the City Committee even at the cost of a little contradiction? No, that is not the reason. Among all the supporters of the combination in New York City they could not find a single man with the experience and authority required for the office of trade union director. That fact says much about the real line-up here. It says almost everything.

Fraternally,
J. P. CANNON

A LETTER TO FARRELL DOBBS

New York, December 15, 1939

Dear Comrade Dobbs,

Last Sunday we had an internal party debate on the Soviet invasion of Finland. This followed by one week the New York City convention about which I have written in another letter. These two events have revealed the profound differences more clearly and have enormously sharpened the factional situation in New York City.

As becomes clearer every day, what is involved is not simply an ordinary discussion in which different opinions are presented, but an irreconcilable struggle in which sides are being taken. You will recall that at the plenum a mere two months ago we characterized the ambiguous resolution of Shachtman as a bridge to the anti-Bolshevik position of Burnham. With the Finnish events this bridge has already been crossed. The author of the minority resolution on Finland was Burnham and, corresponding to the new stage in the development of the struggle, Burnham appeared at the New York membership meeting as the debater for the minority, in place of Shachtman who appeared in this capacity at the beginning of the discussion on the Russian question. This change of pitchers, so to speak, signifies that the ball game is entering the crucial seventh inning. Or, to change the figure, as I remarked in the debate, the attorney is replaced by the principal and the real issues will be clearer now.

The debate had all the tension of a battle. We didn't discuss with each other, we fought each other. We couldn't "discuss" because we didn't proceed from the same premise and couldn't talk on the same plane. I constructed my whole argument around the idea that Roosevelt and Hoover are mobilizing the American and world bourgeoisie for a political and ideological war against the Soviet Union on the pretext of the Finnish events; that this campaign in fact has already advanced to the stage of providing material aid, which can have all the significance of a direct military intervention (Hoover's fund-raising committee, remission of Finnish debt, war materials from Italy, England, etc.) ; and that in these circumstances we must reassert and stand by the two basic points of our thesis on "War and the Fourth International":

1. The main enemy is in our own country—expose and fight the Roosevelt-Hoover combination.

2. Defend the Soviet Union in spite of Stalin against Stalin.

Burnham constructed his whole speech around an attack on the National Committee of the party as capitulators to Stalinism. He denied that the Soviet Union is a workers' state—since he was speaking in his own name and not through an attorney I provoked and demanded of him that he state his position. He declared himself in favor of the defeat of the Red Army.

It was a hard and bitter debate. Two sides. Two camps. Burnham laid aside the professorial urbanity which he never entirely loses in polemics against the class enemy and attacked the National Committee with truculence and even impudence, as though it were indeed the main enemy. He challenged me, with the brutal arrogance of a man who has his opponent in a corner, to go out and face the popular clamor at a public mass meeting on the Soviet invasion of Finland. To all of us he seemed to speak with an unwonted self-assurance and self-confidence, like a man who feels powerful forces behind him.

I, in answer, said that I would be very glad to defend the Soviet Union at a public meeting and hoped one would be arranged in the near future, but that unfortunately my first task was to defend the Soviet Union in our own party. I characterized the whole popular clamor around the question of Finland as primarily an expression of the powerful pressure of the united bourgeoisie on public opinion, mobilized through newspapers, pulpits, radio stations, and other means of communication and information. I said that Stalin to be sure, in this case as always, had done everything possible to alienate the sentiment of the masses and to serve the game of the democratic imperialist masters, but that we shouldn't be thrown off the track and lose sight of the essence of the question on this account.

I characterized—and, by God, I was right!—the offensive against the Soviet Union inside our party as nothing but a craven capitulation to the pressure of bourgeois public opinion. I said that a party which yields to this pressure already before the actual war begins would never be able to stand up when the real heat is turned on. You see, we didn't get along very well together at all.

Burnham wants to undermine the Marxist program of the party and to replace the Marxist political *method* by an empirical approach to every new incident as an independent question. I personally never had any sympathy with Burnham's ideas and conceptions in this respect. But, along with others, as long as Burnham remained an isolated factor unable to assert any decisive influence on the course of the party, I saw no reason to draw our differences with him out to the end. But now, since Burnham speaks as the representative of a numerically strong combination in the party, the situation stands somewhat differently. It would be criminal folly and disloyalty to the Fourth International to yield an inch to this anti-Marxist offensive or to relent for a single moment in the struggle until the program and the methods of Marxism in all fields have re-established an unquestionable hegemony.

In order to leave absolutely nothing unsaid, now that the fight is out in the open in all respects, I intend to write in another letter political and personal characterizations of the three main leaders of the right-wing combination—Burnham, Abern and Shachtman*—and to show that speculation on possible shifts or retreats of one or another of these three people is a false approach to the problem posed by the party crisis. The party membership must be educated to reconquer the positions of Bolshevism in an uncompromising struggle against these people. That is the only way to prepare the party for the war. What any of these individuals, or all of them, may do after the party ranks have consciously asserted themselves—that question, with all its importance, is nevertheless a question of second order.

Fraternally,
J. P. CANNON

---

*Instead of writing these characterizations in letter form, they were set down at length in the document, "The Struggle for a Proletarian Party." See pp. 1-82 of this volume.—*Ed.*

A LETTER TO LEON TROTSKY

New York, Dec. 21, 1939

Dear Comrade Hansen [Trotsky],

Here is one very important question about which we would like to have your opinion by return mail. For some time, Burnham and Shachtman have been pressing to carry the discussion into the public press of the party. Our original decision to publish your second article on the nature of the Soviet State was later reconsidered because the minority demanded the right to answer it also in the *Appeal.**

Next they demanded the right to publish the minority statement on Stalin's invasion of Finland in the *Appeal* with the official statement of the P.C.

Now they announce that they have a long document on the Russian question almost ready which they want to publish in the next number of the *New International.*** We have not yet seen this document, but from all indications it is highly polemical against you as well as against the majority.

The majority of our comrades here, including myself, are opposed to taking the discussion into the public press. Goldman, however, is in favor of it. In view of the difference of opinion, we have decided to consult you since very important issues are involved.

1. Up till now we have felt that if B. and S. carry their struggle into the public press in the present extremely sharp situation, and over such ·fundamental issues, they will be cutting off their own retreat. It would be much more difficult for them to reconcile themselves in one way or another to the party's rejection of their revisionist program once they have advertised it to the world.

2. We come into increasingly sharp conflict with Burnham, and lately also with Shachtman, over some general principles of communist organization involved in this question. They are pressing

---

*The *Socialist Appeal* was the name of the weekly organ of the party at that time. It was later changed back to the original name, *The Militant.*

For Trotsky's "second article on the nature of the Soviet State," see *In Defense of Marxism,* p. 24.—*Ed.*

**The *New International* was the name of the monthly magazine of the party at that time. For an explanation of why the name was changed to *Fourth International,* see "Why We Publish *Fourth International*" in the next section of this volume.—*Ed.*

all the time to establish as the *normal* procedure the right of a minority to contradict the party line in the public press. Implicit, and very frequently now explicit, in every move or proposal of Burnham touching organizational questions is the idea that we must take deliberate measures on every possible occasion to arrest the natural development of the Bolshevik party along the lines of Stalinist bureaucratization. Irrespective of the merits or demerits of the proposals at a given moment, we are entirely opposed to the general assault on the idea of a centralized and disciplined party which regulates its own affairs without the intervention of the general public, and decides for itself when and under what conditions it finds it advisable to make its internal affairs public. In a rather heated argument in the P.C. the other night, Burnham maintained that the right of a minority to publish its views in the press should be assured at any time in the development of the party's activities except during insurrection. I asked, "Why not during the insurrection?"

3. There is no possible question of the democratic party rights of the minority involved in this case. Our internal bulletins publish everything submitted by the minority and reach the entire membership. In addition, there is absolutely no discrimination in the discussion at party branch and membership meetings. The rule everywhere is equal time for the minority. What is really involved in the present demand of the minority is the right to appeal to the public.

4. Goldman maintains that the discussion in the press will serve our cause; that the force of our arguments in the controversy will mobilize the party sympathizers more firmly around the program of the Fourth International. I also think this would be the case. But I insist that if we take this step we must do it with eyes wide open. We must realize that a public discussion can hardly fail to accelerate the movement of Burnham and his satellite, Shachtman, in a direction opposite to ours.

* * *

The situation in New York gets sharper every day. We talk different languages. Nobody, not even the conciliatory Goldman, foresees any possibility of reconciling the conflicting positions. Our decision on the question of opening the discussion in the press must be taken with this state of affairs in mind. We have to make the decision in the next few days, as the magazine is already overdue. We all would appreciate it very highly if you would let us know your opinion immediately.

Fraternally,
J. P. CANNON

A LETTER TO A SEATTLE COMRADE

December 27, 1939

Dear Dick,

I have been sending you regularly copies of caucus correspondence on the internal dispute. Have you been receiving it? . . .

I would be glad to hear your opinion of the Old Man's latest article on the "Petty-Bourgeois Opposition in the Socialist Workers Party" and also on the fight in general.

My opinion in brief is that we now have the fundamental fight with the right-wing tendency that we had a few years ago with the ultra-lefts and that a decisive victory in this struggle is a prerequisite for further progress of the party.

Fraternally,

J. P. CANNON

A LETTER TO THE PARTY MEMBERSHIP

New York, January 3, 1940

To All Locals and Branches:

Dear Comrades,

On the Question of Discussion in the Socialist Appeal

For some time the minority of the Political Committee has been demanding that the public press of the party, including the *Socialist Appeal*, be opened to the minority for the presentation of their position on equal terms with the majority. They demand the right to counterpose [their own program to] the program laid down by national conventions of the party and congresses of the Fourth International.

At the meeting of December 5th, Comrade Burnham presented the following motion: "That in the same issue of the paper where the official party position on the Finnish conflict appears, there also be published the resolution introduced by the minority."

Repeatedly in discussions in the Political Committee, and lately also in branch meetings, the leaders of the minority and their supporters have maintained that a free presentation and defense of another program, as against the official program of the party and the international, in the public press is a normal procedure, and that its denial signifies a suppression of democratic party rights in the spirit of Stalinism.

In this conception of *organization,* as in their *theoretical* and *political* positions, the leaders of the minority demonstrate their antagonism to the principles and traditions of Bolshevism. The demagogic demand for "freedom of the press" represents a petty-bourgeois, anarchistic revolt against revolutionary centralism.

During the pre-convention discussion period the Bolshevik organization system assures full rights and facilities to a minority to present its case, freely and fairly, for the consideration and decision of the party membership. This tradition and unvarying practice of our movement—the best and most honestly democratic tradition and practice the labor movement has ever known—has been fully adhered to in the present discussion. All resolutions and articles submitted by the minority are published without censorship or discrimination in a jointly edited internal bulletin which reaches every party member. At all branch and membership meetings where the disputed questions are under discussion an equal division of time is the uniform rule. No restrictions of any kind are put in the way of the minority getting a fair hearing.

From the point of view of *party democracy*, from the point of view of getting a fair hearing from the entire *party membership*, the minority has no possible ground for any kind of complaint, and has placed no such complaints on record. In assuring and safeguarding this free and democratic discussion, the majority of the National Committee is only according to the minority its party *rights*, as established by the constitution of the party and the traditions of the Bolshevik movement.

With the public press of the party, however, the situation stands differently. If *democracy* holds sway in the *internal* discussion, then *centralism* predominates in the *public* expressions and actions of the party. The public party press is not and cannot be an instrument of discussion under the control of a parity committee. It is, rather, an instrument of the party and its National Committee for the presentation and defense of the official position of the party. In the discussion bulletin the opposition can ask for equal rights with the majority, but the official party publications have the duty to defend the point of view of the party and the Fourth International until they are changed by convention or congress. A discussion in the pages of the official party publications—as provided in the forthcoming issue of the *New International*, for example—can be conducted only within the limits established by the majority of the National Committee. Whoever disputes this rejects the whole conception of a centralized revolutionary party. At the same time he negates party democracy by subjecting the decisions of a majority to the public attack of a minority at whim.

There is a fundamental difference between the honest democratic centralism of a Bolshevik party and the pseudo-democracy of the parties of the reformists and centrists of all shades. The much-advertised public "freedom of discussion" didn't prevent the Socialist Party of Norman Thomas from gagging its revolutionary left wing. On the other hand, the genuine and honest democracy of a Bolshevik party does not assure "freedom" for anarchistic individuals to disavow and attack the party program before the public.

These considerations are self-evident to those comrades who are familiar with the Bolshevik tradition and practice and who desire to uphold it. Different opinions are possible only on the part of those who seek inspiration from other traditions of organization. But it is quite obvious that the attempt of the minority to overthrow the Bolshevik tradition, and break down the right of the party to speak through its press without public contradiction, involves something more than a mere difference of opinion. It is obvious that the leaders of the minority are not content to rest their case with the members of the party and let the party members decide. They want to proclaim their program to the public before the party has endorsed their program.

In view of the insistence with which they present this demand it is proper to ask: What is the source of this impatience? Why can't they wait for the verdict of their own party before appealing to the public? The explanation is all too simple. They want to justify themselves before democratic public opinion. Without waiting for the party convention, and not trusting the party membership to accept their position, they want to shout to all the Eastmans, Hooks and others that they, the opposition, are not as bad as we. They want to make it known that, besides the bad "Trotskyists," there are also some good ones who take a more reasonable—and more popular—view of things.

In their extreme impatience to make these announcements the leaders of the minority are attempting to stampede the inexperienced members of the party and the youth with the demagogic appeal for "democracy." The National Committee answers to the leaders of the minority: Democracy—*party democracy*—is precisely what you shall have. Full and equal rights for the minority in the party discussion—but only there! The *members of the party* and not *the public* will decide these disputes! You must wait for the verdict of the party and you cannot appeal to the public until this party verdict is announced.

The demand of the minority for "equal rights" in the public press of the party is an attack on the Bolshevik principle of centralized party organization. It is a perversion and distortion of its traditions and an unscrupulous attempt to miseducate the party in the spirit of Menshevism. The National Committee declares that it will under no circumstances permit any attacks on the program of the party and the Fourth International to appear in the *Socialist Appeal*—the political-agitational organ of the party. On the contrary, the *Socialist Appeal* will be devoted exclusively to a militant defense of the party position on all questions as long as these positions have not been changed by a convention or a congress.

Political Committee
SOCIALIST WORKERS PARTY
by J. P. CANNON
National Secretary

A LETTER TO THE PARTY MEMBERSHIP

New York, January 3, 1940

To All Locals and Branches:

Dear Comrades,

On Democratic Centralism

Supplementing the Political Committee letter of January 3d, we are calling your attention here to three pertinent references on the subject of democratic centralism as it has been conceived and practiced by our movement in the past and stated in official documents.

1. "Democratic centralism means the right of discussion inside the party, at times and in ways laid down by the party. Democratic centralism also means discipline; it means the subordination of the minority to the majority; it means the centralization of authority, between conventions, in one leading committee selected by the convention; it means that the party always confronts the outside world with a single policy, the policy of the majority of its authoritative bodies. Democratic centralism means that the individual party member always and under all circumstances must subordinate himself in his public action and expressions to the policy and decisions of the party."—From the "Statement of the Political Committee on the Expulsion of Joseph Zack," issued by the Workers' Party under date of June 4, 1935.

2. Replying to and rejecting the demand of the Oehlerites for public discussion, the plenum of the Workers' Party stated: "There is no *principle* which requires that material on controversy within the party must be carried within the public press of the party. Even in pre-convention discussions this is not the case; much less in other periods. It is the province of the National Committee to order such a discussion if it is to take place."—From the "Resolution on the Internal Situation of the Workers' Party, adopted by the October 1935 Plenum."

3. "The plenum . . . will lay down procedure for the pre-convention discussion and arrangements for the convention itself in accordance with the principles of democratic centralism. The rights of the membership will be fully safeguarded. The plenum categorically asserts, however, that it is the prerogative and duty of the plenum and the Political Committee, in accordance with well-established Bolshevik procedure and the constitution of the W.P. itself, to determine what is the correct procedure; what in a given

situation safeguarding the rights of the membership means, and to carry out the provisions of the constitution of the party. No individual or group can arrogate this so-called 'right' to himself or itself."—From the "Resolution on the Internal Situation of the Workers' Party, adopted by the October 1935 Plenum."

Yours fraternally,
POLITICAL COMMITTEE
by J. P. CANNON
National Secretary

A LETTER TO ALL MAJORITY GROUPS

New York, January 3, 1940

Dear Comrades,

We here are of the opinion that the party will benefit in every way if the convention is postponed for at least one month. However, we do not want to take the step here in the Committee without resolutions from the branches, requesting such a postponement.

We request you to introduce resolutions in all branches, asking for a postponement of the convention for at least one month. We list below a list of reasons. You can cite any one or all of them as you see fit in the resolutions you draw up. Please inform us immediately of the adoption of any such resolutions and see that official copies are sent to the National Office without delay.

* * *

Reasons for Postponing the Convention

(1) A month's postponement will assure much better weather for travelling by auto from far distant places. February is still pretty cold. We want at all costs to have a complete representation from the Western branches, and a month's postponement to a time of milder weather should facilitate their travel by car.

(2) We want a discussion in the party on *resolutions* of the two groups. We must demand everywhere that the minority present a resolution stating precisely what the party position will be on the Soviet state and its defense in the event that they receive a majority. Recently they have handed in and also distributed in the party a document of 25,000 words on the Russian question in which they manage to evade these two simple questions. They promise a resolution for the convention, but the membership is entitled to see it and discuss it beforehand. The branch resolution should state that we demand resolutions from the two sides so that members can know what they are voting on. The detailed resolution of the majority is going to be published in the next number of the *New International*.

(3) In view of the fact that Comrade Trotsky in his article on the "Petty-Bourgeois Opposition in the Socialist Workers Party" has raised the question of Marxist philosophy, the branches should ask what the answer of the minority leaders is on this point so that the party membership will be able to judge between the two positions and improve their Marxist education in the process of the discussion.

* * *

All branches are receiving a circular letter from the Political

Committee, replying to the demand of the minority that the columns of the *Appeal* be opened for attacks on the program of the party. In this case we have an excellent opportunity to educate some of the younger and more inexperienced comrades in the meaning of Bolshevik organization.

We propose that resolutions be drawn up on this question in all party branches without exception and that a thoroughgoing discussion take place on the meaning and significance of the two positions. All the necessary arguments are contained in the statement of the Political Committee and in the two letters from Comrade Rork [Trotsky] which you will receive.

We must take the offensive on this point. In no instance have the leaders of the opposition bloc shown their capitulatory attitude towards public opinion more clearly than in their demand of the "right" to tell their troubles to the public before the party membership has decided the disputes.

Incidentally, all comrades who are doing serious work in the mass movement can understand how the agitational value of the *Appeal* will be destroyed if it is converted into a discussion organ at the very moment we are undertaking to defend the Soviet Union against the whole world, including Stalin. It must be pointed out that the campaign of the *Appeal* in defense of the Soviet Union is an *action*. It can be compared to a strike situation, multiplied ten thousand times. A member of a strike committee might consider that a given strike is ill-advised and should be called off for one reason or another, and would have a full right to explain his point of view within the closed limits of a strike committee. But it would be a miserable strike committee indeed which would permit such an individual to carry his fight to the public before the question had been decided in the workers' ranks. And an individual who would resort to such an action would be called something more than miserable.

Fraternally,

J. P. CANNON

A LETTER TO FARRELL DOBBS

[When this letter was written comrade Dobbs was preparing to leave for Mexico City to visit Trotsky.—*Ed.*]

New York, January 3, 1940

Dear Dobbs,

. . . I haven't anything definite that you need to take up with the Old Man that he doesn't already know except what you can tell him from your own personal impressions, etc. The thing here is getting sharper every day. The first letters and articles of the Old Man were taken by these people as a sign of softness and weakness instead of as a warning. His blast on the petty-bourgeois opposition in the party, instead of inducing them to stop, look and listen for a while, has only aroused them to a greater frenzy.

. . . At last night's P.C. meeting we were informed that Shachtman has written an answer entitled "An Open Letter to Leon Trotsky." They should quit politics and read poetry for a while. Alexander Pope warned, "Fools rush in where angels fear to tread." And Shakespeare's Hamlet remarked that "The Almighty had set his canon 'gainst self-slaughter."

With so many people in the world being killed off by the wars and all it seems a pity that others out of the danger zone should embark on an orgy of self-destruction.

Fraternally,
J. P. CANNON

A LETTER TO A SEATTLE COMRADE

New York, January 4, 1940

Dear Dick,

I was very glad to get your letter of December 27th.

It is necessary to devote the maximum attention to the education of the party comrades on the present internal dispute. The coming convention will be in reality the real foundation convention of the American section of the Fourth International. In a broader sense we can say it will represent the real foundation congress of the Fourth International itself. Here we are meeting in concentrated form, in the only country where free democratic discussion is possible at the present time, a concentrated attempt to overthrow the program. If it is firmly repelled here it will represent a milestone in the development of the Fourth International on a world scale.

From this point of view, it is very important that you come to the convention as a delegate. If necessary, we will find some way of helping out with the finances.

According to the constitution, it would be possible for us to have a proxy delegate from the East elected by your branch. But the real purposes of the convention will only be served if the most qualified comrades from every part of the country attend the convention in person.

From this point of view I think you will heartily favor the suggestion that the convention be postponed until the weather breaks a little bit. Therefore, I hope to receive from you by early mail a resolution from the Seattle branch requesting this postponement.

Portland is chartered as a regular branch. It is highly worthwhile and absolutely necessary in fact for you to go down there and see that they get paid up and in shape to send a delegate. I cannot overemphasize the importance of such details as this at the present time. Also, it will be very good for you to contact Vancouver. We have heard that a large majority of the comrades in Toronto support the position of the majority but it is likewise important that Vancouver also take the correct position.

Fraternally,

J. P. CANNON

A LETTER TO A NEW HAVEN COMRADE

New York, January 4, 1940

Dear Frank,

I received your letter of January 3d. In the meantime you should have received some additional material.

It is very gratifying to hear that the majority of the branch has already declared for the majority. The thing to do is to keep hammering away to make it as close to unanimous as possible.

It is not sufficient for us to get a majority at the convention. We've got to get such a strong majority that no adventurer will dare to tamper with the idea of a split.

We are sending a copy of the Old Man's article to ———— as you suggest. It is very important for you to keep in contact with him and try in every way to get his agreement with our position. . . .

We've had an almost similar situation in Boston. The famous leader Donlon, according to a letter from Larry, has resigned from the party because he doesn't want to support red fascism in Russia. That's one of the troubles with the opposition in the party. People who really assimilate their teachings in all their implications can't see any longer the necessity of a revolutionary party.

With best wishes,

Fraternally,
J. P. CANNON

A GRADUATE BURNHAMITE

(An Internal Circular)

By J. P. Cannon

Burnham's theory that the Soviet bureaucracy is a new exploiting class, and "imperialist" to boot, has been taken seriously to heart by one of his Boston converts. D. Lawrence, who was an ardent member of Burnham's opposition bloc, doesn't belong to it any more. He graduated. Burnham convinced him too well; and as a practical man, after he became convinced that the Soviet Union is a new "imperialist" state, he naturally put to himself the question: Why the devil should I bother to argue or quibble about defending such a state in any way or under any circumstances?

Thereupon, he sent a letter of resignation to the Boston branch. The secretary in his official report says: "The branch after hearing the letter and giving it serious consideration and also considering what possible harm he could do our members in the trade unions had a somewhat different idea on the matter of resigning. The E.C. brought in a unanimous recommendation for his expulsion. The branch also unanimously approved the recommendation. The charge which the E.C. presented was on the 'grounds of renegacy from the 4th International'."

Bravo, Boston! Three cheers for the Bolshevik guard of Boston!

A LETTER TO LEON TROTSKY

New York, January 11, 1940

Dear Comrade Trotsky,

Your Open Letter to Burnham was received by Comrade Wright yesterday. He is now at work translating it. As soon as he is finished a copy will be supplied to Comrade Burnham and the document will be promptly published in our internal bulletin.

Your aggressive thrust of the question of the dialectic into the party discussion is producing some quite "dialectical" reactions—in the two camps. The supporters of the minority apparently have been instructed to meet the attack along the following lines:

1. Joke about the question and taunt the supporters of the majority: Since when did you become an expert on philosophy, etc.

2. Dialectical materialism of course is an interesting subject but it should be discussed some other time.

3. It is a bad method to introduce this question during a faction fight. (Did opportunists *ever* in any case to your knowledge fail to object to the "methods" of the Marxists?)

4. It is obviously a factional trick to split the minority by injecting extraneous issues, but since we all agree on our "conclusions" the maneuver will not succeed.

On the other hand, the ranks of the majority have responded with great interest and enthusiasm to your militant intervention on the subject of dialectical materialism *precisely because* it is done in connection with a thoroughgoing political and theoretical struggle. Many of them are turning to the books to study. Spontaneous popular demand called forth a decision to start a class on the subject in the party school under the direction of Comrade Wright who has studied the question seriously. There is general satisfaction and great appreciation of your initiative. Most of our comrades want not only to *win* but to *learn* and they are soaking up the lessons of this struggle like a sponge. Apropos a suggestion in the caucus meeting the other night that the convention might be postponed, one of the best and most promising of our young comrades remarked to those sitting beside him: "I hope the discussion is prolonged; I am learning every day."

Reports from the country are increasingly favorable. What is most gratifying is the virtual unanimity with which the proletarian activists, as well as the older basic cadres of the party, are rallying to the support of the majority. Outside New York and Chicago the party is basically proletarian. I am now receiving the returns from a questionnaire sent to our supporters throughout the country, asking questions as to the membership, social composition and attitude of the branch members on the disputes. These figures are extremely revealing. As soon as the returns are completed I intend to draw up a circular letter analyzing the figures and quoting some of the pertinent comments.

It is extremely interesting—and reassuring—to see how acutely the experienced worker Bolsheviks sensed the real trouble in the party. They *knew* what was the matter, and the various documents and arguments on the majority side only appear to them as rounded-out formulations of their own views. For example, one writes: "Our branch here is 100% for Bolshevik-Leninist methods which is not surprising when you know that the social composition of the branch is proletarian and *completely* so. The article by the Old Man was excellent. It expressed my thoughts on the minority tendency. Our Chicago organization has been stymied by this petty-bourgeois group too long."

Another: "I have not yet seen the article on the 'Petty-Bourgeois Opposition in the Socialist Workers Party' and consequently cannot express myself except to say that if a title means anything it should hit the nail on the head."

Fraternally,
J. P. CANNON

A LETTER TO LEON TROTSKY

New York, January 18, 1940

Dear Comrade Trotsky,

I am enclosing herewith Comrade Burnham's comments on your recent article on the petty-bourgeois opposition. Note the self-revealing first sentence. He shows that he thinks first of all about the reactions of the intellectual camp followers of democratic imperialism. It is unnecessary to point out also that he turns the original dispute with Eastman upside down. Eastman originally claimed to support the whole practical program of Lenin (the "engineering"); at that time, he announced, he simply wanted to make a "revolutionary" revision of Marxism by amputating its "religion" (dialectical materialism). It is amazing how the oppositionists mix up so many simple *facts* as well as ideas.

Resolutions are coming in from practically all the proletarian branches requesting a postponement of the convention in order, among other things, to have a more extended discussion on the questions raised in the first part of your article and Burnham's answer to it. Sneers and wisecracks on the subject of dialectical materialism hold sway among the declassed kibitzers of the Bronx branch (the Shachtman branch) but the proletarians in the party seriously want to know about this "religion," what it is, who is for it, and who is against it, and why.

I think you received a copy of the notice about a "Burnham graduate." Yesterday we received information of another. Robertson, the leader of the minority in Canada—the large majority there is firmly on our side—sent a letter of resignation to the party. The reasons are priceless. First, he does not want to defend the Soviet Union any longer; second, he feels the "despair" of an isolated petty-bourgeois intellectual (he is also by some strange chance a professor); and third, he is very much afraid that an American Soviet government with Cannon at the head of it would be just as ruthless as Stalin. By the way, that is exactly the fear that Burnham expressed almost word for word in a personal conversation with me and Shachtman about the time I wrote you my disturbed letter concerning him two years ago. In that conversation he also told us frankly that he wasn't sure whether the contradictions between his personal life and the responsibilities of a revolutionary leader were subconsciously at the bottom of his differences with us. A few months later Shachtman began to move over into Burnham's orbit. . . .

I am writing to Comrade Dobbs simultaneously. Since he has finally realized his long-deferred visit to you it would be short-sighted to cut the visit short. The length of his stay should be determined by your mutual convenience and desires. We will jog along here in the meantime. I suffer, of course, a great disadvantage and personal annoyance in this situation by the responsibility for administrative details which have to be taken care of somehow. It is like trying to run through a field cluttered with tough vines.

On top of that is the endless speaking. Last night I had to debate once more with Shachtman (on the organization question). I go through such labor with a feeling of physical revulsion; at least two-thirds or three-fourths of the time must be taken up in re-setting Shachtman's "quotations" into their proper context and in explaining how his historical references are falsely and disloyally represented in an opposite sense to their real import. I console myself with the thought that in doing this work I am at least acting the part of a good soldier. In debating with Shachtman I crawl on my belly through the mud for the sake of the Fourth International.

With warmest greetings,

J. P. CANNON

A LETTER TO FARRELL DOBBS

New York, January 18, 1940

Dear Comrade Dobbs,

I just wrote the Old Man that it would be pointless for you to cut your visit short now that it has been realized after so many delays. We will jog along here until you finish everything you have to talk over with him. However, I wish you would let me know what your schedule is and approximately when we can expect you. The convention will undoubtedly be postponed.

If you have time I would also like to get reports from you in rough outline at least of the subjects you are discussing with him and any suggestions or propositions you may have to make on the basis of these discussions. I would advise you to make comprehensive notes after each discussion when the subjects are fresh in your mind for your future consideration and also to refresh your mind when you report to us at more length.

One thing more. Be sure to talk over with the Old Man all questions of an administrative, personal and confidential nature which have concerned his dealings with me and Rose. I have already told him that I expect you will fully participate with us in this aspect of future work; consequently you should take advantage of the conversations face to face to have a thorough understanding about everything. . . .

We are still pounding away in the party fight. A close check-up of the national situation shows that on the basis of the present line-up we can expect a majority of about 5 to 3. They've still got the bulk of the petty-bourgeois elements and we've still got the bulk of the workers, but in spite of everything this is still a workers' party and the workers are the mostest and the toughest.

Fraternally,

J. P. CANNON

A LETTER TO ALL MAJORITY GROUPS

New York, January 19, 1940

Dear Comrades,

The Opposition Leaders Threaten Split

It has become very clear in recent days that the leaders of the opposition bloc are deliberately undertaking to maneuver their supporters into a split from the party and the Fourth International. This tendency has been manifest for some time, but in the most recent period their agitational preparation has taken more concrete forms. It appears that the article of Trotsky on the Petty-Bourgeois Opposition impelled them more deliberately on this course. The rather barren results of Shachtman's tour to the Middle West evidently convinced them finally that it is impossible to get a majority at the convention. The following are the most important facts which have come to our attention:

1. The other night, some comrades have informed us, they held a membership caucus meeting in New York with Shachtman as reporter. There the idea of a split was projected in a half-open, half-diplomatic manner. Shachtman explained that by characterizing them as petty-bourgeois, the majority means to put them in a category of second class citizens in the party. We, he announced, will never submit to this. We have principled differences. There will be no living in the party under Cannon after the convention. They will begin to expel Burnham, Abern, etc., and to remove all our people from posts. Since we are fighting for principles, we must keep our faction together and continue the struggle after the convention. That means we must have an organ of our own. (It was left unclear—perhaps deliberately—whether this means a public or an internal organ.) Cannon will not allow this; thereby he will provoke a split. Such was the gist of his long report.

2. This speech called forth violent reactions and considerable disturbances in the rank and file of the meeting. Three comrades took the floor and protested most vehemently against a split program on the ground that this will disrupt the whole movement of the Fourth International. They especially protested against the ultimative demand for the right to publish an organ after the convention. One comrade in particular (a former Socialist) argued that we have always explained democratic centralism differently. We have always boasted of the tradition of our movement according to which there is the freest discussion before conventions and

strictest discipline afterwards on the basis of the decisions of the majority. How can we go against this without doing violence to our tradition?

On the other hand, Gould, Carter and Garrett took the floor to support the position of Shachtman. Shachtman in his summary replied to the argument of the critics who had opposed an ultimatistic demand for a minority organ after the convention by saying: If Cannon sees that we don't mean it seriously he will not pay any attention to our demand. We can only convince him that we mean it if we actually do mean it. (Psychology!)

3. Along the same line has been the attitude of the opposition leaders towards party duties and even towards Political Committee meetings. Shachtman departed for his tour without authorization or notice to the Political Committee. Letters sent to him by order of the Political Committee, requesting at least that he furnish us with his itinerary, were ignored. One special and one regular meeting of the Political Committee found Shachtman, Abern and Burnham absent without notification. An official request for an explanation from them brought no reply. Shachtman makes no pretense of assuming any responsibility whatever for the production of the *Appeal*, of which he is co-editor. Even more symptomatic is the attitude of Burnham—in the past always very punctilious in the performance of accepted duties. He submits his weekly column or not as he sees fit without informing the managing editor, and usually omits it.

We have information that they have established a separate headquarters for the conduct of their local and national factional work. Burnham and Shachtman never appear at the National Office of the party, and consultation with them on day to day party matters is completely excluded. In addition, it should be mentioned that the national apparatus of the YPSL is to all intents and purposes a faction apparatus of the opposition. It routes organizers for faction work, etc., without any consultation whatever with the National Office of the party.

All in all, we must face the fact that the leaders of the opposition bloc, in their present mood, are moving deliberately towards a split.

How to Combat the Split Program

Already here in New York we have discussed this question several times and have begun our struggle against the split adventure. We give you here an outline from the main points of our approach to the question. It must be borne in mind at the outset that an incipient split is the most dangerous of all things to play with. It is folly to imagine that mere good will and good nature can prevent it. Only well-calculated and ruthless struggle can break up this split as we have broken up others in the past. This premise is incontestable. The methods and the forms of combatting the split, however, are extremely important.

1. First of all, it is necessary to educate and harden our own cadres and to inspire them with a fanatical patriotism for the party and the Fourth International and a determination to defend it under all circumstances. Split adventurers must be shown up in their true light as criminals and traitors to our International. How can one imagine a more perfidious crime than the disruption of the strongest legal section of the Fourth International on the eve of the war?

2. We must make a real campaign to win the rank and file supporters of the minority away from the split program. First of all, this means to convince them that we on our part have no intention whatever to initiate or provoke a split. In all speeches and in private conversations we must remind the comrades that it was the majority which introduced the unity resolution in the Political Committee, with the pledge to the membership that there should be no expulsions on the one side or withdrawals on the other at the party convention. It was we who brought forward the motion to set up a parity commission to examine and regulate grievances. It was we who proposed and provided a joint editorship of the internal bulletin to insure the minority against discrimination or fear of discrimination. On all occasions we state that, for our part, we still stand unconditionally on this resolution and are determined to maintain party unity. Even as a minority at the convention we will remain disciplined and wait for the further development of events to confirm our views and re-establish our majority in the leadership with the support of the vast majority of the party rank and file.

3. On all occasions refer the comrades to the letters of Trotsky and Cannon in Bulletin No. 6 wherein we each speak for unity and against a split even though the convention goes against us.

4. Ask the comrades: What is your complaint? Do you not get a fair hearing in the party discussion? Do you not have free access to the internal bulletin? Are you not given equal consideration with the majority in all respects in the party debates? *Do you think the discussion should be prolonged in order to give you a greater opportunity to win over the majority?* In that case you have only to make a proposal to postpone the convention; the majority will undoubtedly agree to any reasonable proposition along this line.

5. Ask the minority comrades: How can you possibly advance your cause by a split? Surely the workers belonging to the party are the most intelligent and advanced radical workers that can be found at the present time. If you cannot convince them in a prolonged and absolutely free and fair discussion, where, as an independent group, will you find the workers with whom to build a party? Can you visualize a revolutionary party without workers? Are there more advanced, more receptive and more militant workers to be found outside the party? Split leaders in the past who overlooked this point and rushed headlong into an appeal to the 130 million people in the country soon found themselves shouting in a void. The road to the masses is through the vanguard, not over its head.

6. Say to the minority comrades: If, in spite of everything, you really mean to split you should consider carefully the following questions:

a) The first question for every revolutionist is the question of international affiliation. Without a close union of co-thinkers on an international scale a revolutionary movement in our epoch is unthinkable. The split can only be a split away from the Fourth International, for the majority has stated that it will in no case initiate a split even though it remains for the time being in a minority; in no case will the majority leave the Fourth International.

b) Do you think there is political "living space" between the Fourth International and the London Bureau (which means, in the USA, the Lovestoneites)? Do you know any important political group on an international scale that found such a space? As a matter of fact doesn't the evolution of the Lovestone group—the American section of the London Bureau—towards fusion with the Thomas Socialists, who in turn approach the Socialist old guard, show that there is not enough political living space between the Fourth International and the Second?

c) Bear seriously in mind the political fate of others who tried to split the American section of the Fourth International. Weisbord, Field, Oehler, Stamm, etc., were all talented people—collectively, not less so than the leaders of the opposition bloc. In addition, most of them were more serious and more capable of determined struggle and sacrifice for their ideas. Yet all of these people came to the most miserable ends. Field lost his little group of a dozen or so and returned to private life a completely isolated figure. Ditto Weisbord. As for Oehler and Stamm, their original group has split into eight parts and the process goes on uninterruptedly. What do these catastrophic experiences prove? That the leaders of our party were much abler than the split leaders mentioned? Perhaps, but that is not by any means the most important side of the question. The degeneration and decay of each and every group which broke from the Fourth International on an international scale, as well as in the United States, in the course of the past ten years demonstrates conclusively: Outside the Fourth International there is no historic road.

d) A light-minded attitude towards party organization, towards splits and unifications—one of the most characteristic expressions of intellectualism and dilettantism—is a fatal thing. Socialism is inevitable but the struggle for socialism by means of the proletarian revolution must be *organized*. The sole means of organizing the proletarian revolution is the revolutionary party. A petty-bourgeois intellectual or dilettante, who has not assimilated the ideas of Marxism into his blood, is capable of rushing into unifications one day when there is only a seeming agreement and of splits the next day at the first sign of serious disagreement. Not so the workers. The worker joins a party for struggle. He puts his life into it. He takes his time before joining in order to see what a party is doing as well as what it is saying. When such a worker joins a party he takes it very seriously. He gives it his full devotion and recoils fiercely against anyone who takes the party lightly and disregards its discipline.

An intellectual dilettante is capable of joining a party without attaching any great significance to such an action, and of leaving it at the first disagreement, or—more often—the first time someone steps on his toes. The worker, on the other hand, who as a rule will not join a party unless he means business, will not leave it at the first disappointment or when the first doubt enters his mind. No, the worker clings to his party and supports it until all his confidence and hopes in it are exhausted. This is the great factor which underlies the extraordinary tenacity with which thousands of militant workers stick to the Communist Party. Superficial intellectuals are inclined to regard these workers as incurable idiots. Not so. The workers cling to the C.P. in spite of disappointments and doubts and misgivings only because they do not see any other party. This sentiment of seriousness, devotion, sacrifice, tenacity—horribly abused and betrayed by the Stalinist fakers—is a sentiment that in its essence is profoundly revolutionary. Don't be hasty to leave your party. That is a sign of petty-bourgeois impatience and instability, not of proletarian revolutionary responsibility.

* * *

Threats Are Useless

7. All the above arguments and others of a similar nature are always supplemented in our discussions, both at meetings and in private conversations, with the following: If the talk about a split is meant as a threat to scare us, then it would be better to lay aside the threats. We are not afraid of threats. We shall continue to characterize the minority politically as we see it, and call it by its right name. We shall continue a merciless political struggle against their revisionist ideas under all circumstances.   The dispute must be fought out within the framework of the party and the Fourth International, according to the method of democratic centralism. That means the fullest freedom and discussion, without organization discrimination on the one side or threats on the other. The party membership must decide the dispute at the convention. The minority must be subordinated to the majority. The unity of the party must be secured on that basis.

Fraternally yours,
J. P. CANNON

A LETTER TO A ROCHESTER COMRADE

New York, January 22, 1940

Dear Comrade,

I am writing you this additional note as a personal letter.

Aside from the general considerations of the official letter I am enclosing—to which I am sure no one can object—I may say that we of the majority consider that every extension of party activity outside the narrow circle, which results in the recruitment of new workers, is bound to strengthen our tendency.

We base ourselves squarely on the conception of a proletarian party, in composition as well as in program. In our opinion it is precisely the unfavorable social composition of the party in New York—a state of affairs derived from many causes peculiar to the metropolis—that gives the present faction dispute its intense atmosphere and strengthens revisionist tendencies.

The present sickness of the party cannot be cured without an improvement in the social composition of the party. A few hundred more workers who take the class struggle more seriously and who discuss, not for the sake of discussion, but in order to decide and to act will very soon restore a normal internal atmosphere in the party and call the undisciplined and unrestrained intellectuals to order.

I personally thought the Boston branch acted correctly in not giving Lawrence the "honor" of resigning. His letter of resignation was a slanderous insult to the party and made it clear that he leaves us as an enemy to work against us in the trade unions. Of course the personal character of Lawrence was an additional reason to prompt the action of the Boston comrades. The Russian question for him was not simply a point of disagreement, but also a pretext for getting out of the line of fire. I, of course, do not attribute this motivation to all the comrades of the minority. But such people naturally gravitate towards them and they do nothing to repel them.

Yes, I personally think the teachings of Burnham, which are anti-Marxist and anti-Bolshevik, are a preparatory school for desertion of the revolutionary movement. You will see from the enclosed circular that there is a second "graduate" already. There will be others, mark my words.

From this it does not follow that there is any ground to expel Burnham from the party. The thing is to combat and refute his anti-Marxist teachings. This we are doing to the best of our ability and not without success. As far as the proletarian militants of the party are concerned, an overwhelming majority supports the program of the Fourth International against Burnham's attempt to revise it.

Our party is democratic not only in the formal but in the real sense of the word. If anybody thinks he can improve the program or propose a better one he has a full right to bring his propositions forward in the course of the pre-convention discussion. Any proposal to expel him for this would be absurd. That would be the negation of democracy. That would be equivalent to passing a definitive judgment in advance of the convention, which alone has the right to decide. Up to the convention there is only a struggle of opinions and all opinions must have free play.

However, if it is shown that one disciple of Burnham after another draws the conclusion that he can no longer function as a member of the revolutionary party we have a right to cite these facts as an argument against his teachings. What kind of a program is it that leads people to desert the fight?

I assume you know that the joint declaration on party unity sent to the branches some weeks ago was introduced on the initiative of the majority. According to this resolution, we stand against any expulsions of comrades at the convention for the opinions they have defended in the discussion, and also against any withdrawals of a minority. After the convention there remains only the obligation on the part of the minority, whichever side it may be, to respect the decisions of the convention and to observe discipline in public action.

We repeat on every occasion that we intend fully to abide by this declaration if we find ourselves in a minority at the convention. Only if both sides take such a serious and responsible attitude toward party unity can we demonstrate our capacity to build a serious revolutionary party in spite of the inevitable differences of opinion which arise from time to time.

I hope that all the Rochester comrades are following the discussion bulletins with the greatest attentiveness. Two more articles by Comrade Trotsky will appear in new bulletins soon together with an article by Comrade Burnham. These documents will still further clarify the principle questions in dispute.

I know very well that politically inexperienced comrades have a tendency to get impatient with the prolonged discussion and to consider it a waste of time and energy. But this is a short-sighted view. The questions in dispute at the present time go to the very heart of our principled program. How can the dispute be resolved by the collective decision of the party members without the most thoroughgoing discussion? If this takes time and energy away from practical work we have to charge it off as an unavoidable part of the overhead costs of the democratic self-education of the party membership.

Nobody can give the proletarian vanguard a party able to lead the struggle for power. They must create it themselves. The present discussion is in my judgment one of the most important events in the creation of the American section of the Fourth International. We will all know more when it is finished and we will know it more firmly because of the discussion.

The important thing is to keep up the constructive work of the party while the discussion is in progress. I would be very glad to hear your personal appreciation of the internal struggle as it has unfolded so far and also the opinions of the other individual comrades of the Rochester branch.

Fraternally,
J. P. CANNON

A LETTER TO OSCAR COOVER

New York, January 22, 1940

Oscar Coover
Minneapolis, Minn.

Dear Oscar,

I notice in your minutes of January 11th a reference to a letter from Shachtman and an answer from you. I would appreciate very much if you would send me copies of these documents.

You must know that the opposition is circulating a lot of slanderous agitation and cheap school boy sneers against the Twin Cities organization. They represent it as a conglomeration of provincial scissorbills that is cut off from the life of the party by a Chinese wall. They say Shachtman wanted to go to Minneapolis but couldn't get a passport, etc.

There are two more articles by the Old Man on the fire. One, an open letter to Burnham and two, an answer to Shachtman's document.

Fraternally,
J. P. CANNON

A LETTER TO C. THOMAS

New York, January 22, 1940

C. Thomas
San Francisco, Cal.

Dear Thomas,

I received the copy of Bill's letter of January 20th.

The most important thing in the Bay Section is to moderate the atmosphere a bit so that the important political disputes can break through. I think it is very important for you to return to the Bay Section for a while even if you have to cut your trade union mission short.

You should even try to talk to Sam Meyers and show him that he is on the road to hell. Burnham comes out openly more and more as a shrewd opponent of the doctrine and traditions of our movement. Meyers, who used to take pride in his Marxist education, should take a week or two out to think things over and pull himself up short.

As you will see from the enclosed circular, we already have a Burnham graduate number two. The leader of the minority in Canada has just walked out of the Fourth International and—purely incidentally of course—out of the line of fire for the duration of the war.

Please tell the comrades not to get nervous about rumors. The proletarian majority caucus is as solid as a rock from Coast to Coast. The only sailor we know who supports the revisionists is ————. We expected that. We also expect that the minority leaders are perfectly capable of supporting any kind of a screwball trade union policy in exchange for a few votes. The seaman comrades should give a thought to this when they consider the question of "regime." They had a good sample of our regime in the handling of the maritime dispute. In the auto dispute there was a sample of the regime of the opposition. For any serious comrade these two examples alone are decisive. They epitomize the whole question.

Two more blasts from the Old Man are coming out soon. One is an open letter to Burnham; the other is a reply to Shachtman. In the latter document, which he informs us is already written and is now being revised, he indicates that he will put Shachtman's pseudo-learning and cheap juggling of quotations and historic incidents out of their context under the Marxist microscope.

Many comrades who are taken in by this phony document of Shachtman's will be surprised to see what kind of a bug it turns out to be under the glass.

Let me know if you will return to Frisco as soon as possible and when.

Fraternally,
J. P. CANNON

A LETTER TO ALL MAJORITY GROUPS

Confidential

New York, January 24, 1940

Dear Comrades,

Measures to Combat a Split

Enclosed herewith is a letter we received from Cornell [Trotsky]* about the ways and means of combatting the split program of Burnham and Co.

There can be no doubt that they are working along this line. How shall we combat it? In a previous letter, Trotsky remarked that it is difficult to hinder adult individuals who want to commit suicide. I might add that, as experience shows, it is equally difficult to stop a man who has an inner compulsion to get out of the line of fire. However, our problem is the problem of conducting our struggle in such a way as to hamper an organized split and reduce its size while keeping our own forces intact and militant.

This requires a combination of measures. On the one hand, the struggle on the political front must take on an even more aggressive and merciless character. We cannot admit even a suggestion of any conciliation or compromise in this respect. But we can and should supplement the ruthless political fight with all the necessary organizational flexibility.

The general sentiment of the leading comrades here is in favor of the proposals indicated in Cornell's [Trotsky's] letter. However, we do not want to move on these points until we hear your opinions.

One of the great factors we must take into account now is the impatience of the worker elements with a prolongation of the discussion and their impulses—soundly proletarian revolutionary—to clamp down on the petty-bourgeois windbags rather than to make concessions to them. If we decide on the course of organizational concessions, as we feel sure the majority of you will agree, we must be doubly careful to explain the thing fully to the rank and file of our supporters as soon as the announcement is made officially.

We all know that the worker who is busy in the class struggle, to say nothing of the shop—two fields of activity which occupy very little of the time of the professional discussion mongers—are as a rule very impatient with too much palaver. This will be our salvation when we get a few hundred more workers in the party.

---

*See *In Defense of Marxism*, pp. 101-102.—*Ed.*

But right now, when the task is to draw the lessons of the present dispute out to the end, and to isolate the would-be splitters, this impatience can operate against us.

The worker comrades have to see the faction fight as an unavoidable part of the revolutionary struggle for the consolidation of cadres. We didn't balk at more than a year's factional struggle in the S.P. in order to win over a few hundred people. We needed them in order to turn more effectively to mass work. The present struggle must be seen in that same light fundamentally. In addition, one of the most important positive results of the factional fight inside the S.P.—perhaps the most important—was that in the process of winning over and partly educating a few hundred new people we also demolished the opportunist party of Thomas and Co. This is also an extremely important element of the tactic of combatting the split.

If some people are bent on breaking with the Fourth International we can hardly prevent it. But we must take off our coats and roll up our sleeves and do a thorough, workman-like job of smashing the attempt to set up a serious organizational rival to the S.W.P. This requires patience as well as militancy, and organization concessions as well as political intransigence. If we do a bad and hasty job and permit Burnham and Co. to make a deep split, we will then have the problem of continuing the struggle between two organizations for a time. That would seriously interfere with all practical mass work. It is better to be patient and try to finish the job inside the party.

Please keep this letter confidential and let us know right away your opinion.

Fraternally,
J. P. CANNON

A LETTER TO BILL MORGAN

New York, January 25, 1940

Bill Morgan
San Francisco, Cal.

Dear Bill,

. . . You did right to retreat on the organization question of the Bay Area Committee. It would be foolish for us to concentrate the fight around such a question when we have such advantages on the political and theoretical side.

. . . I am going to take up the question of the membership status of seamen and other comrades who fall far behind in their dues for one reason or another. I think it is best to get some kind of a general ruling from the P.C. In any case, however, do not make factional discriminations or distinctions on these questions. We proceed always by rules and let the chips fall where they may. I personally favor the idea of a special rule which would allow all comrades who have not been stricken from the rolls to pay up their back dues and regain full status, within a definite time limit.

. . . Above all, don't let the fight reach the boiling point over incidental and organizational questions. That is the only kind of politics Trimble knows apparently. Ours is a different brand.

Fraternally,
J. P. CANNON

P.S. I have heard several reports about some agitation against the Minneapolis comrades. I wish you would send me details of anything you hear along this line. I think the petty-bourgeois faction is taking hold of the hot end of a poker when they start a fight against our leading proletarian center.

A LETTER TO C. THOMAS

New York, January 25, 1940

C. Thomas,
San Francisco, Cal.

Dear Thomas,

I wrote you the other day about returning to the Bay Area to concentrate on party work for a while.

I get the impression from letters of Morgan that things are not in a good way there. There is too much tension and struggle over secondary and incidental questions.

Our aim must be to break through all this to the political and theoretical questions and educate the comrades in the process. Above all, we must not carry our concentration on practical work to the point of leaving the maritime fraction open to factional demoralization.

If the petty-bourgeois opposition gets a foothold in the maritime fraction it will cancel out all your work in the canneries and every place else. You must make up your mind to devote the necessary time and attention to preventing this.

Fraternally,
J. P. CANNON

A LETTER TO ALL MAJORITY GROUPS

New York, January 25, 1940

Dear Comrades,

Convention Postponement

At last night's Political Committee meeting it was decided to postpone the convention till April 5th. Numerous branches had requested such a postponement. Shachtman voted for the motion. The other members of the minority abstained. The postponement does not become officially effective, however, until the non-resident members of the National Committee have cast their votes. However, there is no doubt that a majority of the National Committee will concur in the decision.

This postponement will give you time to open up a new stage of the discussion and to organize our forces more systematically and thoroughly. Trotsky's open letter to Burnham, together with an article by Burnham against Trotsky, comes out in a printed bulletin in two or three days. These two documents should be the basis for a new development of the discussion. Following that, we have word from Comrade Trotsky that another long article in reply to Shachtman is already written and will be here soon.

In addition, we are mimeographing now an excellent document by Comrades Wright and Hansen, entitled "The Shachtman School of Quotations." In this document the whole fraudulent, pseudo-learned manipulation of quotations and historic incidents and quotations out of context, which distinguishes the political method of Shachtman, and which has confused some inexperienced comrades, is treated to a thorough examination and exposure. We also have a substantial document by Comrades Clarke and Gordon which dissects the lengthy bulletin of the opposition bloc on the Russian question. There is also a Marxist analysis of the Russian question and the political method of the opposition by Comrade Murry Weiss.

You will have no lack of material for the systematic education of our own people and for beginning a new Marxist offensive against the revisionists and their contemptible attorneys.

The best method in our opinion is to have regular educational meetings of our own caucus where the various documents are analyzed and discussed. On the basis of this procedure the individual comrades can be equipped with the necessary arguments for individual propaganda among the minority comrades.

The publishing facilities of the National Office bogged down a bit under the sheer weight of material that had to be published. If you bear in mind that we have already published eight internal bulletins; that number nine is on the press; and that we already have material for three or four more; you will realize what a strain the National Office has been put to on the technical side alone.

However, we are in a discussion now that is really determining the future of the Fourth International in this country, and not only in this country. Weeping and wailing will not help. The only thing to do is to settle down for a thorough job that will put an end definitely to any attempt to revise Marxism in our movement.

Fraternally,

J. P. CANNON

A LETTER TO MURRY WEISS

New York, January 25, 1940

Dear Murry,

I am very glad to hear that you have possibilities of influencing the Akron comrades. For our part it is O.K. for you to devote all the necessary time to this if the Youngstown comrades are in agreement.

The conquest of the Abernite fortress in Akron would be a major victory for the party. There are not many left, you know. Lynn long ago passed over to the side of the majority almost unanimously, and now it appears Chicago is also definitely lost to the opposition. Out of the six delegates from the four branches, we appear to be assured of four.

The opposition has created some confusion and is apparently making a little headway in California. If we get any word of a move by Shachtman to go to California we intend to ship you out there to combat him. Hold yourself in readiness for a quick summons in this respect. And keep me informed all the time where we can reach you in short order.

Otherwise, there is no contemplated interference from here with the concentration on the Ohio District.

Please let me know every nuance of development.

Fraternally,
J. P. CANNON

A LETTER TO C. CHARLES

New York, February 1, 1940

C. Charles, Organizer
Los Angeles, California
Dear Comrade,

I received your letter of January 29, reporting the motion passed by the city-wide Red Card meeting at Los Angeles on January 28.

The motion as you report it reads: "Motion to inquire of the National Secretary the reason for the removal of Shachtman from the *Appeal* on the grounds of retrenchment only to add two weeks later Clarke and Goldman to the payroll."

It is obvious that the Los Angeles comrades have been misinformed. The minutes of the Political Committee on the *Socialist Appeal*, at its meeting November 28, read as follows:

"Motion by Cannon: That during the period of the financial emergency the staff of the *Appeal* be reduced to one paid editor and one business manager and that all other labor be organized on a voluntary basis.—*Carried.*

"Motion by Cannon: That Comrade Shachtman continue as the sole paid editor.

"Motion by Shachtman: That Comrade Morrow be retained as the sole paid editor during the emergency.—*Carried.*

"Motion by Shachtman: That Morrow and Shachtman be designated as editors of the paper.—*Carried.*"

From this official record it will be clear to you that Comrade Shachtman was not "removed" from the *Appeal* but retired as a paid worker on his own motion and at his own request, and that he retains the status of co-editor of the paper.

Comrade Clarke was appointed to the post of general press manager to replace Comrade Abern who resigned this position to take up the post of city organizer in New York. There was no removal and no addition to the payroll. On the contrary, the overhead payroll of the publications has been substantially reduced since then by the substitution of voluntary workers in technical capacities for others previously paid small amounts. There have been no removals and no increasing of payrolls.

As for Comrade Goldman, this question must be separated from the press question since his duties are connected with the administration of the National Office.

At the meeting of December 12 Comrade Goldman was appointed

Assistant Secretary to work in the National Office at a salary of $15.00 per week. Nobody objected and nobody could object to this modest proposal. The total administrative and technical staff of the National Office of the party consists of Comrades Cannon, Goldman and one stenographer.

Yours fraternally,
J. P. CANNON

A LETTER TO ALL MAJORITY GROUPS

New York, February 2, 1940

Dear Comrades,

Comrade Goldman is going to assist in the work of the National Office for the next period. I am going to take a little time out to catch up with some of the organizational falsifications by which the opposition bloc is trying to divert attention from the principled issues.

I enclose herewith a copy of a letter sent today to Comrade Charles.* As I understand, this same misrepresentation is being broadcasted generally and is being taken seriously by some inexperienced comrades. Any questions of this kind which are used as arguments by the supporters of the opposition should be promptly brought before the branch in the form of a motion to ask official information from the National Office.

Up to now we have steadfastly refused to follow the trail of the opposition on minor issues of organization. The reason for this policy was that we considered it necessary to break through with the principled questions first. We suffered somewhat from this procedure insofar as inexperienced comrades allowed themselves to become disoriented over the secondary questions, rumors, gossip, etc. Nevertheless, the main objective was achieved.

In the next phase of the discussion we can take up the organization question in its proper subordinate place. Our aim here also will be first of all to show that the dispute over the organization question springs not at all from abuses and grievances, but from fundamentally different conceptions of party organization. In this setting we will also clear aside a great deal of the rubbish, half truths, and downright misrepresentations over little "incidents."

The facts about the "removal" of Shachtman as revealed by the official records of the Political Committee should be an eye-opener as a beginning.

Yours fraternally,

J. P. CANNON

---

*The reference is to the letter printed on the preceding two pages.—*Ed.*

A LETTER TO THE PARTY MEMBERSHIP

New York, February 3, 1940

To All Locals and Branches:
Dear Comrades,

"New International"

The January-February number of the *New International*, delayed because of financial difficulties, is just coming off the press and is devoted to an exposition of the Russian question from the point of view of the program of the Fourth International.

Originally the Political Committee provided that documents of the two points of view represented in the National Committee be published. The minority submitted their statement, entitled, "What Is at Issue in the Dispute on the Russian Question," and also the "Open Letter to Comrade Trotsky" by Max Shachtman. On the majority side the article of Comrade Trotsky, entitled, "A Petty-Bourgeois Opposition in the Socialist Workers Party"; the resolution of the National Committee and other relevant documents were submitted.

The comrade in charge of technical preparation of the issue informed the Political Committee that the publication of all these documents would require a magazine almost triple the usual 32 pages. This was manifestly out of the question from the financial standpoint—the two preceding issues of the magazine had been reduced to 16 pages for these reasons.

In addition, the Political Committee considered it necessary to reconsider the decision from the point of view of the general interest of the party. That is, while allowing an objective presentation of the position on each side, factional polemics must be eliminated from the public organ.

At the Political Committee meeting of January 9th the Political Committee adopted the following motion:

"That the discussion in the *New International* be confined to an objective presentation of the two points of view on the Russian question without internal factional polemics. That the documents of the majority be edited from this point of view and the article of Trotsky, entitled "A Petty-Bourgeois Opposition in the Socialist Workers Party" be eliminated from this point of view. That the minority be requested to make an objective presentation of their position in not more than 5,000 words to fit space requirements. That all documents submitted by both sides which do not conform to these regulations be printed at once in the internal bulletins without any changes or editing."

The minority comrades refused to accept this proposition and submitted no material for publication under the provisions of the motion.

Yours fraternally,

J. P. CANNON
National Secretary

A LETTER TO ALL MAJORITY GROUPS

New York, February 3, 1940

Dear Comrades,

Forthcoming "New International"

Enclosed herewith is a copy of a circular sent today to all locals and branches on the forthcoming issue of the *New International*.

Our decision to eliminate factional polemics from the *New International* was motivated by the following considerations:

1. It became obvious that the publication of the violent factional polemics on each side would work an injury to the party and accelerate the tendencies of the minority towards a split. By committing themselves to such fantastic positions and violent attacks before the public, they would be cutting off their own retreat—and retreat is their only salvation from an impossible position.

2. The great majority of the resolutions and letters from the proletarian branches—and the proletarian branches, not the petty-bourgeois student youth, are for us the barometer—protested most strenuously against carrying the factional dispute into either the *New International* or the *Appeal*.

3. The two articles submitted by the minority, together with articles of corresponding length on the majority side, would have required a publication of such size and consequently such a staggering expense as to be out of the question for an institution already bankrupt. (Of course such earthly considerations do not trouble the petty-bourgeois politicians of the opposition in the least. They float in the air far above the battle—especially the vulgar battle with creditors threatening suit, landlords threatening eviction, etc.)

It is indicated that the opposition is going to make a fight in the branches over the "injustice" of offering them a mere 5,000 words to present their point of view in an objective manner.

It is above all necessary for our comrades everywhere to take an aggressive and militant stand on this question as in the case when the issue of the *Socialist Appeal* was before the branches. This same fundamental issue is involved and it would be entirely false to take a defensive position. It is advisable to read over again the statement of the Political Committee on the question concerning the *Appeal*. The same reasons hold good now with double force.

The opposition is in frantic haste to make their appeal to the democratic public before the verdict of the party convention. We, on the other hand, are doubly determined to bind them to the rules of democratic centralism and compel them to submit to the judgment of the party first.

Fraternally,

J. P. CANNON

A LETTER TO A ST. LOUIS COMRADE

New York, February 6, 1940

Dear Comrade,

I got your letter of February 2d. By this time you will have had the answer to the momentous question of the penny pamphlet. I think I sent you a copy of my answer to the Los Angeles local on a point of similar character, concerning removals, etc.

You are right in your statement that these are not political questions. They are dragged in and inflated in order to divert discussion from the principled questions and to catch inexperienced people. Moreover, every one of their accusations along this line is false. There is no merit in a single one of them. I am beginning to work now on a comprehensive document on the question of party organization. In the course of this work, and putting things in their proper proportion, I will answer these accusations.

I was very much interested to note your reference to the conflict between the Spokane local and the General Executive Board of the I.W.W. in 1913. I was an organizer of the I.W.W. at that time and remember the incident very well. Even at that time, 27 years ago, I was a firm believer in centralized organization and a member of St. John's faction of centralizers against the decentralizers.

In the summer of 1913 I was leading, together with Frank Little, a rather important strike on the ore docks in Duluth and Superior. I remember that Fred Heselwood gave our strike a big play in the *Industrial Worker*. I was also well acquainted with Leheney who was sent out to Spokane to take over the editing of the paper by the General Executive Board. . . .

There is another very big document by Trotsky, in answer to Shachtman, which has just been translated. It is simply devastating.

I hope we gain the majority in St. Louis and I am glad to note that you have formed a majority caucus. This is absolutely necessary. I would like to get from you a report as to how things stand insofar as the line-up of the comrades is clearly established by this time.

As I understand it, your organization is divided into two branches and will have a delegate from each branch. Therefore, I would like to get a report of the status of each branch.

Fraternally,
J. P. CANNON

A LETTER TO A FRESNO COMRADE

New York, February 6, 1940

Dear Comrade,

I would like to know your impressions of the party struggle. I have a special personal interest in the attitude of the California comrades. Since I spent a whole year there I shouldn't like to think that young comrades who were influenced in any way by me at that time should turn out to be Menshevik revisionists, as the crisis approaches.

Comrade Charles wrote me that you agree with the majority. Please let me know your opinion precisely and that of other comrades with whom you are in contact.

Fraternally,
J. P. CANNON

A LETTER TO MURRY WEISS

New York, February 6, 1940

Murry Weiss
Youngstown, Ohio

Dear Murry,

As I wrote you yesterday, we have decided in favor of your going to California and remaining there up to the convention. It is important, however, that you get formal release from the branch. At tonight's P.C. meeting we will introduce a motion to relieve you of your responsibilities provided it is agreeable to the branch.

California is by far the most important sector now. The comrades write that ———— is out there and that the "organizational" question is disturbing many comrades. That is somewhat strange —but inexperienced people are always caught on this hook and some people never learn from experience. Just consider: I spent an entire year in California and in general had far more influence on the "regime" of our faction in the Socialist Party than I could possibly exert on the regime of the last P.C., in which I was one member against six of the present minority.

Isn't it logical to ask the California comrades to give some consideration to their own experience at first hand with the "Cannon regime" and weigh it against the fantastic stories about events alleged to have occurred 3,000 miles away which cannot be verified and which never had any influence in the life of the California organization?

To be sure, the P.C., under my instigation, did intervene very energetically in the San Francisco local faction situation. But that was to oppose the bureaucratism of Trimble and others and to protect the party rights of a minority with which—as you know from my letters to you—we had no political sympathy. Doesn't it seem to you that this case alone has an important bearing on the real nature of the regime from the standpoint of the California comrades?

Another thing: Sam Meyers, I hear, is doing a lot of beefing about the regime of Cannon, the one-man dictatorship and so forth and so on. But how did Meyers judge the Cannon regime when he saw it operating under his nose in 1936-37? Under date of November 23, 1936, Sam Meyers wrote to Larsen, who was at that time National Secretary of our faction:

"Comrade Cannon here sees the situation as it is and works like a realist. He does not overestimate people. He feels his way carefully, utilizing everyone and does not put a period where a question mark is necessary. He gets results with an amazing rapidity. . . .

"The arrival of Comrade Cannon gave us an opportunity to estimate our strength. His experience and leadership improved the situation manifold. It was like having all the elements of a powerful solution and along with it, a chemist who knows how to mix it. As you know, I changed places with Charles after the W.P. convention so that I was away from L.A. When I visited L.A. on the day of one of Comrade Cannon's last lectures of a series of six it was difficult to find a seat in the hall and there was such a spirited jubilation that the cafes around the hall after the lecture resembled nothing so much as Fourteenth St., N.Y.

"This 'resurgent Socialism' has taken California Socialism a long way in a short time. It was at that time that *Labor Action** began to be born. It is no surprise that some of the comrades cannot accustom themselves to the idea in so short a time.

"Our connection with the waterfront also worked in our favor. Here I must acknowledge that my reports on the waterfront were somewhat faulty in giving too negative a picture. I was blinded by skepticism and could not see the real character of the problem. I was blinded by my lack of confidence in Comrade ———. Here too, Comrade Cannon saw a little farther. Of course, experience, ability and *authority* were indispensable in this case. I find myself writing like a Soviet journalist (I mean in my eulogy of Cannon) but of course, with greater sincerity."

As you see, Comrade Sam is somewhat inclined to exaggeration in praise as well as in blame. However, at that time he was writing about what he saw himself; now he is talking about what he heard.

Now that Comrade Goldman is back in the office to give me a hand there, I am assembling material to sit down and write a comprehensive document on the balance sheet of the party discussion and the organization question. In passing, I will take up each and every one of the half truths, distortions and falsifications of the opposition's drawn-out Winchellized column on "Bureaucratic Conservatism." But I will do my best to show that what is really at stake in all this dispute over the organization question is the con-

---

*This refers to the periodical published in California, with comrade Cannon as editor in 1936-37 during the stay of the Trotskyists in the Socialist Party.—*Ed.*

flict over conceptions of Leninist centralism and petty-bourgeois looseness.

I am anxious to know how you have arranged the California trip from a personal point of view. Since you will be back in New York for the convention and our plan is for you to remain in the East for another period, you have to take this into consideration.

I would like to know what was your impression of the latest document of the Old Man which we sent to Preis and asked him to turn over to you—"From a Scratch to the Danger of Gangrene."* It seemed to me something like taking a twenty-pound sledge hammer to smash a flea.

Fraternally,
J. P. CANNON

---

*See *In Defense of Marxism*, pp. 103-148.—*Ed.*

A LETTER TO GRACE CARLSON

New York, February 9, 1940

Dear Grace,

I received your letter of January 15th and note that your time is all taken up with the fight with the bosses and the capitalist courts. I suppose this is what qualifies you as "backward elements" in the minds of the Bronx kibitzers.

There is quite a campaign in the party against Minneapolis-St. Paul instigated by Burnham and Shachtman. They claim it is a walled-off medieval city to which they can't get a passport. But I don't think they are really worried about getting in. It is the problem of getting out again that really worries them.

I have heard a good many high school boys and girls expressing disapproval of the Twin Cities movement in recent weeks and half started to turn loose on them many times. Then I decided I might as well be real mean and wait till Dobbs gets here and then turn them over to him.

I have made, according to my count, 43 speeches so far in this tussle and I am beginning to get somewhat bored with the sound of my own voice. The worst of it is that with many of these people here, speeches by Cannon and even articles by Trotsky don't do any good. It is like lecturing on the art of swimming on dry land. We will have to chuck them into the water (the mass movement) and then look around to see what happens. Those who manage somehow or other to stay on top will be O.K. . . .

As ever,

J. P. CANNON

A LETTER TO LEON TROTSKY

(Copies to All Groups of the Majority)

New York, February 20, 1940

Dear Comrade Cornell [Trotsky],

It is now the unanimous opinion of the leading comrades here that the split which the opposition leaders have been preparing is no longer to be avoided. Our tactics in the struggle from now on must take this as the point of departure. Last Sunday night's general membership meeting in New York removed the last doubt that any of us entertained on the question.

The debate occurred between Shachtman and Goldman. The latest article of Trotsky—"From a Scratch to the Danger of Gangrene"—had been published and we awaited the public reactions of Shachtman and of the opposition comrades generally to this last warning to halt. There was no sign even of an understanding of the political meaning of this solemn document. Shachtman—true to himself—spent his whole time twisting and squirming around those points in the document which dealt with him personally, ignoring the fundamental principle sections, and joking—above all joking—in a manner which even for Shachtman was exceptionally clownish. The opposition followers, especially the high school and college students, enjoyed the jokes immensely. As for the speech of Goldman—they did not even listen. They laughed and joked among themselves and engaged in buzzing conversations most of the time. It is safe to say that every serious comrade left the meeting cursing under his breath and saying to himself: It is really time to call a halt. There is no more profit in this discussion.

In reply to Goldman's point-blank question as to whether the opposition intends to demand the right to a public organ of its own as a splitting ultimatum, Shachtman, without giving a direct reply, gave an airy and facetious exposition of the "well-known traditions" in which the publication of separate organs by the Bolsheviks and Mensheviks, the Trotskyists and others was taken as a matter of course. He conveyed the impression with many grimaces and quips that anyone who doubts the necessity of repeating all this experience, and starting all over again as if nothing happened in the meantime, is simply stupid. The college students especially enjoyed this part of the performance. Some of them, it seems, are students of history.

Meanwhile—*right during the meeting*—Demby sat in a corner

collecting money for the caucus treasury and many bills of no small
denomination passed across the table.   (We were threatened with
a strike at the print shop last week because we couldn't pay the
printer's wages.)   The collections were obviously being taken to
finance the national conference of the opposition to be held, as I
understand, in Cleveland this weekend. This is not a gathering of
a few national leaders, but a full-fledged conference, with delegates
from all districts, and is manifestly designed to organize and prepare the split.   The very fact of the holding of this conference on
such a scale, taken together with the attitude expressed at Sunday
night's meeting; the latest document of Burnham, "Science and
Style," which exceeds all others in impudence and disdain and
class hatred of the proletarian majority; Abern's letter to Trotsky
which threatens a split in as frank a manner as Abern knows how
to speak; the complete abstention of the opposition leaders from
all participation in party work; the campaign against Trotsky as a
fool, a liar and a crook—any high school student in the opposition
will tell you that Trotsky has made all kinds of mistakes in the
past and that as far back as the controversy over Max Eastman and
Lenin's testament he showed he had no moral scruples—all this
must lead to the inevitable conclusion: Any further attempts to restrain the petty-bourgeois tendency and to assimilate and reeducate
them within the framework of a common organization are utopian.
The petty-bourgeois opposition is bent on a break.   It is necessary
without any further delay to acknowledge the reality and to prepare our lines of battle accordingly.

There is another side of the question too.   The discussion has
become completely degenerated.   It is no longer possible to produce
anything more than a laugh or a sneer in the New York branches
if one attempts an exposition of the Russian question from the
point of view of the Marxist theory of the State.   Meeting after
meeting in the branches is taken up with disputes initiated by the
Abern City Committee on practical differences of tenth-rate importance.   Along with this there is the complete neglect and even
sabotage of daily party work.   It was discovered, for example, that
Shachtman's Bronx branch had not distributed a single copy of the
Appeal for five weeks.

It is necessary to acknowledge that the discussion has exhausted
itself. We have before us a first-class demonstration of "the petty
bourgeoisie gone mad." All of us now feel sorry that we postponed
the convention, since the prolongation of the discussion is obviously producing disintegration and demoralization.   Of course we
could not know that beforehand.   We all shared the hope that the

last document of Trotsky would at least have a sobering effect and prompt the oppositionists to stop and consider their future course. And here I think we all made a common error. It is this: We did not realize how deeply petty-bourgeois panic and petty-bourgeois corruption permeate the ranks of the opposition as well as the leadership.

On the other side, there is a factor of no less importance that we dare not underestimate. The serious worker elements in the party have had enough and more than enough of this horseplay. We have received several ominous warnings of this development. Just think: eleven thick bulletins have already been published and the material for two more is on hand. For such a brief space of time, this is already the most voluminous party discussion in the history of mankind. In several letters we have been informed that active workers are fed up with this flood of material and beginning to grumble. The workers have made up their minds firmly about the merits of the dispute and about the character of the leaders as revealed in the crisis. They don't want to talk forever. They want to act.

Even the suggestion of permitting a limited continuation of the discussion after the convention—which was contained in a confidential letter of Cornell [Trotsky] and relayed to our most responsible people—brought a storm of opposition from the field. One comrade wrote very cogently: "I am very much afraid that if we continue this business after the convention the workers will simply walk away and leave their address behind so we can look them up if and when we mean business." The Minneapolis incident can be taken as a danger signal. Shachtman from Chicago wrote to the Minneapolis comrades, asking for an informal meeting to discuss the party disputes. They answered him bruskly that they saw no need of such a meeting. They did not ask my advice on this procedure. If they had done so, it is possible that I would have suggested to them that they hold a meeting in order to thrust aside extraneous arguments about democracy, etc. Such arguments have been made against the Minneapolis comrades by Shachtman in a factional circular, but the Minneapolis comrades remain unmoved. They have read and studied all the bulletins and discussed them in meeting after meeting; they know Shachtman; and they don't want to hear anything more from Shachtman. Now, when the most advanced and experienced and responsible proletarian comrades in the party take this attitude and make no bones about it, it is time for us to realize that the proletarian elements in general want to bring this discussion to a conclusion and get down to work.

We are coming right up against the necessity for a decision and a line of action which will put our conception of the "organization question" to a test in life, not in the pages of the opposition's fiction serials. My own opinion is very definite and I will state it frankly: It is impossible to build a combat party with a tolerant attitude towards splits. In the discussion every democratic right must be assured and has been assured. Every reasonable organization concession must be made in the interests of preserving unity and educating the party in a normal atmosphere. But we must not sanctify permanent demoralization. We must not permit anybody to make an endless discussion club out of the party. Those who go beyond these bounds and take the road of split are no longer to be considered as comrades discussing a difference of opinion, but as enemies and traitors. They must be fought without mercy and without compromise on every front. We will never instil a real party patriotism into the ranks unless we establish the conception that violation of the party unity is not only a crime but a crime which brings the most ruthless punishment in the form of a war of political extermination against those who commit it.

I personally have no use for the French system of organization. I know very well, especially after my experience there, all the many factors which contributed to the unfortunate results in France. Many of these perhaps were insurmountable. But I have for long been deeply convinced that the light-minded attitude towards unifications on the one side and splits on the other contributed heavily to the failures which occurred so often when good prospects for successes were at hand.

It is possible that the opposition leaders, counting on our fear of a scandal and Trotsky's well-known and extraordinary patience, really imagine that they will bluff us into permitting the spectacle of two public organs, advocating two different and contradictory policies. If that is so—and if I have my way—they will meet a cruel disillusionment. What do I propose? I propose to call their bluff. I will advise the worker delegates at the convention to say firmly that we want a party not a play house, that we want one program and one press that defends it. If the opposition will not accept this fiat of the party majority—and their present frenzy excludes the possibility of them accepting it—and take the road of split, then war to the knife begins.

Shachtman has been circulating an anecdote that I, in the earliest days of the discussion, proposed to him a "friendly split." This only shows that this jokesmith does not understand the broadest and most obvious sarcasm. For me the vanguard party of the proletariat is a combat organization aiming at the conquest of power on the basis of a clearly defined program. Another party with another program—that I can understand only as an enemy. To be sure, there are exceptional cases where comrades having the same fundamental program can divide into separate organizations to facilitate a division of labor—like entrists and non-entrists, for example—and still, at least theoretically, maintain friendly relations and avoid mutual polemical attacks. We know cases of two separate parties of different origin beginning to approach each other and establishing friendly cooperative relations preparatory to fusion. That was the case, as you recall, with the American Trotskyists and the Muste organization. But even to think of having a friendly attitude towards a group that splits from a party of the Fourth International on programmatic questions, and on the eve of war to boot—that is simply monstrous.

* * *

I fully agree that even now, faced with a certain split being organized by the opposition, we must do everything within reason to show that the splitters have no just grievances in the organizational sphere; that the split takes place over principled political questions and not at all over bureaucratic injustices. I fully agree with your remarks that our organizational methods are not fixed and final and applied rigidly in all cases. The fact that we gave up our organization and even our press for a time in order to penetrate into the Socialist Party should convince all the comrades that we are flexible enough in our "organization methods"; that we can make even the most sweeping concessions *when we have something to gain politically which can later be crystallized organizationally.*

I personally do not rule out in principle the idea, in certain cases, of permitting a minority to have its own internal bulletin. I would go even further and say that such a concession could in exceptional cases even be extended to the permission of a separate public organ for a time—*if the composition and general nature of the dissident group were such as to give some reasonable hope that it would learn and change under the impact of events.* But the present opposition is not that kind of a group—and this is the essence of the whole question. The opposition is petty-bourgeois to the core in its ranks as well as in its leadership. Except for stray individuals who do not decide the course, it is not connected with the labor movement, and does not learn anything from experiences in the class struggle. Because it is not proletarian it has not assimilated the discipline and respect for organization which is more or less natural for a worker. Taken as a whole, the minority, as is so glaringly demonstrated in the discussion, never assimilated the basic principles of Marxism as a guide to action in the class struggle. How else could one account for the fantastic departure from everything that is elementary in such a short time?

Under these conditions, a prolongation of the discussion with this group after the convention or an attempt to maintain the fiction of unity with two separate public organs would only demoralize the proletarian section of the party by compelling it to squander its time and energy in the most barren field. I am profoundly convinced that the present hodge-podge program of the opposition represents only the first stages of its fundamental break with Marxism. It is by no means a finished expression of the real tendencies inherent not only in the leadership, but, again I repeat, in its ranks.

The two groups in the party will begin moving in opposite directions from the first day of the split. The moment the opposition is freed from the formal restraints of membership in a common party with us, the "experimental science" of Burnham will begin to assert in full scope its real anti-proletarian and anti-revolutionary meaning. This would also be manifested, even if not at such an accelerated pace, if our proletarian majority should be so foolhardy at the convention as to permit the experiment with two public organs. It can be said with certainty in advance, that the tendencies in that case would not grow together but apart. The result of the experiment would only be to discredit the party as an organization that doesn't know its own program, doesn't know how to keep its ranks united and lacks the resolution to make a definitive split.

*   *   *

The day after the split should mark a sharp turn in our orientation and in the character of our work in general. As a matter of fact, the split will be more of a scandal than a loss. The basic cadres of the party throughout the country will remain virtually unaffected. The same is true of all our trade union groups. Only individual trade union comrades here and there have wandered into the minority by mistake. The same is even true of the youth—that is, the real youth. The opposition has the bulk of the petty-bourgeois students; of that there is no doubt. But the young sailors, steel workers and others, are on our side almost to a man. Our ranks will have had enough discussion to last for a while and there will be a general all around impulse to get down to practical work. With the coming of Dobbs to the center our trade union work in particular can get a big impulse and receive for the first time a systematic direction and development.

One of our first tasks should be to reshape the character of the *Appeal* from top to bottom as a bona fide workers' paper that is accessible to the rank and file worker and understandable to him. We will be in a position to turn our backs completely on the soul-sick intellectuals and sophisticated radicals and make an earnest and determined effort to penetrate into new proletarian circles. Even here in New York there are a great many workers. Unfortunately, we didn't reach very many of them yet. I am afraid we must admit that we have spent too much time and too many years explaining the fine points to sophisticated radicals and have not carried on enough persevering activity in the workers' neighborhoods. . . .

* * *

We must not wear our lives out trying to convince intellectuals and petty-bourgeois smart alecks who don't want to be convinced, or who are not prepared to act seriously even when they agree fundamentally. I am very much afraid that here in New York at least the party activity—including my own—has been too much concentrated on this barren soil. . . .

We must change all this after the convention and take drastic steps to reshape the whole nature of our activity in New York. That will be far more profitable for the party and far more satisfying than trying to explain to over-wise college boys and girls that the question of the class character of the state is an important point and that Trotsky really didn't raise the question of dialectical materialism as a factional trick.

* * *

If we now recognize that the opposition is determined to carry through the split and that we cannot prevent it, but perhaps at best only prolong the agony a while at the cost of demoralization and disintegration and get a worse split in the end—if that is the case, as we all here feel, then we should reconsider our previous attitude towards the publication of the most important documents in the controversy in the *New International*. Previously, as you know, my objection to this was motivated chiefly on the ground that the publication of the sharp polemical documents would compromise the opposition hopelessly before the public and cut off their retreat.

That reason doesn't hold in the new situation. If we are going to have a split we should make a sharp right-about-face in our tactics on this point and begin to prepare the sympathizing public for the split. We had a discussion in our committee yesterday about this matter, but did not come to final conclusions. I personally am of the opinion that we will be at a disadvantage if we have to begin explaining the split the day after it happens. That would take an enormous amount of time and energy and space in our press. It would be better to publish the most important documents before the convention so that the whole case and the basic issues of the split are known to our sympathizers. That will clear the decks, so to speak. Then, following the convention, we can devote a few sharp and not too lengthy summary articles to the splitters, and let them talk among themselves thereafter. We will have more serious things to do.

I would be very glad to know your opinion on the points in this letter.

Fraternally,
J. P. CANNON

A LETTER TO LEON TROTSKY

New York, February 22, 1940

Dear Comrade Cornell [Trotsky],

I just saw your letter of February 19th to Goldman.

I think by now practically all of the leading comrades here agree that we shall publish the most important documents from both sides in a special number of the *New International*. Along with this, I think we can draw up a general letter to the party which will be designed to put some more obstacles in the path of the splitters. However, we must be absolutely clear in our own minds as to what is going to happen. The split will not be prevented and we must prepare for it on all fronts.

One extremely important point which I did not touch on in my other letter is the situation in the International. . . .

The Canadian section supports the majority with practical unanimity. The one supporter of the minority in the leadership, Robertson, resigned from the movement with a shameful capitulatory statement.

I understand the Mexican section also supports the program. A sailor comrade from California who recently returned from a voyage to China where he contacted our people, reports that the Chinese section entirely supports the majority, having fought this issue out some time ago.

From Europe we hear nothing. Held sent us a resolution adopted by himself, Neureth and a third emigre, together with four Scandinavian comrades. It is a very bad statement on the Finnish events. I presume you have received a copy. Of course Held does not accept the fundamental position of the minority on the Russian question, but they exploit the resolution against us. This is somewhat ironic. The polemics of Held in the *New International** against Shachtman's article on Luxemburg were extremely interesting. It could even be said that they foreshadowed the struggle which has now broken out in full force on the question of the party organization.

Fraternally,
J. P. CANNON

---

*See *New International* of February, 1939.—*Ed.*

A LETTER TO OSCAR COOVER

New York, February 22, 1940

Oscar Coover
Minneapolis, Minn.

Dear Oscar,

I received your note of February 19th with the copy of Comrade E——'s letter.

His remarks on the Russian question are very pertinent. It doesn't bear out the impression that Shachtman and Co. are trying to convey that the Minnesota people are a bunch of illiterate farmers who can't read and who are not permitted to hear anything from the professorial leaders of the minority.

Instead of Shachtman travelling to Minnesota to teach a comrade who can explain the Russian question in such a concise Marxist manner as E—— did, there would be more sense in them bringing E—— to New York to make a speech to them. But that would be a waste of time and carfare too. People who can't learn anything even from the last big document of the Old Man don't offer much hope.

Fraternally,
J. P. CANNON

A TELEGRAM TO THE MINORITY CONFERENCE*

NEW YORK, FEBRUARY 24, 1940

I. BERN
C/O CHELSEA HOTEL
1815 EAST 9TH STREET
CLEVELAND, OHIO

TO THE MINORITY CONFERENCE, DEAR COMRADES:

WE ADDRESS YOUR CONFERENCE ON ONE POINT ONLY: PARTY UNITY. WE ON OUR PART REPEAT OUR PREVIOUS DECLARATION THAT IF WE ARE IN THE MAJORITY AT THE CONVENTION WE WILL OPPOSE ANY EXPULSIONS. IF WE ARE IN THE MINORITY WE WILL MAINTAIN UNITY AND DISCIPLINE. WE ASK YOUR CONFERENCE TO MAKE A SIMILAR DECLARATION. ON THAT BASIS, IF WE ARE IN THE MAJORITY WE ARE WILLING TO MAKE EVERY REASONABLE PROVISION OR ORGANIZATIONAL CONCESSION CONSISTENT WITH THE PRINCIPLES AND METHODS OF BOLSHEVIK ORGANIZATION TO GUARANTEE THE PARTY RIGHTS OF THE MINORITY AFTER THE CONVENTION.

THE MAJORITY OF THE P.C.
BY J. P. CANNON

---

*See pp. 14, 173 ff. of this volume; and *In Defense of Marxism*, pp. 152 ff.—*Ed.*

A LETTER TO LEON TROTSKY

New York, February 29, 1940

Dear Comrade Rork [Trotsky],

I just received your letter of February 27th.

We have not yet received from the minority any report of their conference proceedings. All we have is the informal reports of individual comrades which we have not been able to check against any documents.

I gather, however, from all these reports that their demand is for the right to publish a separate organ of their own after the convention.

I was told that Comrades ——— and ——— appeared at their conference and issued a statement—whether "in the name of the International" or not, I do not know—and stated that in their opinion the demand for the separate organ was justified under the circumstances.

We sent a telegram to the conference as follows:

"To the Minority Conference, Dear Comrades:

"We address your conference on one point only: Party Unity. We on our part repeat our previous declaration that if we are in the majority at the convention we will oppose any expulsions. If we are in the minority we will maintain unity and discipline. We ask your conference to make a similar declaration. On that basis, if we are in the majority we are willing to make every reasonable provision or organizational concession consistent with the principles and methods of Bolshevik organization to guarantee the party rights of the minority after the convention.

"The Majority of the P.C.
"by J. P. CANNON."

Up till today we have received neither an acknowledgment nor an answer to our telegram.

We also distributed to all the delegates your letter, "Back to the Party."

Comrade Stuart, secretary of the E.C., received the proposals of Crux, Fischer and Munis only after the conference had begun and all delegates had left New York. However, he immediately transmitted copies of the letter to the conference, addressed to Shachtman, Lebrun and Johnson, with the statement that both he and I agreed with the proposals. This was last Saturday. Up to today—Thursday—he has not received any acknowledgment from any of those addressed.

We are proceeding with the publication of the next number of the *New International* as indicated. We are also proceeding with every necessary step of self-defense and preparation. At the same time, you have no need whatever to fear any precipitous acts on our part or any failure to make an absolutely clear record of efforts to prevent a split by every reasonable means. We now await the resolutions of the minority conference and will determine our answer after we have studied them.

I don't know whether you fully appreciate the character and tendencies of the present opposition as it is revealed by such incidents as their failure to come to the party office from one end of the week to the other; the failure to give us a formal statement of their conference demands after four days; the neglect of all the party duties and routine and financial obligations. In my experience I have never yet encountered such a thoroughly irresponsible petty-bourgeois tendency.

A half-serious politician, even if he were deliberately planning a split, would be afraid to encourage such irresponsible attitudes for fear that the new organization would be poisoned with them at the beginning. Even at the time of our split with the Socialist Party we made a better formal record, up to the very end, in responsibility for the routine activities of the party.

Perhaps a part of the impatience of the worker comrades is due to their inexperience with drawn-out theoretical controversy. However, the feeling of impatience with the present opposition is practically universal in our ranks, no less so on the part of the most theoretically qualified comrades. There is a pretty general feeling that even the small percentage of them that are not more or less deliberately breaking with our movement under a cloud of dust and controversy will require a few sharp experiences to wake them up.

If they are permitted to have a public organ after the convention it will simply mean that we have in reality two parties. The opposition would have its own treasury, its own headquarters, its own distributing staff, etc. At the same time our own activities would be paralyzed by the continuation of the dispute with them in common branches. I don't know anyone in our ranks that is willing to consider such a perspective for a movement.

As far as the majority is concerned, the split will represent no serious rupture whatsoever. The separation on the psychological plane is as profound as on theoretical, political and organizational planes.

We will keep you informed of all developments and as always will be glad to have your opinion on every point that you consider important.

Fraternally,
J. P. CANNON

A CIRCULAR LETTER TO THE PARTY MEMBERSHIP

New York, March 5, 1940

Dear Comrades,

An Answer to the Splitters

Under separate cover you have already received a copy of the "Resolution on Party Unity" adopted by the Cleveland conference of the opposition. This "resolution" was handed to us by the representatives of the opposition at the P.C. meeting the other day. Evidently they want our answer. We shall not keep them waiting. Here is our answer:

I. Formal Declaration of Split

This resolution is in fact a political declaration of the split which the conference itself was designed to prepare in an organizational sense. The resolution declares, "The nature of the differences is such that it does not permit a solution merely by the procedure, normal in the movement, of having the convention minority submit to the decision of the convention majority." By that declaration they reject in advance the only possible solution of a party dispute by the *democratic* method of majority rule. They say in effect that for them the decisions of a democratically organized party convention have no meaning and they declare in advance their refusal to accept the decisions of the convention. As far as they are concerned, the convention might as well not be held unless they can have their way.

Unless we are prepared to throw overboard the Leninist principle of democratic centralism; unless we are ready to turn the principle upside down and compel the majority to submit to the minority—we have to recognize the declaration of the opposition for what it really is: the formal declaration of a split. Nothing remains but to recognize reality and take all the necessary measures to protect the integrity of the party and declare a merciless and uncompromising war on the splitters.

II. Peculiar Kind of "Unity"

The resolution demands for the minority "the right to publish a political journal of its own." And to leave no room for doubt that they mean a completely independent publication, they add: "Such a journal can only be published upon the responsibility and under the control of the tendency itself." And then, to make their position crystal clear, they state that this "solution" of the difficulty "is the only concrete one that can be made." Under these conditions, and only under these conditions, they assure us the "unity of the party" can be preserved. That is to say, if the majority will authorize and "legalize" a split, the party can have the fiction of formal unity by way of compensation. We do not believe a single member of the majority will entertain such a proposition for a moment.

III. Democratic Centralism Annihilated

At the very best, the resolution of the opposition can be described as an attempt to annihilate the democratic centralism of a revolutionary party in favor of the notorious and ill-fated "all inclusive party" of Norman Thomas. But history has already passed a cruel judgment on this conception of party organization. It would be insane folly to repeat the experiment. If the convention should sanction such a scheme of organization it would simply mean that the "united" party would be paralyzed internally by a permanent faction fight and deprived of all external striking power.

For the opposition to have its own press, "published upon the responsibility and under the control" of the opposition, could mean only that it must have its own treasury, its own staff, and its own apparatus of distribution. But things could not possibly stop even there. If the opposition is granted the right to attack the party program and defend another in print, there is no plausible reason why they should be denied the right to do the same thing orally. There is no logical ground to prevent them from holding public meetings "upon the responsibility and under the control" of the autonomous faction. There would be no means of enforcing discipline in the execution of the party program upon the members of a faction which has been granted the right to attack the program in public. In short, the minority would have all the rights of a party of their own, plus the privilege of paralyzing the official party from within and discrediting it before the working class public.

This is precisely what is intended by the hypocritical "unity" resolution of the minority. It is a scheme to carry out their split and achieve complete freedom of action for themselves in such a way as to do the most damage and bring the greatest possible discredit to the party. This is fully in line with the conscious design of Burnham, who has already proclaimed the downfall of the Fourth International in his infamous document on "Science and Style," to bring about the maximum possible disruption of our movement before taking his formal departure.

IV. *Another of "Shachtman's Precedents"*

It is to be assumed that Shachtman's contribution to the resolution is the paragraph on "precedents" from the history of the Bolshevik party of Lenin and of the Fourth International. We know from the article of Comrades Wright and Hansen on the "Shachtman School of Quotations," and from Trotsky's answer to Shachtman's "Open Letter," how Shachtman perverts and falsifies historical incidents to serve factional ends. The historical references in the resolution under discussion are worth just as much and just as little as the others. It is precisely from Lenin's Bolshevik party that we learned the theory and practice of democratic centralism. Lenin's party had a single program and subordinated the party press to the service of the program. It is from Bolshevism that we learned to conduct free discussions, not for the sake of discussing in permanence, but in order to decide and to act unitedly on the basis of the decision of the majority.

We are approaching the end of a six-months' discussion, and none was ever freer or more democratic. We are on the eve of the convention which will conclude the discussion with a decision. From that we shall proceed to discipline in action on the basis of the decision. That is in the real tradition of Bolshevism. The "tradition" which the opposition invokes are those of Menshevism, of pre-war social democracy, of the "all inclusive party." To attempt to pass this off in the name of Lenin and his party of democratic centralism is to practice fraud on the inexperienced and uninformed members of the party and the youth.

Equally fraudulent is the reference to "many similar instances" in the history of the Fourth International. There are no such instances. The Fourth International and its predecessor, the International Left Opposition, never sanctioned different publications advocating antagonistic programs on fundamental questions. Just the contrary. The International Left Opposition took shape on a world scale in the course of an irreconcilable struggle for a single program and against groupings (with their publications) which, while pretending agreement "in general," advocated antagonistic programs. The International Left Opposition continued to exist and to grow and to expand as the world movement of the Fourth International not only by uniting revolutionary elements around a common program, but also by openly repudiating all groups and all publications advocating a different program. This was the case with Urbahns in Germany; Van Overstraaten in Belgium; Souvarine, Monatte and Paz in France; Weisbord and Field in the United

States, etc. They lie about the Fourth International, they pervert
its history, when they say the Fourth International gave its blessing
to publications which opposed its program.

The temporary experiment sanctioned by the Executive Committee of the Fourth International in the case of the French section
a year ago has nothing in common with the proposal of the opposition. The differences in the French section occurred exclusively
over *tactics*; both groups adhered to a common *program* on the
principle questions as laid down by the Congress of the Fourth International. One group of the POI (our French section) wanted
to maintain the complete independence of the organization. The
other group wanted to join the PSOP to work as a Bolshevik fraction within it. The Executive Committee of the Fourth International was strongly in favor of the "entrist" position, but did not
desire in the beginning to impose this tactic on the opposing comrades by disciplinary measures. Under these conditions, the Executive authorized a *division of labor* whereby one group would continue its independent activity with its own press and the other group
would join the PSOP and publish a journal *as a fraction of the
PSOP* in favor of the program of the Fourth International.

There was no question whatever of two different *programs*.
The only difference between the two publications was that the
journal of the independent group addressed its propaganda primarily to workers outside the PSOP, while the journal of the
entrist faction addressed its propaganda in favor of the same
programmatic ideas primarily to the members of the PSOP. But even
this experiment was strictly limited in time. It was discontinued a
few months later after a test of experience with work in the two
fields.

This "analogy" of Shachtman's, like all the others, is false
to the core and is criminally distorted and misapplied. Their
scheme compares not at all *to the relations established between
the two groups of Fourth Internationalists in France*—the entrists and the majority of the POI—but, by a dishonest twist,
*to the relations between the entrist faction of Bolshevik-Leninists
and the majority of the PSOP*. If, like all liberal philistines,
the Burnhamites argue that they should have the same "rights"
in a Trotskyist party of the Fourth International that the Rous
group of Fourth Internationalists enjoyed for a time in the
Pivertist party of the London Bureau, we answer: The Pivert party
pretended to be an "all inclusive party" and could not conveniently
refuse these rights to the Fourth Internationalists, since they were
also enjoyed by Free Masons, and all kinds of opportunists and

social patriots. We, on the other hand, don't pretend to be an "all inclusive party," and nobody shall make such a madhouse out of our organization.

On this point we shall ask the convention to reaffirm the section of the organization resolution drafted by Shachtman and Cannon and adopted at the foundation convention of the SWP in Chicago:

"The revolutionary Marxian party rejects not only the arbitrariness and bureaucratism of the C.P., but also the spurious and deceptive 'all-inclusiveness' of the Thomas-Tyler-Hoan party, which is a sham and a fraud. Experience has proved conclusively that this 'all-inclusiveness' paralyzes the party in general and the revolutionary left wing in particular, suppressing and bureaucratically hounding the latter while giving free rein to the right wing to commit the greatest crimes in the name of socialism and the party."

V. Split Disastrous to Splitters

The "unity" resolution of the Burnhamite splitters makes the assertion—the wish is father to the thought—that "a split would prove disastrous to the American section and to the International as a whole." We remain unimpressed by this forecast of calamity. If those who seek to terrorize us in this way would take a backward glance at the history of our party they would discover that threats of split have always been a menace only to those who uttered them. It cannot be otherwise with the present opposition, the most miserable of all those impatient petty-bourgeois groupings which tried to impose their demands upon the majority with threats of split. There has never yet been an opposition in our movement so heterogeneous, so far removed from Marxism and the spirit of the proletarian revolution, so weak in proletarian composition and so lacking in leaders with the necessary political firmness, devotion, singleness of purpose and capacity to sacrifice.

The threat of such an opposition to split from our party and set up an independent organization presents the prospect of a truly ludicrous spectacle. We have done everything in our power throughout the discussion to save the supporters of the opposition from this sad experience, and to preserve the unity of the party. We shall continue to work in this spirit, to make every reasonable concession, to provide every guarantee for the party rights of the minority after the convention consistent with the principles and methods of Bolshevik organization, that is, with the requirements of a combat party of the proletarian revolution.

But so far—and no further! Nobody shall transform our party into a perpetual talking shop. Nobody shall make a playhouse out of the party. Nobody shall be allowed to obstruct the proletarianization of the party. The convention must make it obligatory for all party members to connect themselves in one way or another with a workers' environment and recruit fresh elements from the proletariat in the course of class struggle activities.

That is the only way to save the party and prepare it for its great historic mission. Those who try to block this course will be defeated. Those who try to disrupt our movement by a treacherous split on the eve of the war will be smashed, as enemies and traitors deserve to be smashed.

After six months of discussion, as free and democratic as any party has ever known, the party is approaching the convention and the decision. Let every comrade in the party, regardless of what his opinion has been, face seriously once more and finally the inescapable rules of democratic centralism: The unconditional right of the party majority to decide the disputed questions and the unconditional duty of every party member to accept the decision. Only in this way can the unity of the party be preserved and common political work for the future made possible. There is no other road.

The slogan of split is the slogan of class betrayal. Its purpose is to disrupt the Fourth International on the eve of the war. But it will fail in its purpose. The only "disaster" will be the one that overtakes those criminals who, on the eve of the war, dare to direct such a treacherous blow at the only revolutionary movement in the whole world. The Fourth International will survive it in spite of all the Burnhams and Aberns plus the Shachtmans.

THE NATIONAL COMMITTEE MAJORITY

A LETTER TO C. CHARLES

New York, March 6, 1940

C. Charles, Organizer
Los Angeles Branch
(Copy to all California Branches)
Dear Comrade:

Concerning Johnson

I hear that Johnson is in California promoting the split program of the opposition and giving sermons on the organization question. I hope the comrades who value the unity of the party will give him a suitable reception. Here is a first class example of an irresponsible adventurer in our movement who deserves to be handled without gloves. Let me tell you a few things about him.

Johnson was appointed director of a party department under the supervision of the P.C. He leaves town and turns up in California without so much as notice to the Political Committee of his departure, to say nothing of permission. This is no doubt a sample of the "organizational methods" which the petty-bourgeois opposition recommends to the party. I am sure that every serious worker in the party will repudiate and condemn such light-minded irresponsibility. The procedure of Weiss in returning to California stands in marked contrast to that of Johnson. He did not venture to leave his post as *branch organizer* at Youngstown until he received the formal and official approval of both the P.C. and the Youngstown branch. There is a difference in the men and in the method. The method of Weiss is better, more responsible, more revolutionary. . . .

Our party, like every other, also has its share of inexperienced members who are inclined to mistake oratorical and literary facility for the qualities of revolutionary leadership. Cruel disappointments await such young comrades. But perhaps some of them will learn from their experience to demand better credentials next time. . . .

I hear that Johnson, the disorganizer, is going to lead a discussion of the Los Angeles comrades on the organization question. This impudence can only be based on the assumption that any kind of quackery can prosper in Southern California. But I know another California—the California of a group of resolute Trotskyists who have shown in practice that they know how to organize a party and do serious work in the mass movement. Instead of lecturing such comrades on "organization" Johnson should go to school to them. . . .

I greatly regret that I cannot be present when Johnson elucidates these questions. They go to the heart of the issue. It may seem impolite and even "bureaucratic" of me to put the questions so bluntly and so concretely. But that is the only way to bring the discussion of the organization question down to earth. Engels was fond of the proverb: "The proof of the pudding is in the eating." The organizational puddings Johnson has cooked up to date have not been very digestible.

With Trotskyist greetings,

J. P. CANNON

A LETTER TO LEON TROTSKY

New York, March 7, 1940

Dear Comrade Rork [Trotsky],

We received and discussed your letter of February 29th regarding the International Executive Committee.

We are all in agreement with your proposal. We think the best way would be for the S.W.P. to issue the call for the conference and to sponsor it and in the near future we will try to determine the most feasible approximate date at the earliest possible time after our convention.

We will contact the Canadian section and are assured of their complete support. After the ignominious departure of the Canadian Burnham (Robertson) the few comrades in Canada who had wavered on the fundamental question drew the necessary conclusions and the latest report we had is that they are all now unanimous in support of the program.

In the meantime, we think it would be a good idea for the Coyoacan delegation to begin work on the manifesto. The publication of the manifesto immediately after the conference will undoubtedly become the rallying call for all the sections of the Fourth International.

We learned yesterday that the Argentine section had published our Finnish resolution in their paper. We have not heard from them directly, but we must conclude from this act that they are in agreement with us. The Argentine section, together with the Mexican, can go a long way to dissipate the pretensions of Lebrun. We have no direct contact with the Brazilian section. . . .

However, in a letter from the Brazilian section which came last fall, it was stated that one or two of the prominent leaders (journalists, I think) had turned bad at the beginning of the war crisis and had been expelled and the section reorganized. This would seem to indicate that the rank and file of the Brazilian section can be depended upon.

As for the English section, we have not succeeded in getting any direct report from them, nor can we learn whether they receive our publications or letters. However, in the latest number of their paper, dated last October, they state categorically their position in favor of defending the Soviet Union in spite of Stalin and even use almost the exact formulas contained in our press. I think it can be considered an absolute certainty that the English section will completely repudiate ————. It is only a question of establishing communication in some way and providing the possibilities for them to get the necessary information and to declare their position.

We likewise have not been able to get any direct information from the Belgian section. We know, however, that Vereecken criticizes them for defending the Soviet Union and we conclude from that that the Belgian section is on the right line.

We are going to make renewed attempts in every way to establish direct communication with them. We have not gotten word now for several months. However, from such information as we have now it is quite clear that the International as a whole will rally round the war manifesto of our conference. If the splitters, aided by Johnson and Lebrun, attempt to represent themselves as the Fourth International this pretense cannot last for any great length of time.

I don't know whether I mentioned in a previous letter that a sailor comrade who had returned from China reported that the entire section with the exception of one individual supported the official position of the Fourth International. They told him they couldn't understand why the minority in our party is so large, since they themselves had discussed this question a long time ago and settled it quite decisively. . . .

* * *

Under separate cover we are sending you our answer to the resolution adopted by the minority national conference. It is being distributed on a wide scale in the party, with the object of making clear to any wavering elements, who draw back from the prospect of a split, that there is no possibility of bargaining with us on the question of two parties in one and two public journals.

The oppositionists are telling our comrades all over the country that you will intervene at the last moment in favor of their demands for an independent journal of their own. It is quite possible that even some of the leaders believe this and it is the most important argument by which they reassure the wavering elements in their ranks. It would be very good to disillusion the oppositionists on this point. It is the one best way now to compel the wavering elements who shrink from leaving the party to stop and consider their course before it is too late.

Dobbs is here and he is already rapidly integrating himself into the work. As you perhaps observed, he has the precious qualities of enthusiasm and confidence and imparts these sentiments to others.

Our ranks are firmly united from one end of the country to the other. There is not a trace of pessimism or hesitation. On the contrary, there are unanimous expressions of satisfaction about the great lessons learned in this struggle and over the fortunate circumstance that the party was able to have its showdown struggle with unreliable leaders before the real test begins.

The lectures of Wright and Warde on dialectical materialism are being conducted with remarkable success and appreciation by the comrades.

Fraternally,
J. P. CANNON

A LETTER TO MURRY WEISS

New York, March 7, 1940

Murry Weiss
Los Angeles, California

Dear Murry,

... I have today written a letter to the Los Angeles organization about Johnson. You should go after him hammer and tongs along the line of this letter, and pull a few feathers from this peacock. You are also receiving by air mail our answer to the split resolution of the Cleveland conference of the minority and also the Old Man's answer in the form of a letter to Dobbs. These new developments—the program of split, completely overshadowed the organizational details which were the subject of discussion earlier, and your speech must take this into account in its emphasis.

I think it would be useful for you also to present the organization question from the point of view of the California experience. In a previous letter to the group I dwelt at some length on this. After all, the test of all organizational theories is the practice. The California comrades had a solid year's experience with our "regime." They have also had some experience with the Trimble regime.

I am working on my document on the organization question, but I am continually interrupted and never get a chance to do any sustained work. Our comrades must understand that everything is now poised for the split, and conduct a struggle accordingly. No compromise and no quarter—must be our slogan. This is the only way to impress the wavering comrades with the fact that they must decide finally which way they are going.

It is absurd for us to take a defensive position on the organization question. By God, we built the best section of the whole Fourth International by our methods. We know what the French and English methods produced. Johnson is a first class exponent of these methods, and it is not by accident that he is with the minority and belongs to the same school.

If I get a chance to send you more material between now and the convention date, I will do so.

Comradely greetings,
Fraternally,
J. P. CANNON

A LETTER TO ALL MAJORITY GROUPS

New York, March 8, 1940

Dear Comrades,

Prepare for the Split

Along with this letter or under separate cover you will receive our mimeographed reply to the split resolution of the Cleveland conference of the opposition. We decided to mimeograph this for widespread distribution in the party. The reason: to make it clear to any wavering elements of the opposition, to anyone in the ranks still inspired by sentiments of loyalty to the party, and to any others who may think they may bluff us into permitting an independent "journal" of the opposition attacking our program—that there is nothing doing, and that as far as we are concerned the "negotiations" on this point are finished before they start.

It is extremely important that you conduct a concentrated campaign along these lines. This is the only way to save for the party a small part of the deluded supporters of the petty-bourgeois opposition.

In the meantime the most important thing is to make all necessary organizational preparations for the inevitable split. See that all membership lists, lists of sympathizers, contacts and so forth are in safe hands. Have all supporters of the majority prepared for resolute action the moment the split becomes a formal reality.

It is important to impress upon any comrades playing with the idea of split that it can only mean the beginning of a merciless war with us. Some of them undoubtedly are playing with the idea that they can split the party and still maintain some kind of friendly and comradely relations with us. It must be made clear to them that friendship ceases when the party is attacked.

The International

The opposition leaders are deluding some of their followers with the story that they have the support of the Fourth International. This is pure nonsense. All the sections of the Fourth International which are known to have declared themselves are standing by the position of the majority. The Canadian section is unanimous; likewise the Mexican. Yesterday we saw the paper of the Argentine section which printed our resolution on Finland. This is a decisive test as to their attitude, although we have no direct mail reports from them yet.

We note in the bulletin of the London Bureau that Vereecken attacks our Belgian section for defending the Soviet Union in Finland. This is an indirect confirmation of other reports we have had that the Belgian section, the strongest proletarian section in Europe, is on our side. We have heard no direct communication from England on account of the censorship. But the last number of their organ which we saw in October repeated our formulas about the defense of the Soviet Union. One thing we can be absolutely sure of is that the English section will repudiate ———— and leave him hanging in mid-air with all his pretensions.

The same thing applies to ————. He is the Latin-American representative, but with Mexico and Argentina disavowing him he is also shown up as a phony, representing nobody but himself. The paper of the Australian section supports the position of the majority. A sailor comrade who returned from China reported that the entire Chinese section with the exception of one individual supports the official program. *Also, it is not without importance that the Russian section supports our position.*

We plan to call a conference of genuine representatives of all available sections immediately after the convention and publish an anti-war manifesto in their name. Any pretensions the traitors may make to being the representatives of the Fourth International will be knocked into a cocked hat. There is no question whatever that practically all the functioning sections of the International throughout the world will rally around the anti-war manifesto of the conference called by our party.

Warning Against Provocations

From all sections of the country we get reports of the growing impatience of the proletarian sections of the party with the petty-bourgeois opposition and its provocations. We must expect that an opposition of this kind will do everything in its power to dirty up our house before they leave it. They can be expected to try to create some scandals in order to bring discredit on our movement. Therefore, it is necessary to warn all comrades to be on guard against provocations. Do not under any circumstances engage in any physical encounters which can be utilized to scandalize our movement. Observe all formalities of organization and do not deprive the oppositionists of any of their normal rights up to the moment of the convention and the split.

Check carefully the membership lists in connection with elections for delegates. In this regard be governed by one inflexible rule. Do not permit any irregularities whatever on one side or the other. Don't give the opposition a single vote they are not entitled to and don't try to make any claims for the majority to which we are not justly entitled.

Finances

I think all of us understand that this struggle is the fundamental crisis and test of the Fourth International in this country, of its ability to survive and face the war. The fact that some unreliable leaders showed their colors in time to be dealt with properly is a great advantage. But just because the crisis is of such a fundamental nature all comrades must realize the necessity for making extraordinary sacrifices to enable the party to cope with the problem. It is needless to tell you that we are operating here under great difficulties in the face of the sabotage of the minority and the general paralysis of party work.

All delegates should come to the convention with enough money to take care of themselves. The assistance which out of town delegates have been accustomed to in normal times cannot be depended upon in this situation. If we have a few dollars on hand here we will be lucky and we will need that for party work and the struggle against the splitters, beginning the day after the convention.

Please bear this in mind and collect all the funds you need to finance your delegate.

Fraternally,
J. P. CANNON

A LETTER TO MURRY WEISS

New York, March 8, 1940

Murry Weiss
Los Angeles, Cal.

Dear Murry,

I got your letter of February 29th.

We are most of all glad to hear that the caucus is getting organized on a military basis. That is the most important thing now. The opposition is heading straight for a split and we must organize our forces to smash it. That is the alpha and omega of revolutionary strategy from now on.

I think you are quite right in stating that Burnham's impudent document on "Science and Style" is a blow at the remnants of Shachtman's independence. That I think is the real purpose of it. He is just giving these traitors to Marxism advance notice of what he will serve up for them and make them take after they set up an independent organization of their own.

Incidentally, it is an excellent lesson in principled politics, or rather, the fatal consequences of experimenting with unprincipled politics. I think you could give the comrades a whole lecture on this point, using the latest incident as a supplement to similar incidents in the past history of our movement.

George Clarke has written a long document on the auto crisis which should go onto the mimeograph today or tomorrow. It is a complete history of the affair and will be quite an eye-opener to the Los Angeles rank and file comrades who were taken in on this and similar questions. Its subtitle certainly describes the document: "The Petty-Bourgeois Leaders Before the Test of the Class Struggle."

As you know I was away in France at the time. I heard a great deal about the affair in snatches but I never realized what a horrible mess was made of things by these so-called leaders until I read the whole connected and integrated story as written by Clarke.

The "independent" position of the Everett group is a transparent fraud. Soviet defeatism is a position of class betrayal and its advocates belong with the other traitors. I got the impression from previous letters that there was a tendency in the ranks of the majority to temporize with this group. I don't think that's correct. I read Everett's document and think you estimate him correctly when you say he is just a Burnhamite who wants a house of his own. I think it should be made perfectly clear in our caucus that there can be no talk of any kind of conciliation with the Everett tendency. They are not shooting in the same direction that we are. Consequently they cannot be allies in any sense of the word whatever.

It is possible that the Los Angeles Everettites may hesitate at a split. They should be smoked out on this without delay. If they decide to remain in the party naturally we will make a distinction between them and the splitters. But we will not conciliate with their tendency in any way, shape or form. Nor will we continue the discussion with them after the convention.

You speak about the "Menshevik spirit and conception" of the oppositionist leaders. Trotsky in a letter to Chris Andrews the other day remarked that "our Russian Mensheviks were revolutionary heroes in comparison to Burnham and Company."

I note the reactions of Ted to the first page of Burnham's document. Every worker in the party was similarly revolted. I don't know who was this international figure who stopped to admire the beauty of the cop's sabers flashing in the sun instead of plunging into the fight. But from the way he describes him he belongs in the opposition caucus. Comrades around here think he is referring to Glenner, that fourflusher who is trying to palm himself off as some kind of international leader, and rationalizing his personal demoralization into a political program. Give short shrift to these birds, Murry.

I agree with your proposals to work out party propositions in the caucus for presentation in branch meetings, etc. As a matter of fact the comrades must consider the majority caucus from now on as *the* party and they must take the whole responsibility upon themselves already now in preparation for the split which is sure to come at the convention. . . .

Fraternally,
J. P. CANNON

P.S. I just this minute opened a letter from Trotsky to Dobbs. He fully supports our stand in openly and flatly rejecting the demand of the minority for a public organ. You will receive a copy perhaps in the next mail or so.

A LETTER TO C. CHARLES

New York, March 12, 1940

C. Charles
Los Angeles, Cal.
Dear Charley,

I received your letter of March 7th and I am awaiting with some impatience a report of the debates with Johnson and the reaction of the comrades to the biographical material I sent on this fly-by-night expert on the organization question.

There is no sense in taking time to write an answer to Lebrun. Even historians of the movement will have to dig a long while through the mass of material already printed to get to anything that is written now. The party is water-logged with the discussion.

It is important to keep pounding away on the minority on the split question to shatter their morale in confronting this decisive break with our movement. I agree with your comments on the minority. I don't care what the Los Angeles comrades do with the official status of Johnson. As far as we are concerned, he is 3,000 miles away from his post of duty without authorization and what he does or does not do is not our affair.

I received the copy of ——'s letter on China. You will receive a copy of a letter from the Brazilian section which shows that the opposition claims about that are mainly the bunk.

Fraternally,
J. P. CANNON

P.S. Now that Dobbs is here and has taken a good many duties and worries off my hands I am pounding away every day on my document on the organization question. I am afraid it is going to be a book before I get through. Of course it will not have any influence in the present discussion and is not so intended. People who can be lined up on organization questions when fundamental principles are at stake are not the kind of material we want at this time in the majority ranks. My document is designed to deal with this method of politics fundamentally and to be a sort of manual for the party in the future.

A LETTER TO ALL MAJORITY GROUPS

New York, March 15, 1940

Dear Comrades,

Trade Union Discussion at the Convention

We intend to have a real thoroughgoing trade union discussion at the convention. We must not permit the faction struggle to put it off the agenda this time. Regardless of what the opposition does or does not do we intend to utilize the opportunity of this convention to bring out the whole problem of the trade union work—our policy, our experiences and our plans—in the most thoroughgoing discussion we ever had to date.

Comrade Dobbs is preparing a comprehensive convention report on the trade union question in general.* He will illustrate it by all kinds of examples drawn from experiences in practical trade union work. We also plan to have outstanding comrades in the different trade union fields give supplementary reports on their work. I think we can count on very instructive and interesting reports from Minneapolis, the maritime fraction, the auto fraction and from the steel fraction.

We don't know yet how long we'll be stalled up in the fight with the opposition, but we intend to have this trade union discussion regardless. All delegates should plan to stay an extra day if necessary for this trade union discussion. All branches and locals which have comrades participating actively in trade union work should try to have at least one trade unionist on the delegation in order to enrich this discussion with every possible variety of experience.

Fraternally,
J. P. CANNON

---

*Comrade Dobbs worked up the material for this highly important report into a pamphlet *Trade Union Problems*, which is still available. Pioneer Publishers.—*Ed.*

A LETTER TO LEON TROTSKY

New York, March 16, 1940

Dear Comrade Cornell [Trotsky],

Our statement flatly rejecting the ultimatum of the Cleveland conference and your supplementary letter along the same line seem to have disoriented the minority.

Many comrades were persuaded to support the demand for a public organ as a clever bargaining point which might be discussed and result in some compromise. The fact that the leadership put it in ultimatistic form and that we rejected it out of hand—thus leaving no room for "negotiations"—has greatly disturbed a considerable number of rank and file minorityites and has perhaps raised some doubts in their minds as to the strategical wisdom of their leadership.

Both here in New York and in other parts of the country they have been approaching our comrades with the suggestion that we discuss the matter and perhaps achieve a settlement, not on the basis of an independent journal, but on the space allotment in *The New International*. I think many of these suggestions are inspired by the leadership. However, there is noticeable a distinct hesitation of many rank and file minorityites before the cold prospect of a definitive split.

Another significant development occurred in the Bronx branch the other night. Two comrades, who have been with the minority from the beginning and who are counted as amongst the most fanatical, suddenly changed their position and announced their support of the majority. One of them, a very active comrade in the branch work, read a statement to this effect: I have been studying Comrade Trotsky's article, "From a Scratch to the Danger of Gangrene" as well as other documents. This reconsideration and further study of the dispute have brought me to the conclusion that the majority is correct on all the principled points; that the minority under the influence of Burnham is moving in the direction of Menshevism; and that the leaders of the opposition are deliberately preparing a split. For these reasons I have changed my position and announce my support of the majority.

This declaration caused considerable consternation in the Bronx stronghold of Shachtman-Abern. All the more so since the comrade in question has been an *Abernite*. He came to us from the Socialist Party, had no previous serious political experience, was drawn into the social gossip circles by Max Sterling, poisoned with all the "dope" of a personal nature and completely disoriented.

We are letting the opposition stew in its own juice for the time being. We think the best strategy is to let the idea sink deeply into the minds of the rank and file of the opposition that it is impossible to negotiate with us on the basis of any ultimatums and that they cannot entertain the hope that we will legalize a split by authorizing the publication of an independent journal.

The latest circular of the opposition coming after our statement rejecting their ultimatum complains that "Cannon" has seized their ultimatistic demand for an independent public journal as a "pretext" to push them out of the party. Apparently it has not yet occurred to them to disarm Cannon by removing the "pretext."

The agitation initiated by Shachtman against Minneapolis has apparently had boomerang effects. There has been a noticeable tendency to qualify their criticism and to make elaborate explanations that the Minneapolis comrades are very good in their way, that they have the highest respect for them, etc., etc.

The ultimate results of the fight in the party are wholly progressive. We are all beginning to realize on second thought that the postponement of the convention was very advantageous in spite of the continued irritations and growing impatience of the rank and file comrades with the discussion. The smoking out of Burnham was a major victory. In general, all the profound differences are more fully ripened and the decision of the convention can be all the firmer.

As I view it, we are already three-fourths or four-fifths through the most decisive and radical new stage in the evolution and development of the American section. It has been demonstrated to the hilt that the proletarian cadres of the party stand four-square on the basis of orthodox Bolshevism and cannot be diverted from it.

Simultaneously, a leadership of the party intimately connected with the proletarian ranks and directly expressing its revolutionary sentiments has been more firmly consolidated than ever before. Up till now the leadership has always been a coalition of the proletarian and the unripened petty-bourgeois tendencies. The party as a whole reflected this unstable equilibrium which was frequently upset by the moods and caprices of people who were considered as an indispensable section of the leadership.

In this fight, such people have not only lost terribly in prestige and authority; they have lost the power to seriously disturb the party or to impede a radical transformation of its activities in a proletarian direction. The proletarian ranks are so firmly consolidated against them that the Hamlet question—to split or not to split—is pretty much their own personal affair. The party will move forward on sure feet in either case.

Last night we had a quite startling demonstration of this. Comrade Dobbs has already integrated himself into the party work and is especially taking hold of the trade union end of it. Last night he called the first of what are to be regular meetings of the party trade unionists in New York to discuss the practical aspects of their work and to exchange experiences. The meeting was quite successful and aroused considerable enthusiasm among the trade union comrades. A small number of minorityites were present and seemed to be quite astounded at the nonchalance with which we are proceeding to outline and organize future plans for practical work without regard for the fact that the "catastrophe" of a split is in the offing. Among other things, this meeting was a direct and powerful blow at the will of the rank and file minorityites to split.

Comrade Dobbs has already drawn up a comprehensive questionnaire which will establish the exact number of trade unionists in the party, their location, experiences, etc., and lay the ground for a better coordination of the work on a national scale. Simultaneously, with the help of some of our research comrades, he is preparing a comprehensive survey of the geographic and industrial distribution of the American proletariat as a basis for a more concrete consideration by the convention—as he expresses it, "to fit the small gear of available party forces in the most efficient manner to the large gear of the mass movement."

At the end of the internal party fight we are thus coming back to the original slogan, the serious application of which will be the best assurance against any recurrence of the petty-bourgeois disease: Deeper into the mass movement of the proletariat.

Fraternally yours,

J. P. CANNON

DOCUMENTS OF
THE   STRUGGLE

EDITOR'S NOTE:

While in the preceding section of this book, the struggle against the petty-bourgeois opposition is reflected in the letters written by Comrade Cannon, in the following section the struggle—from its inception, through its most critical stages of the discussion up to the climax at the convention and the split following the convention—is faithfully reproduced through documents.

The first of these documents, "Speech on the Russian Question," is in point of fact also one of the first political documents of the Trotskyist majority, being preceded only by Leon Trotsky's "The USSR in War," which is dated September 25, 1939, and which arrived in New York a few days before the above-mentioned speech of Cannon on October 15, 1939. Of Cannon's sixty-odd speeches on Bolshevik political and organizational issues involved in the eight months' struggle, it is the only one which has been preserved. No stenograms were taken down of the others primarily because the entire limited resources and tiny apparatus of our party were strained to the utmost at the time.

The remaining documents in this section pertain to questions of organization, discipline and party press. They are either self-explanatory or accompanied with adequate notes.

The political questions decided by the National Convention of the Socialist Workers Party on April 5-8, 1940 are dealt with exhaustively in the book, *In Defense of Marxism*, by Leon Trotsky.

DOCUMENTS OF
THE STRUGGLE

SPEECH ON THE RUSSIAN QUESTION*

*(New York Membership Meeting of the Socialist Workers Party,
October 15, 1939)*

The Russian question is with us once again, as it has been at every critical turning point of the international labor movement since November 7, 1917. And there is nothing strange in that. The Russian question is no literary exercise to be taken up or cast aside according to the mood of the moment. The Russian question has been and remains the question of the revolution. The Russian Bolsheviks on November 7, 1917, once and for all, took the question of the workers' revolution out of the realm of abstraction and gave it flesh and blood reality.

It was said once of a book—I think it was Whitman's "Leaves of Grass"—"who touches this book, touches a man." In the same sense it can also be said, "Who touches the Russian question, touches a revolution." Therefore, be serious about it. Don't play with it.

The October revolution put socialism on the order of the day throughout the world. It revived and shaped and developed the revolutionary labor movement of the world out of the bloody chaos of the war. The Russian revolution showed in practice, by example, how the workers' revolution is to be made. It revealed in life the role of the party. It showed in life what kind of a party the workers must have. By its victory, and its reorganization of the social system, the Russian revolution has proved for all time the superiority of nationalized property and planned economy over capitalist private property, and planless competition and anarchy in production.

---

*Published in *The New International* of February 1940.—*Ed.*

A Sharp Dividing Line

The question of the Russian revolution—and the Soviet state which is its creation—has drawn a sharp dividing line through the labor movement of all countries for 22 years. The attitude taken toward the Soviet Union throughout all these years has been the decisive criterion separating the genuine revolutionary tendency from all shades and degrees of waverers, backsliders and capitulators to the pressure of the bourgeois world—the Mensheviks, Social Democrats, Anarchists and Syndicalists, Centrists, Stalinists.

The main source of division in our own ranks for the past ten years, since the Fourth Internationalist tendency took organized form on the international field, has been the Russian question. Our tendency, being a genuine, that is, orthodox, Marxist tendency from A to Z, has always proceeded on the Russian question from theoretical premises to political conclusions for action. Of course, it is only when political conclusions are drawn out to the end that differences on the Russian question reach an unbearable acuteness and permit no ambiguity or compromise. Conclusions on the Russian question lead directly to positions on such issues as war and revolution, defense and defeatism. Such issues, by their very nature, admit no unclarity, no compromise, because it is a matter of taking sides! One must be on one side or another in war and revolution.

The Importance of Theory

But if the lines are drawn only when political conclusions diverge, that does not at all signify that we are indifferent to theoretical premises. He is a very poor Marxist—better say, no Marxist at all—who takes a careless or tolerant attitude toward theoretical premises. The political conclusions of Marxists proceed from theoretical analyses and are constantly checked and regulated by them. That is the only way to assure a firm and consistent policy.

To be sure, we do not decline cooperation with people who agree with our political conclusions from different premises. For example, the Bolsheviks were not deterred by the fact that the left S.R.s were inconsistent. As Trotsky remarked in this connection, "If we wait till everything is right in everybody's head there will never be any successful revolutions in this world" (or words to that effect). Just the same, for our part we want everything right in our own heads. We have no reason whatever to slur over theoretical formulas, which are expressed in "terminology." As Trotsky says, in theoretical matters "we must keep our house clean."

Our position on the Russian question is programmatic. In brief: The theoretical analysis—a degenerated Workers' State. The political conclusion—unconditional defense against external attack of imperialists or internal attempts at capitalist restoration.

Defensism and Defeatism

Defensism and defeatism are two principled, that is, irreconcilable positions. They are not determined by arbitrary choice but by class interests.

No party in the world ever succeeded in harboring these two antipathetic tendencies for any great length of time. The contradiction is too great. Division all over the world ultimately took place along this line. Defensists at home were defeatists on Russia. Defensists on Russia were defeatists at home.

The degeneration of the Soviet state under Stalin has been analyzed at every step by the Bolshevik-Leninists and only by them. A precise attitude has been taken at every stage. The guiding lines of the revolutionary Marxist approach to the question have been:

See the reality and see it whole at every stage; never surrender any position before it is lost; the worst of all capitulators is the one who capitulates before the decisive battle.

The International Left Opposition which originated in 1923 as an opposition in the Russian party (the original nucleus of the Fourth International) has always taken a precise attitude on the Russian question. In the first stages of the degeneration of which the Stalinist bureaucracy was the banner bearer the opposition considered it possible to rectify matters by methods of reform through the change of regime in the Communist Party of the Soviet Union. Later, when it became clearer that the Communist Party of Lenin had been irremediably destroyed, and after it became manifest that the reactionary bureaucracy could be removed only by civil war, the Fourth International, standing as before on its analysis of the Soviet Union as a workers' state, came out for a political revolution.

All the time throughout this entire period of 16 years the Bolshevik-Leninists have stoutly maintained, in the face of all slander and persecution, that they were the firmest defenders of the workers' state and that in the hour of danger they would be in the front ranks of its defense. We always said the moment of danger will find the Fourth Internationalists at their posts defending the conquests of the great revolution without ceasing for a moment our struggle against the Stalinist bureaucracy. Now that the hour of danger is at hand—now that the long-awaited war is actually knocking at the door—it would be very strange if the Fourth International should renege on its oft-repeated pledge.

"Conservatism" on the Russian Question

Throughout all this long period of Soviet degeneration since the death of Lenin, the Fourth Internationalists, analyzing the new phenomenon of a degenerating workers' state at every turn, striving to comprehend its complications and contradictions, to recognize and defend all the progressive features of the contradictory processes and to reject the reactionary—during all this long time we have been beset at every new turn of events by the impatient demands of "radicals" to simplify the question. Thrown off balance by the crimes and betrayals of Stalin, they lost sight of the new system of economy which Stalin had not destroyed and could not destroy.

We always firmly rejected these premature announcements that everything was lost and that we must begin all over again. At each stage of development, at each new revelation of Stalinist infamy and treachery, some group or other broke away from the Fourth International because of its "conservatism" on the Russian question. It would be interesting, if we had the time, to call the roll of these groupings which one after another left our ranks to pursue an ostensibly more "revolutionary" policy on the Russian question. Did they develop an activity more militant, more revolutionary, than ours? Did they succeed in creating a new movement and in attracting newly awakened workers and those breaking from Stalinism? In no case.

If we were to call the roll of these ultra-radical groups it would present a devastating picture indeed. Those who did not fall into complete political passivity became reconciled in one form or another to bourgeois democracy. The experiences of the past should teach us all a salutary caution, and even, if you please, "conservatism," in approaching any proposal to revise the program of the Fourth International on the Russian question. While all the innovators fell by the wayside, the Fourth International alone retained its programmatic firmness. It grew and developed and remained the only genuine revolutionary current in the labor movement of the world. Without a firm position on the Russian question our movement also would inevitably have shared the fate of the others.

The mighty power of the October revolution is shown by the vitality of its conquests. The nationalized property and the planned economy stood up under all the difficulties and pressures of the capitalist encirclement and all the blows of a reactionary bureaucracy at home. In the Soviet Union, despite the monstrous mismanagement of the bureaucracy, we saw a tremendous development of the productive forces—and in a backward country at that—while capitalist economy declined. Conclusion: Nationalized and planned economy, made possible by a revolution that overthrew the capitalists and landlords, is infinitely superior, more progressive. It shows the way forward. Don't give it up before it is lost! Cling to it and defend it!

The Class Forces,

On the Russian question there are only two really independent forces in the world. Two forces who think about the question independently because they base themselves, their thoughts, their analyses and their conclusions, on fundamental class considerations. Those two independent forces are:

(1) The conscious vanguard of the world bourgeoisie, the statesmen of both democratic and fascist imperialism.

(2) The conscious vanguard of the world proletariat.

Between them it is not simply a case of two opinions on the Russian question, but rather of two camps. All those who in the past rejected the conclusions of the Fourth International and broke with our movement on that account, have almost invariably fallen into the service of the imperialists, through Stalinism, social and liberal democracy, or passivity, a form of service.

The standpoint of the world bourgeoisie is a class standpoint. They proceed, as we do, from fundamental class considerations. They want to maintain world capitalism. This determines their fundamental antagonism to the U.S.S.R. They appreciate the reactionary work of Stalin, but consider it incomplete, insofar as he has not restored capitalist private property.

Their fundamental attitude determines an inevitable attempt at the start of the war, or during it, to attack Russia, overthrow the nationalized economy, restore a capitalist regime, smash the foreign trade monopoly, open up the Soviet Union as a market and field of investments, transform Russia into a great colony, and thereby alleviate the crisis of world capitalism.

The standpoint of the Fourth International is based on the same fundamental class considerations. Only we draw opposite conclusions, from an opposite class standpoint.

Purely sentimental motivations, speculation without fundamental class premises, so-called "fresh ideas" with no programmatic base—all this is out of place in a party of Marxists. We want to advance the world revolution of the proletariat. This determines our attitude and approach to the Russian question. True, we want to see reality, but we are not disinterested observers and commentators.

We do not examine the Russian revolution and what remains of its great conquests as though it were a bug under a glass. *We have an interest! We take part in the fight!* At each stage in the development of the Soviet Union, its advances and its degeneration, we seek the basis for revolutionary action. We want to advance the world revolution, overthrow capitalism, establish socialism. The Soviet Union is an important and decisive question on this line.

Our standpoint on the Russian question is written into our program. It is not a new question for us. It is 22 years old. We have followed its evolution, both progressive and retrogressive, at every stage. We have discussed it and taken our position anew at every stage of its progressive development and its degeneration. And, what is most important, we have always *acted* on our conclusions.

The Decisive Criterion

The Soviet Union emerged from the October revolution as a workers' state. As a result of the backwardness and poverty of the country and the delay of the world revolution, a conservative bureaucracy emerged and triumphed, destroyed the party and bureaucratized the economy. However, this same bureaucracy still operates on the basis of the nationalized property established by the revolution. That is the decisive criterion for our evaluation of the question.

If we see the Soviet Union for what it really is, a gigantic labor organization which has conquered one-sixth of the earth's surface, we will not be so ready to abandon it because of our hatred of the crimes and abominations of the bureaucracy. Do we turn our backs on a trade union because it falls into the control of bureaucrats and traitors? Ultra-leftists have frequently made this error, but always with bad results, sometimes with reactionary consequences.

We recall the case of the International Ladies' Garment Workers Union here in New York. The bureaucrats of this union were about as vile a gang of labor lieutenants of the capitalist class as could be found. In the struggle against the left-wing in the middle twenties they conspired with the bosses and the A. F. L. fakers. They expelled the left-wing locals and used hired thugs to fight them and to break their strikes. The difference between them and Stalin was only a matter of opportunity and power. Driven to revolt against the crimes of these bureaucrats the left-wing, under the influence of the Communist Party in the days of its Third Period frenzy, labelled the union—not merely its treacherous bureaucracy —as a "company union."

But this same "company union," under the pressure of the workers in its ranks and the increasing intensity of the class struggle, was forced to call a strike to defend itself against the "imperialist" attack of the bosses. Workers who had kept their heads, supported ("defended") the strike against the bosses. But the Stalinists, trapped by their own hastily-improvised theory, having already denounced the union as a company union, renounced support ("defense") of the strike. They denounced it as a "fake" strike. Thus their ill-considered radicalism led them to a reactionary position. They were denounced, and rightly, throughout the needle trades market as strike breakers. To this day they suffer the discredit of this reactionary action.

To defend the Soviet Union as a gigantic labor organization against the attacks of its class enemies does not mean to defend each and every action of its bureaucracy or each and every action of the Red Army which is an instrument of the bureaucracy. To impute such a "totalitarian" concept of defense to the Fourth International is absurd. Nobody here will deny defense of a bonafide trade union, no matter how reactionary its bureaucracy. But that does not prevent us from discriminating between actions of the bureaucracy which involve a defense of the union against the bosses and other actions which are aimed against the workers.

The United Mine Workers of America is a great labor organization which we all support. But it is headed by a thoroughgoing scoundrel and agent of the master class who also differs from Stalin only in the degrees of power and opportunity. In my own personal experience some years ago, I took part in a strike of the Kansas miners which was directed against the enforcement of a reactionary labor law, known as the Kansas Industrial Court Law, a law forbidding strikes. This was a thoroughly progressive action on the part of the Kansas miners and their president, Alex Howat. Howat and the other local officials were thrown into jail. While they were in jail, John L. Lewis, as president of the national organization, sent his agents into the Kansas fields to sign an agreement with the bosses over the head of the officers of the Kansas district. He supplied strike breakers and thugs and money to break the strike while the legitimate officers of the union lay in jail for a good cause. Every militant worker in the country denounced this treacherous strike-breaking action of Lewis. But did we therefore renounce support of the national union of mine workers? Yes, some impatient revolutionaries did, and thereby completely disoriented themselves in the labor movement. The United Mine Workers retained its character as a labor organization and only last Spring came into conflict with the coal operators on a national scale. I think you all recall that in this contest our press gave "unconditional defense" to the miners' union despite the fact that strikebreaker Lewis remained its president.

The Longshoremen's Union of the Pacific Coast is a bona fide organization of workers, headed by a Stalinist of an especially unattractive type, a pocket edition of Stalin named Bridges. This same Bridges led a squad of misguided longshoremen through a picket line of the Sailors' Union in a direct attempt to break up this organization. I think all of you recall that our press scathingly denounced this contemptible action of Bridges. But if the Longshoremen's Union, headed by Bridges, which is at this moment conducting negotiations with the bosses, is compelled to resort to strike action, what stand shall we take? Any ordinary class-conscious worker, let alone an educated Marxist, will be on the picket line with the Longshoremen's Union or "defending" it by some other means.

Why is it so difficult for some of our friends, including some of those who are very well educated in the formal sense, to understand the Russian question? I am very much afraid it is because they do not think of it in terms of struggle. It is strikingly evident that the workers, especially the more experienced workers who have taken part in trade unions, strikes, etc., understand the Russian question much better than the more educated scholastics. From their experiences in the struggle they know what is meant when the Soviet Union is compared to a trade union that has fallen into bad hands. And everyone who has been through a couple of strikes which underwent crises and came to the brink of disaster, finally to emerge victorious, understands what is meant when one says: *No position must be surrendered until it is irrevocably lost.*

I, personally, have seen the fate of more than one strike determined by the will or lack of will of the leadership to struggle at a critical moment. All our trade union successes in Minneapolis stem back directly to a fateful week in 1934 when the leaders refused to call off the strike, which to all appearances was hopelessly defeated, and persuaded the strike committee to hold out a while longer. In that intervening time a break occurred in the ranks of the bosses; this in turn paved the way for a compromise settlement and eventually victorious advance of the whole union.

How strange it is that some people analyze the weakness and defects in a workers' organization so closely that they do not always take into account the weakness in the camp of the enemy, which may easily more than counter-balance.

In my own agitation among strikers at dark moments of a strike I have frequently resorted to the analogy of two men engaged in a physical fight. When one gets tired and apparently at the end of his resources he should never forget that the other fellow is maybe just as tired or even more so. In that case the one who holds out will prevail. Looked at in this way a worn-out strike can sometimes be carried through to a compromise or a victory by the resolute will of its leadership. We have seen this happen more than once. Why should we deny the Soviet Union, which is not yet exhausted, the same rights?

The Danger of a False Position

We have had many discussions on the Russian question in the past. It has been the central and decisive question for us, as for every political tendency in the labor movement. That, I repeat, is because it is nothing less than the question of the revolution at various stages of its progressive development or degeneration. We are, in fact, the party of the Russian revolution. We have been the people, and the only people, who have had the Russian revolution in their program and in their blood. That is also the main reason why the Fourth International is the only revolutionary tendency in the whole world. A false position on the Russian question would have destroyed our movement as it destroyed all others.

Two years ago we once again conducted an extensive discussion on the Russian question. The almost unanimous conclusion of the party was written into the program of our first convention:

(1) The Soviet Union, on the basis of its nationalized property and planned economy, the fruit of the revolution, remains a workers' state, though in a degenerated form.

(2) As such, we stand, as before, for the unconditional defense of the Soviet Union against imperialist attack.

(3) The best defense—the only thing that can save the Soviet Union in the end by solving its contradictions—is the international revolution of the proletariat.

(4) In order to regenerate the workers' state we stand for the overthrow of the bureaucracy by a political revolution.

But, it may be said, "Defense of the Soviet Union, and Russia is a Workers' State—those two phrases don't answer everything." They are not simply phrases. One is a theoretical analysis; the other is a political conclusion for action.

The Meaning of Unconditional Defense

Our motion calls for unconditional defense of the Soviet Union against imperialist attack. What does that mean? It simply means that we defend the Soviet Union and its nationalized property against external attacks of imperialist armies or against internal attempts at capitalist restoration, without putting as a prior condition the overthrow of the Stalinist bureaucracy. Any other kind of defense negates the whole position under present circumstances. Some people speak nowadays of giving "conditional" defense to the Soviet Union. If you stop to think about it we are for conditional defense of the United States. It is so stated in the program of the Fourth International. In the event of war we will absolutely defend the country on only one small "condition": that we first overthrow the government of the capitalists and replace it with a government of the workers.

Does unconditional defense of the Soviet Union mean supporting every act of the Red Army? No, that is absurd. Did we support the Moscow Trials and the actions of Stalin's G.P.U. in these trials? Did we support the purges, the wholesale murders of the forces in Spain which were directed against the workers? If I recall correctly, we unconditionally defended those workers who fought on the other side of the barricades in Barcelona. That did not prevent us from supporting the military struggle against Franco and maintaining our position in defense of the Soviet Union against imperialist attack.

It is now demanded that we take a big step forward and support the idea of an armed struggle against Stalin in the newly occupied territories of old Poland. Is this really something new? For three years the Fourth International has advocated in its program the armed overthrow of Stalin inside the Soviet Union itself. The Fourth International has generally acknowledged the necessity for an armed struggle to set up an independent Soviet Ukraine. How can there be any question of having a different policy in the newly occupied territories? If the revolution against Stalin is really ready there, the Fourth International will certainly support it and endeavor to lead it. There are no two opinions possible in our ranks on this question. But what shall we do if Hitler (or Chamberlain) attacks the Sovietized Ukraine before Stalin has been overthrown? This is the question that needs an unambiguous answer. Shall we defend the Soviet Union, and with it now and for the same reasons, the nationalized property of the newly annexed territories? We say, yes!

That position was incorporated into the program of the foundation congress of the Fourth International, held in the summer of 1938. Remember, that was after the Moscow Trials and the crushing of the Spanish revolution. It was after the murderous purge of the whole generation of Bolsheviks, after the People's Front, the entry into the League of Nations, the Stalin-Laval pact (and betrayal of the French workers). We took our position on the basis of the economic structure of the country, the fruit of the revolution. The great gains are not to be surrendered before they are really lost. That is the fighting program of the Fourth International.

The Stalin-Hitler Pact

The Stalin-Hitler pact does not change anything fundamentally. If Stalin were allied with the United States, and comrades should deny defense of the Soviet Union out of fear of becoming involved in the defense of Stalin's American ally, such comrades would be wrong, but their position would be understandable as a subjective reaction prompted by revolutionary sentiments. The "defeatism" which broke out in our French section following the Stalin-Laval pact was undoubtedly so motivated and, consequently, had to be refuted with the utmost tolerance and patience. But an epidemic of "defeatism" in the democratic camp would be simply shameful. There is no pressure on us in America to defend the Soviet Union. All the pressure is for a democratic holy war against the Soviet Union. Let us keep this in mind. The main enemy is still in our own country.

What has happened since our last discussion? Has there been some fundamental change in Soviet economy? No, nothing of that kind is maintained. Nothing happened except that Stalin signed the pact with Hitler! For us that gave no reason whatever to change our analysis of Soviet economy and our attitude toward it. The aim of all our previous theoretical work, concentrated in our program, was precisely to prepare us for war and revolution. Now we have the war; and revolution is next in order. If we have to stop now to find a new program it is a very bad sign.

Just consider: There are people who could witness all the crimes and betrayals of Stalin, which we understood better than anybody else, and denounced before anybody else and more effectively— they could witness all this and still stand for the defense of the Soviet Union. But they could not tolerate the alliance with fascist Germany instead of imperialist England or France!

The Invasion of Poland

Of course, there has been a great hullaballoo about the Soviet invasion of Polish Ukraine. But that is simply one of the consequences of the war and the alliance with Hitler's Germany. The contention that we should change our analysis of the social character of the Soviet state and our attitude toward its defense because the Red Army violated the Polish border is even more absurd than to base such changes on the Hitler pact. The Polish invasion is only an incident in a war, and in wars borders are always violated. (If all the armies stayed at home there could be no war.) The inviolability of borders—all of which were established by war—is interesting to democratic pacifists and to nobody else.

Hearing all the democratic clamor we had to ask ourselves many times: Don't they know that Western Ukraine and White Russia never rightfully belonged to Poland? Don't they know that this territory was forcibly taken from the Soviet Union by Pilsudski with French aid in 1920?

To be sure, this did not justify Stalin's invasion of the territory in collaboration with Hitler. We never supported that and we never supported the fraudulent claim that Stalin was bringing "liberation" to the peoples of the Polish Ukraine. At the same time we did not propose to yield an inch to the "democratic" incitement against the Soviet Union on the basis of the Polish events. The democratic war mongers were shrieking at the top of their voices all over town. We must not be unduly impressed by this democratic clamor. Your National Committee was not in the least impressed.

In order to penetrate a little deeper into this question and trace it to its roots, let us take another hypothetical example. Not a fantastic one, but a very logical one. Suppose Stalin had made a pact with the imperialist democracies against Hitler while Rumania had allied itself with Hitler. Suppose, as would most probably have happened in that case, the Red Army had struck at Rumania, Hitler's ally, instead of Poland, the ally of the democracies, and had seized Bessarabia, which also once belonged to Russia. Would the democratic war mongers in that case have howled about "Red Imperialism"? Not on your life!

I am very glad that our National Committee maintained its independence from bourgeois democratic pressure on the Polish invasion. The question was put to us very excitedly, point-blank, like a pistol at the temple: "Are you for or against the invasion of Poland?" But revolutionary Marxists don't answer in a "yes" or "no" manner which can lump them together with other people who pursue opposite aims. Being for or against something is not enough in the class struggle. It is necessary to explain *from what standpoint* one is for or against. Are you for or against racketeering gangsters in the trade unions?—the philistines sometimes ask. We don't jump to attention, like a private soldier who has met an officer on the street, and answer, "against!" We first inquire: who asks this question and from what standpoint? And what weight does this question have in relation to other questions? We have our own standpoint and we are careful not to get our answers mixed up with those of class enemies and pacifist muddleheads.

Some people—especially affected bosses—are against racketeering gangsters in the trade unions because they extort graft from the bosses. That side of the question doesn't interest us very much. Some people—especially pacifist preachers—are against the gangsters because they commit violence. But we are not against violence at all times and under all circumstances. We, for our part, taking our time and formulating our viewpoint precisely, say: We are against union gangsterism because it injures the union in its fight against the bosses. That is our reason. It proceeds from our special class standpoint on the union question.

So with Poland: We don't support the course of Stalin in general. His crime is not one incident here or there but his *whole* policy. He demoralizes the workers' movement and discredits the Soviet Union. That is what we are against. He betrays the revolution by his whole course. Every incident for us fits into that framework; it is considered from that point of view and taken in its true proportions.

The Invasion of Finland

Those who take the Polish invasion—an incident in a great chain of events—as the basis for a fundamental change in our program show a lack of proportion. That is the kindest thing that can be said for them. They are destined to remain in a permanent lather throughout the war. They are already four laps behind schedule: There is also Latvia, and Estonia, and Lithuania, and now Finland.

We can expect another clamor of demands that we say, pointblank, and in one word, whether we are "for" or "against" the pressure on poor little bourgeois-democratic Finland. Our answer —wait a minute. Keep your shirt on. There is no lack of protests in behalf of the bourgeois swine who rule Finland. The *New Leader* has protested. Charles Yale Harrison has written a tearful column about it. The renegade Lore has wept about it in the *New York Post*. The President of the United States has protested. Finland is pretty well covered with moral support. So bourgeois Finland can wait a minute till we explain our attitude without bothering about the "for" or "against" ultimatum.

I personally feel very deeply about Finland, and this is by no means confined to the present dispute between Stalin and the Finnish Prime Minister. When I think of Finland, I think of the thousands of martyred dead, the proletarian heroes who perished under the white terror of Mannerheim. I would, if I could, call them back from their graves. Failing that, I would organize a proletarian army of Finnish workers to avenge them, and drive their murderers into the Baltic Sea. I would send the Red Army of the regenerated Soviet Union to help them at the decisive moment.

We don't support Stalin's invasion only because he doesn't come for revolutionary purposes. He doesn't come at the call of Finnish workers whose confidence he has forfeited. That is the only reason we are against it. The "borders" have nothing to do with it. "Defense" in war also means attack. Do you think we will respect frontiers when we make our revolution? If an enemy army lands troops at Quebec, for example, do you think we will wait placidly at the Canadian border for their attack? No, if we are genuine revolutionists and not pacifist muddleheads we will cross the border and meet them at the point of landing. And if our defense requires the seizure of Quebec, we will seize it as the Red Army of Lenin seized Georgia and tried to take Warsaw.

Foreseen in Program of Fourth International

Some may think the war and the alliance with Hitler change everything we have previously considered; that it, at least, requires a reconsideration of the whole question of the Soviet Union, if not a complete change in our program. To this we can answer:

War was contemplated by our program. The fundamental theses on "War and the Fourth International," adopted in 1934, say:

"Every big war, irrespective of its initial moves, must pose squarely the question of military intervention against the U.S.S.R. in order to transfuse fresh blood into the sclerotic veins of capitalism. . . .

"*Defense of the Soviet Union* from the blows of the capitalist enemies, irrespective of the circumstances and immediate causes of the conflict, is the elementary and imperative duty of every honest labor organization."

Alliances were contemplated. The theses say:

"In the existing situation an alliance of the U.S.S.R. with an imperialist state or with one imperialist combination against another, in case of war, cannot at all be considered as excluded. Under the pressure of circumstances a temporary alliance of this kind may become an iron necessity, without ceasing, however, because of it, to be of the greatest danger both to the U.S.S.R. and to the world revolution.

"The international proletariat will not decline to defend the U.S.S.R. even if the latter should find itself forced into a military alliance with some imperialists against others. But in this case, even more than in any other, the international proletariat must safeguard its complete political independence from Soviet diplomacy and thereby also from the bureaucracy of the Third International."

A stand on defense was taken in the light of this perspective.

A slogan of defense acquires a concrete meaning precisely in the event of war. A strange time to drop it! That would mean a rejection of all our theoretical preparation for the war. That would mean starting all over again. From what fundamental basis? Nobody knows.

There has been much talk of "independence" on the Russian question. That is good! A revolutionist who is not independent is not worth his salt. But it is necessary to specify: Independent of whom? What is needed by our party at every turn is class independence, independence of the Stalinists, and, above all, independence of the bourgeoisie. Our program assures such independence under all circumstances. It shall not be changed!

RESOLUTION ON PARTY UNITY*

*A Proposal for a Joint Statement to the Party Membership, to be
Signed by the Leading Representatives of Both Groups in the P.C.*

Submitted to the Political Committee, November 7, 1939, by
J. P. Cannon for the N.C. Majority.

In view of the fears expressed by some comrades that the present
internal discussion can lead to a split, either as a result of expulsions by a majority or the withdrawal of a minority, the leading
representatives of both sides declare:

(1) It is necessary to regulate the discussion in such a way as
to eliminate the atmosphere of split and reassure the party members
that the unity of the party will be maintained. Toward this end both
sides agree to eliminate from the discussion all threats of split or
expulsions.

(2) The issues in dispute must be clarified and resolved by
normal democratic processes within the framework of the party and
the Fourth International. After the necessary period of free discussion, if the two sides cannot come to agreement, the questions in
dispute are to be decided by a party convention, without, on the
one side, any expulsions because of opinions defended in the pre-
convention discussion, or any withdrawals on the other side.

(3) Both sides obligate themselves to loyal collaboration in the
daily work of the party during the period of the discussion.

(4) The internal bulletin is to be jointly edited by two editors,
one from each side.

(5) A parity commission of four—two from each side—is to
be constituted. The function of the parity commission is to investigate all organization complaints, grievances, threats, accusations, or
violations of discipline which may arise out of the discussion and
report same to the Political Committee with concrete recommen-
dations.

---

*The N.C. minority (Burnham-Shachtman-Abern and others) voted
for this resolution at the time. All of the provisions in it were strictly
fulfilled and enforced by the N.C. majority but violated shamelessly and
disloyally by the leaders and members of the opposition. *In Defense
of Marxism* (pp. 63-69 ff.) contains further details and clarifying material on this aspect of the struggle.—*Ed.*

CONVENTION RESOLUTIONS

(The National Convention of the Socialist Workers Party convened on April 15, 1940, after more than six months of democratic discussion on all the disputed questions. The following four resolutions pertaining to questions of organization and discipline were adopted by the convention in the final sessions on April 8th.—*Ed.*)

THE ORGANIZATION PRINCIPLES UPON WHICH THE PARTY WAS FOUNDED*

(Resolution Adopted by the Convention)

The third convention of the Socialist Workers Party reaffirms the resolution adopted by the Founding Convention of the S.W.P. "On the Internal Situation and the Character of the Party," as follows:

The Socialist Workers Party is a revolutionary Marxian party, based on a definite program, whose aim is the organization of the working class in the struggle for power and the transformation of the existing social order. All of its activities, its methods and its internal regime are subordinated to this aim and are designed to serve it.

Only a self-acting and critical-minded membership is capable of forging and consolidating such a party and of solving its problems by collective thought, discussion and experience. From this follows the need of assuring the widest party democracy in the ranks of the organization.

The struggle for power organized and led by the revolutionary party is the most ruthless and irreconcilable struggle in all history. A loosely-knit, heterogeneous, undisciplined, untrained organization is utterly incapable of accomplishing such world-historical tasks as the proletariat and the revolutionary party are confronted with in the present era. This is all the more emphatically true in the light of the singularly difficult position of our party and the extraordin-

---

*This resolution was drafted originally by Cannon and Shachtman in the struggle against Menshevik principles of organization advanced by Burnham and others in the party discussion preceding the National Convention of December 1937-January 1938; and was adopted by this convention. In the struggle of 1939-1940 Shachtman went over to Burnham's position on the organization question and joined him in a general attack on the basic Leninist principles. The majority of the convention, maintaining the old principles, consequently reaffirmed the old resolution, partly drafted by Shachtman, against the contentions of the petty-bourgeois opposition as a whole on the organization question.—*Ed.*

ary persecution to which it is subject. From this follows the party's unconditional demand upon all its members for complete discipline in all the public activities and actions of the organization.

Leadership and centralized direction are indispensable prerequisites for any sustained and disciplined action, especially in the party that sets itself the aim of leading the collective efforts of the proletariat in its struggle against capitalism. Without a strong and firm Central Committee, having the power to act promptly and effectively in the name of the party and to supervise, coordinate and direct all its activities without exception, the very idea of a revolutionary party is a meaningless jest.

It is from these considerations, based upon the whole of the experience of working class struggle throughout the world in the last century, that we derive the Leninist principle of organization, namely, democratic centralism. The same experience has demonstrated that there are no absolute guarantees for the preservation of the principle of democratic centralism, and no rigid formula that can be set down in advance, a priori, for the application of it under any and all circumstances. Proceeding from certain fundamental conceptions, the problem of applying the principle of democratic centralism differently under different conditions and stages of development of the struggle, can be solved only in relation to the concrete situation, in the course of the tests and experience through which the movement passes, and on the basis of the most fruitful and healthy inter-relationship of the leading bodies of the party and its rank and file.

The Responsibilities of Leadership

The leadership of the party must be under the control of the membership, its policies must always be open to criticism, discussion and rectification by the rank and file within properly established forms and limits, and the leading bodies themselves subject to formal recall or alteration. The membership of the party has the right to demand and expect the greatest responsibility from the leaders precisely because of the position they occupy in the movement. The selection of comrades to the positions of leadership means the conferring of an extraordinary responsibility. The warrant for this position must be proved, not once, but continuously by the leadership itself. It is under obligation to set the highest example of responsibility, devotion, sacrifice and complete identification with the party itself and its daily life and action. It must display the ability to defend its policies before the membership of the party, and to defend the line of the party and the party as a whole before the working class in general.

Sustained party activity, not broken or disrupted by abrupt and disorienting changes, presupposes not only a continuity of tradition and a systematic development of party policy, but also the continuity of leadership. It is an important sign of a serious and firmly constituted party, of a party really engaged in productive work in the class struggle, that it throws up out of its ranks cadres of more or less able leading comrades, tested for their qualities of endurance and trustworthiness, and that it thus insures a certain stability and continuity of leadership by such a cadre.

Continuity of leadership does not, however, signify the automatic self-perpetuation of leadership. Constant renewal of its ranks by means of additions and, when necessary, replacements, is the only assurance that the party has, that its leadership will not succumb to the effects of dry-rot, that it will not be burdened with deadwood, that it will avoid the corrosion of conservatism and dilettantism, that it will not be the object of conflict between the older elements and the younger, that the old and basic cadre will be refreshed by new blood, that the leadership as a whole will not become purely bureaucratic "committee men" with a life that is remote from the real life of the party and the activities of the rank and file.

Responsibilities of Membership

Like leadership, membership itself in the party implies certain definite rights. Party membership confers the fullest freedom of discussion, debate and criticism inside the ranks of the party, limited only by such decisions and provisions as are made by the party itself or by bodies to which it assigns this function. Affiliation to the party confers upon each member the right of being democratically represented at all policy-making assemblies of the party (from branch to national and international convention), and the right of the final and decisive vote in determining the program, policies and leadership of the party.

With party rights, the membership has also certain definite obligations. The theoretical and political character of the party is determined by its program, which forms the lines delimiting the revolutionary party from all other parties, groups and tendencies in the working class. The first obligation of party membership is loyal acceptance of the program of the party and regular affiliation to one of the basic units of the party. The party requires of every member the acceptance of its discipline and the carrying on of his activity in accordancc with the program of the party, with the decisions adopted by its conventions, and with the policies formulated and directed by the party leadership.

Party membership implies the obligation of one hundred per cent loyalty to the organization, the rejection of all agents of other, hostile groups in its ranks, and intolerance of divided loyalties in general. Membership in the party necessitates a minimum of activity in the organization, as established by the proper unit, and under the direction of the party; it necessitates the fulfillment of all the tasks which the party assigns to each member. Party membership implies the obligation upon every member to contribute materially to the support of the organization in accordance with his means.

A Party of Revolutionary Workers

From the foregoing it follows that the party seeks to include in its ranks all the revolutionary, class conscious and militant workers who stand on its program and are active in building the movement in a disciplined manner. The revolutionary Marxian party rejects not only the arbitrariness and bureaucratism of the Communist Party, but also the spurious and deceptive "all-inclusiveness" of the Thomas-Tyler-Hoan Socialist Party, which is a sham and a fraud. Experience has proved conclusively that this "all-inclusiveness" paralyzes the party in general and the revolutionary left wing in particular, suppressing and bureaucratically hounding the latter while giving free rein to the right wing to commit the greatest crimes in the name of socialism and the party. The S.W.P. seeks to be inclusive only in this sense: that it accepts into its ranks those who accept its program and denies admission to those who reject its program.

The rights of each individual member, as set forth above, do not imply that the membership as a whole, namely, the party itself, does not possess rights of its own. The party as a whole has the right to demand that its work be not disrupted and disorganized, and has the right to take all the measures which it finds necessary to assure its regular and normal functioning. The rights of any individual member are distinctly secondary to the rights of the party membership as a whole. Party democracy means not only the most scrupulous protection of the rights of a given minority, but also the protection of the rule of the majority. The party is therefore entitled to organize the discussion and to determine its forms and limits.

All inner-party discussion must be organized from the point of view that the party is not a discussion club, which debates interminably on any and all questions at any and all times, without arriving at a binding decision that enables the organization to act, but from the point of view that we are a disciplined party of revolutionary action. The party in general not only has the right, therefore, to organize the discussion in accordance with the requirements of the situation, but the lower units of the party must be given the right, in the interests of the struggle against the disruption and disorganization of the party's work, to call irresponsible individuals to order and, if need be, to eject them from the ranks.

The decisions of the national party convention are binding on all party members without exception and they conclude the discussion on all these disputed questions upon which a decision has been taken. Any party member violating the decisions of the convention, or attempting to revive discussion in regard to them without formal authorization of the party, puts himself thereby in opposition to the party and forfeits his right to membership. All party organizations are authorized and instructed to take any measures necessary to enforce this rule.

THE ORGANIZATIONAL CONCLUSIONS OF THE PRESENT DISCUSSION

(Resolution Adopted by the Convention)

The Bolshevik party of Lenin is the only party in history which successfully conquered and held state power. The S.W.P., as a combat organization, which aims at achieving power in this country, models its organization forms and methods after those of the Russian Bolshevik party, adapting them, naturally, to the experience of recent years and to concrete American conditions.

The S.W.P. as a revolutionary workers' party is based on the doctrines of scientific socialism as embodied in the principal works of Marx, Engels, Lenin and Trotsky and incorporated in the basic documents and resolutions of the first four congresses of the Communist International and of the conferences and congresses of the Fourth International.

The S.W.P. rejects the contention of social democrats, skeptics and capitulators disillusioned in the Russian revolution, that there is an inevitable and organic connection between Bolshevism and Stalinism. This reactionary revision of Marxism is a capitulation to democratic imperialism. It is capable of producing only demoralization and defeat in the critical times of war and revolution.

The rise of reaction on a world scale, accompanied and produced by the disastrous course of Stalinism in the working class movement, has catapulted all centrist groups and parties (Lovestoneites, Socialist Party, London Bureau) away from Bolshevism and in the direction of social democracy. In whole or in part, all of these groups attempt to identify Bolshevism with Stalinism. Without exception these groups are all in a state of collapse and passing over to the side of the class enemy.

Petty Bourgeoisie Transmits Skepticism

This tendency (Souvarinism) has manifested itself in leading circles of our party (Burnham) and in certain sections of the membership. Their skeptical criticisms of Bolshevism express their petty-bourgeois composition and their dependence on bourgeois public opinion. The petty bourgeoisie is a natural transmission belt carrying the theories of reaction into the organizations of the working class.

Those who seek to identify Bolshevism with Stalinism concern themselves with a search for guarantees against the Stalinist degeneration of the party and the future Soviet power. We reject this demand for insurance as completely undialectical and unrealistic. Our party, in the first instance, is concerned with the struggle for state power, and therefore with creating a party organization capable of leading the proletarian struggle to this goal. There are no constitutional guarantees which can prevent degeneration. Only the victorious revolution can provide the necessary preconditions for preventing the degeneration of the party and the future Soviet power. If the party fails to carry through and extend the revolution the degeneration of the party is inevitable.

Insofar as any guarantees are possible against the degeneration of the proletarian party, these can be obtained only by educating the party in firm adherence to principles and by a merciless struggle against all personal and unprincipled clique combinations within the party. The outstanding example of this clique formation is the Abern group which is based solely on personal loyalties and on rewards of honor and place within the party for those whose primary loyalty is to the clique. The history of the Fourth International in this country amply reveals that such a clique, with its utter disregard for principles, can become the repository for alien class influences and agents of enemy organizations seeking to disrupt the Fourth International from within. The S.W.P. condemns the Abern clique as hostile to the spirit and methods of Bolshevik organization.

REVOLUTIONARY CENTRALISM

To overthrow the most powerful capitalist ruling class in the world, the S.W.P. must be organized as a combat party on strong centralist lines. The resolution adopted at the founding convention gave a correct interpretation of the principle of democratic centralism. Its emphasis was placed on the democratic aspects of this principle. The party leadership has faithfully preserved the democratic rights of the membership since the founding convention. It has granted the widest latitude of discussion to all dissenting groups and individuals. The duty of the incoming National Committee is to execute the decisions of the convention, arrived at after the most thorough and democratic discussion, and to permit no infringement upon them.

Conditions, both external and in the internal development of the party, demand that steps now be taken towards knitting the party together, towards tightening up its activities and centralizing its organization structure. For the work of penetrating into the workers' mass movement, for the heavy struggles to come against capitalism, for the onerous conditions of war, it is imperative that a maximum of loyalty be required of every leader and every member, that a maximum of activity be required, that a strict adherence to discipline be demanded and rigidly enforced.

THE PRESS

The party press is the decisive public agitational and propagandist expression of the Bolshevik organization. The policies of the press are formulated on the basis of the fundamental resolutions of the congresses and conferences of the International, the conventions of the party, and decisions of the National Committee not in conflict with such resolutions. Control of the press is lodged directly in the hands of the National Committee by the convention of the party. The duty of the editors is loyally to interpret the decisions of the convention in the press.

Control of Public Discussion

The opening of the party press to discussion of a point of view contrary to that of the official leadership of the party or of its programmatic convention decisions must be controlled by the National Committee which is obligated to regulate discussion of this character in such a way as to give decisive emphasis to the party line. It is the right and duty of the National Committee to veto any demand for public discussion if it deems such discussion harmful to the best interests of the party.

The petty-bourgeois opposition in our party demonstrates its hostility to Bolshevik organization by its demand that the minority be granted the right to transform the press into a discussion organ for diametrically opposite programs. By that method it would take the control of the press out of the hands of the National Committee and subordinate it to any temporary, anarchistic combination which can make itself heard at the moment.

By the same token, the demand of the petty-bourgeois opposition for an independent public organ, expounding a program in opposition to that of the majority of the party, represents a complete abandonment of democratic centralism and a capitulation to the Norman Thomas type of "all-inclusive" party which is inclusive of all tendencies except the Bolshevik. The granting of this demand for a separate organ would destroy the centralist character of the party, by creating dual central committees, dual editorial boards, dual treasuries, dual distribution agencies, divided loyalties and a complete breakdown of all discipline. Under such conditions the party would rapidly degenerate into a social democratic organization or disappear from the scene altogether. The convention categorically rejects the demand for a dual organ.

LEADERSHIP

To build the combat organization capable of conquering state power, the party must have as its general staff a corps of professional revolutionists who devote their entire life to the direction and the building of the party and its influence in the mass movement. Membership in the leading staff of the party, the National Committee, must be made contingent on a complete subordination of the life of the candidate to the party. All members of the National Committee must devote full-time activities to party work, or be prepared to do so at the demand of the National Committee.

In the struggle for power, the party demands the greatest sacrifices of its members. Only a leadership selected from among those who demonstrate in the struggle the qualities of singleness of purpose, unconditional loyalty to the party and revolutionary firmness of character, can inspire the membership with a spirit of unswerving devotion and lead the party in its struggle for power.

The party leadership must, from time to time, be infused with new blood, primarily from its proletarian sections. Workers who show promise and ability through activity in the union movement and its strike struggles should be elevated to the leading committees of the party in order to establish a more direct connection between the leading committee and the workers' movement, and in order to train the worker-Bolshevik for the task of party direction itself.

The party must select from its younger members those qualified, talented and promising elements who can be trained for leadership. The road of the student youth to the party leadership must not and cannot be from the class room of the high school and college directly into the leading committee. They must first prove themselves. They must be sent without high-sounding titles into working class districts for day-to-day work among the proletariat. The young student must serve an apprenticeship in the workers' movement before he can be considered as candidate for the National Committee.

PROLETARIANIZE THE PARTY

The working class is the only class in modern society that is progressive and truly revolutionary. Only the working class is capable of saving humanity from barbarism. Only a revolutionary party can lead the proletariat to the realization of this historic mission. To achieve power, the revolutionary party must be deeply rooted among the workers, it must be composed predominantly of workers and enjoy the respect and confidence of the workers.

Without such a composition it is impossible to build a programmatically firm and disciplined organization which can accomplish these grandiose tasks. A party of non-workers is necessarily subject to all the reactionary influences of skepticism, cynicism, soul-sickness and capitulatory despair transmitted to it through its petty-bourgeois environment.

To transform the S.W.P. into a proletarian party of action, particularly in the present period of reaction, it is not enough to continue propagandistic activities in the hope that by an automatic process workers will flock to the banner of the party. It is necessary, on the contrary, to make a concerted, determined and systematic effort, consciously directed by the leading committees of the party, to penetrate the workers' movement, establish the roots of the party in the trade unions, the mass labor organizations and in the workers' neighborhoods and recruit worker militants into the ranks of the party.

Steps to Proletarianize the Party

To proletarianize the party, the following steps are imperative:

1. The entire party membership must be directed towards rooting itself in the factories, mills, etc., and towards integrating itself in the unions and workers' mass organizations.

2. Those members of the party who are not workers shall be assigned to work in labor organizations, in workers' neighborhoods and with the worker-fractions of the party—to assist them and learn from them. All unemployed members must belong to and be active in organizations of the unemployed.

Those party members who find it impossible after a reasonable period of time to work in a proletarian milieu and to attract to the party worker militants shall be transferred from party membership to the rank of sympathizers. Special organizations of sympathizers may be formed for this purpose.

Above all the student and unemployed youth must be sent into industry and involved in the life and struggles of the workers. Systematic, exceptional and persistent efforts must be made to assist the integration of our unemployed youth into industry despite the restricted field of employment.

Lacking connection with the workers' movement through failure or inability to get jobs in industry or membership in unions, the student and unemployed youth are subject to terrific pressure from the petty-bourgeois world. A large section of the youth membership of the S.W.P. and Y.P.S.L. adopted the program of the Fourth International, but brought with them the training and habits of the social democratic movement, which are far removed from the spirit of the proletarian revolution.

These student elements can transform the program of the Fourth International from the pages of books and pamphlets into living reality for themselves and for the party only by integrating themselves in the workers' movement and breaking irrevocably from their previous environment. Unless they follow this road they are in constant danger of slipping back into their former social democratic habits or into complete apathy and pessimism and thus be lost for the revolutionary movement.

3. To attract and to hold workers in the ranks of the party, it is necessary that the internal life of the party be drastically transformed. The party must be cleansed of the discussion club atmosphere, of an irresponsible attitude toward assignments, of a cynical and smart-aleck disrespect for the party.

Organizing Real Campaigns

Party activity must be lifted out of dragging, daily routine and reorganized on the basis of campaigns which are realistically adjusted to the demands and direction of the workers' movement. These campaigns must not be sucked out of the thumb of some functionary in a party office, but must arise as a result of the connections of the party with the workers' movement and the indicated direction of the masses in specific situations.

All party agitation campaigns, especially in the next period, must be directed primarily at those workers' groups and organizations in which we are attempting to gain a foothold and attract members. General agitation addressed to the working class as a whole or the public in general must be related to those specific aims.

The press must gear its agitation into the activity conducted among specific workers' groups so as to transform the party paper from a literary organ into a workers' organizer. The integration of the party into the workers' movement, and the transformation of the party into a proletarian organization, are indispensable for the progress of the party. Successful achievement of this internal transformation is a thousand times more important than any amount of empty phrases about "preparation of the party for war." This transformation is, in fact, the only real preparation of the party for war, combined of course with the necessary technical adjustments in organization forms.

The S.W.P. must adhere to the principles and program of the

Fourth International, transform itself into a democratically centralized Bolshevik organization, integrate itself into the workers' movement. On that basis, and on that basis alone, can the party meet the test of the war, survive the war and go forward to its great goal—the establishment of a Workers' Republic in the United States.

RESOLUTION ON DISCIPLINE

(Resolution Adopted by the Convention)

Having heard the declaration made to the convention by the representative of the minority to the effect that, regardless of the decision of the convention, the minority will publish a paper of its own in opposition to the press of the party, the convention states:

1. The threat is an attempt of a petty-bourgeois minority to impose its will upon the party in opposition to the principles of democratic centralism which alone can assure the unity of a revolutionary combat party. The convention categorically rejects the ultimatum of the minority and declares that any attempt on the part of any individual or group to execute it and to issue or distribute any publication in opposition to the official press of the party is incompatible with membership in the party.

2. All party organizations are instructed to expel from the party any member or members violating this convention decision. The National Committee or its Political Committee are empowered and instructed by the convention to expel any regular or alternate member or members of the N.C. or P.C. who may participate in any such violation. The N.C. or P.C. is instructed to immediately expel and reorganize any party unit or executive committee failing to act promptly in the execution of the above instructions in regard to any member or members under its jurisdiction who may violate the convention decisions.

SUPPLEMENTARY RESOLUTION ON THE ORGANIZATION QUESTION

(Resolution Adopted by the Convention)

In order to assure the concentration of the party membership on practical work under the most favorable internal conditions, to safeguard the unity of the party and to provide guarantees for the party rights of the minority, the convention adopts the following special measures:

1. The discussion in the party branches on the controversial issues is to be concluded with the convention decisions and the reports of the delegates to their branches. It may be resumed only by authorization of the National Committee.

2. In order to acquaint the party sympathizers and the radical labor public with all aspects of the disputes, and the opinions of both sides, the N.C. shall publish in symposium form the most important articles on the Russian question and the organization question. These symposia shall be jointly edited and each side may select the articles it wishes to publish.

3. As an exceptional measure in the present circumstances, the discussion may be continued in literary form if the representatives of either side, or both, so desire. Articles dealing with the theoretical-scientific aspects of the disputed questions may be published in *The New International*. Political discussion articles are to be published in a monthly Internal Bulletin, issued by the N.C., under joint editorship of the convention majority and minority.

4. The N.C. shall publish all resolutions considered by the convention, those rejected as well as those adopted. Editorial comment shall be restricted to defense of the adopted positions.

5. The decisions of the party convention must be accepted by all under the rules of democratic centralism. Strict discipline in action is to be required of all party members.

6. No measures are to be taken against any party member because of the views expressed in the party discussion. Nobody is obliged to renounce his opinion. There is no prohibition of factions. The minority is to be given representation in the leading party committees and assured full opportunity to participate in all phases of party work.

THE SUSPENSION OF THE BURNHAM-SHACHTMAN-ABERN GROUP

(Statement of the National Committee*)

The readers of the *Appeal* are already familiar with the resolutions adopted by the recently concluded national convention of our party. These resolutions (published last week) made extremely liberal provisions for the participation of the leaders of the minority in party work. The resolutions offered them the opportunity to continue the discussion in defense of their point of view in the Internal Bulletin and in *The New International*, on the condition that they refrain from issuing an independent publication in opposition to the press of the party.

These decisions of the convention have been rejected by the leaders of the minority. This conduct left the National Committee no alternative, under the instructions of the convention, but to suspend the minority leaders from the party until such time as they signify their readiness to abide by the convention decisions. This action was taken by the National Committee, at its meeting held on April 16, in order to protect the party against disruption. At the same time the terms of the suspension leave the way open for the suspended members to reconsider the question and return to their places in the party leadership and in its editorial boards on the basis of the convention decisions.

---

*Published in the *Socialist Appeal*, April 20, 1940.—*Ed.*

THE CONVENTION OF THE SOCIALIST WORKERS PARTY*

The special convention of the Socialist Workers Party, held in New York, April 5-8, summed up the internal discussion which has been in progress ever since the outbreak of the war in Europe. The task of the convention was to determine whether the party shall maintain its allegiance to the program of the Fourth International; that is, whether it shall continue to exist as a revolutionary organization or begin to degenerate along the lines of reconciliation with democratic imperialism. The convention accomplished its task in a revolutionary fashion. By the decisive vote of 55 to 31, the delegates from the branches reaffirmed their allegiance to the program and rejected the revisionist improvisations of the opposition.

The victory of the proletarian revolutionary tendency was in reality far more decisive than these figures indicate. More than half of the delegates of the opposition came from New York branches which are predominantly petty-bourgeois in composition. Outside New York the delegates stood three to one behind the majority of the National Committee in its defense of the program. But even these figures do not adequately portray the weakness of the opposition in the proletarian ranks of the party. Among the genuine worker elements of the party, those members connected with the mass movement and directly engaged in the class struggle, the position of the majority of the National Committee prevailed by not less than ten to one. The opposition started and finished as a purely literary tendency, making big pretensions, but without any serious base of support in the proletarian ranks of the party.

The decision of the party came at the end of a thoroughgoing, democratic party discussion which left not a single question unclarified. The discussion was formally opened early in October and continued uninterruptedly for six months. It is highly doubtful that any party discussion anywhere was ever so extensive, so complete and so democratically conducted as this one. Thirteen big internal bulletins were published by the National Committee during the discussion, with the space about equally divided between the factions; and there was an unrestricted distribution of factional documents, besides those published in the official bulletins. In addition, there were innumerable debates and speeches in party membership meetings. Such an extensive and drawn-out discussion may

---

*A summary article published in *Fourth International*, May 1940.— Ed.

appear to be abnormal, even for a democratic organization such as ours which settles all disputed questions by free and democratic discussion. So it was. But the controversy which preoccupied our members in this instance, went far beyond the usual differences of opinion as to the best methods of applying the program. The revisionist opposition attacked the program itself.

Their position at bottom represented a fundamental break with the programmatic concepts, traditions and methods embodied in the Fourth International. Consequently it was necessary to carry the fight out to a definitive conclusion. The result justified the extraordinary amount of time and attention devoted to the dispute. The internal fight was imposed upon the party by the war. Disoriented by the war, or rather by the approach of war, a section of the leadership turned their backs on the program, which had been elaborated in years of struggle in preparation for the war. Overnight, they forgot the principles which they had defended jointly with us up to the very day of the signing of the Stalin-Hitler pact. These soldiers of peace had evidently assimilated the ideas of Bolshevism only as a set of literary formulas. They wrote endlessly, and sometimes cleverly, in favor of them. But the moment the formulas were put to the test of life—or rather the threat of such a test, for America has not yet entered into the war—the literary exponents crumpled miserably and shamefully. And with amazing speed.

Even a revolutionary party is not free from the pressure of its bourgeois environment. In the case of Burnham and Shachtman this pressure was reflected in its crudest form. Stalin in alliance with the brigands of French imperialism, and prospectively with the United States, was acceptable to democratic public opinion; his frame-up trials and purges and his bloody work in Spain were passed over as the peccadillos of an eccentric "democrat." During all this time—the time of the Franco-Soviet pact—all the leaders of the opposition fully agreed with us that the defense of the Soviet Union is the elementary duty of every workers' organization. When the same Stalin "betrayed" the imperialist democracies by making an alliance with Hitler Germany, he became anathema to the bourgeois democrats. Immediately, as if by reflex action, our heroic Burnham, and after him Shachtman and the others, disavowed the defense of the Soviet Union by the world proletariat as an "outmoded" idea. That is the essence of the dispute they started in the party, and its immediate causes. All the rest of their explanations are literary trimming.

Fortunately the proletarian militants of the party took their program more seriously, and showed they are capable of adhering to it without regard to external pressure. Our eleven years' struggle for a proletarian party—which has also been an unceasing struggle against alien tendencies within our own ranks—was recapitulated in our six months' discussion. The convention drew a balance from this whole experience, and put an end to all speculation about the course of the party. It recorded the determined will of the proletarian majority to face the war with the same program that had been worked out in years of international collaboration in anticipation of the inevitable war. It showed clearly that, in spite of all obstacles and difficulties, the party has become predominantly proletarian in composition. Thereby it has reenforced its proletarian program.

Our convention had more than national significance. The Fourth International, as a whole, like all other organizations in the labor movement, was put to a decisive test by the outbreak of the war. Fortuitous political circumstances have delayed the entry of U.S. imperialism into the war. This provided our party with a more favorable opportunity for a free and democratic discussion of the issues posed by the war crisis than was enjoyed by any other section of our International. Our party was also the best equipped by past experience and training to carry out this discussion in all its implications, from all sides, and to the very end. In addition, outstanding representatives of several other important sections of our International were able to participate directly in the literary discussion in our party. The discussion in the S.W.P. became in effect a discussion for the entire Fourth International and was followed with passionate interest by the members of all sections.

It was clear from the beginning that the issues at stake were international in character and that our decisions would have fateful consequences for our movement on a world-wide scale. Thus our convention, formally and nominally a convention of the Socialist Workers Party, was in its political import a veritable Congress of the Fourth International. Under war conditions, and the consequent illegality of many of the sections, a formally organized World Congress, composed of representative delegations, could not be held. Our convention had to serve as temporary surrogate for the World Congress. Politically, there can be no doubt that it had this meaning for all the other sections.

The discussion initiated in our party was transferred into the other sections; and one after the other, they began to take positions on the dispute. In every case where we have been able to establish communication under war conditions, and have direct knowledge of their position, the sections have supported the majority of our party. The international report at our convention disclosed that the Canadian, Mexican, Belgian, German, Argentine, Chinese, Australian and Russian sections have all declared categorically in support of the position of the majority of our party. The other sections, with whom communication is faulty or who have not formerly recorded their position, indicate the same tendency. After our convention there can no longer be the slightest doubt that the overwhelming majority of the members and sections of the Fourth International remain true to their banner—to the doctrine and program of revolutionary Marxism. The decision is made. The revisionist movement of Burnham and Co. can no longer hope for success in our movement, nationally or internationally. The Fourth International remains, after the first test of the war, firm in its programmatic position—the only revolutionary organization of the workers' vanguard in the entire world.

From beginning to end, and in all respects, the two factions in the S.W.P. confronted each other in a classic struggle of the proletarian against the petty-bourgeois tendency. This line of demarcation was unmistakably evident in the class composition of the factions and in their general orientation, as well as in the programs they defended.

Despite the extraordinary preoccupation of the entire party with the theoretical dispute, the convention, on the initiative of the majority, devoted two whole sessions and part of a third to discussion of the trade union question and mass work in general. Led by the informed and inspiring report of Farrell Dobbs, the discussion of the delegates on this point revealed that our party in many localities and industries is already deeply integrated in the mass movement of the workers, and that its whole orientation is in this direction. The reports of the delegates showed that even during the six months' discussion, when the literary panic-mongers were crying havoc and discovering nothing but weaknesses and failures, the proletarian supporters of the majority were busy in many sections with their trade union work; burrowing deeply into the mass movement and establishing firm bases of support for the party there. The opposition at the convention was greatly compromised and discredited by the fact that it virtually abstained from participation in this extensive discussion. They had nothing to say and nothing to report. Here again the petty-bourgeois composition of the opposition, and its lack of serious interest in mass work, were flagrantly manifest.

The report and discussion on the trade union question and mass work dealt a knockout blow to the calamity howlers, pessimists and quitters who have been attributing to the movement their own weak-

ness, cowardice and futility. The convention resounded with proletarian optimism and confidence in the party. The trade union
report and discussion, following the decisive reaffirmation of the
proletarian program, engendered a remarkable enthusiasm. It was
clear from this discussion that the turn of the party toward mass
work is already well under way and that the proceedings of the
convention could not fail to give it a powerful acceleration.

If any came to the convention with the usual discouragement
over a heated factional fight and the prospect of a split, there was
no evidence of it. In the camp of the proletarian majority there
was not a trace of pessimism, or discouragement, or doubt that the
party is going forward to the accomplishment of its historic goal,
and that the period ahead of us will be one of expansion and growth
and integration in the mass movement. They approached the factional situation in the convention with the calm assurance of people
who have made up their minds and know precisely what they want.
When the leaders of the petty-bourgeois opposition, defeated in the
convention, hurled the threat of split, it was received without a
ripple of agitation. The demand of Burnham and Shachtman for
the "right" to publish a press of their own in opposition to the
press of the party—that is, to make a split in the hypocritical guise
of unity; to attack the party in the name of the party—was rejected
out of hand by the majority of the convention. The minority was
confronted with a clear alternative: either to accept the decision
of the majority under the rules of democratic centralism or go their
own way and unfurl their own banner.

The majority did everything possible to preserve unity, and
even made extraordinary concessions to induce the minority to turn
back from their splitting course before it was too late. Their party
rights as a minority were guaranteed by a special resolution at
the convention. This resolution went to the extreme length of sanc-
tioning a continuation of discussion of the decided questions in the
Internal Bulletin, and a discussion of the theoretical aspects of
the question in *The New International*. At the same time, the convention resolution decreed that discussion in the branches must
cease, and that all attention and energy of the party membership
be concentrated on practical mass work in the next period.

The minority was given proportional representation on the National Committee and a period of time to make up their minds
whether to remain in the party or not under the terms and conditions laid down. The minority leaders rejected the convention decision, launched their own publication, and began a public attack
on the program of the party and the Fourth International. Thus, by

their own decision and actions, they placed themselves outside the ranks of the party and the Fourth International. Their political degeneration is inevitable; nobody has ever yet found a revolutionary road outside the Fourth International. But that is their own affair. Our discussion with them, which was fully adequate, is now concluded.

We are looking forward, not backward. Our task is a deeper penetration of the workers' mass movement on the basis of the convention decisions. That is our way to prepare for the war. In this course we are assured of the support of the overwhelming majority of the sections of the Fourth International. With a correct program, and the assurance of international collaboration and support, we have every reason to be confident of our future.

WHY WE PUBLISH "FOURTH INTERNATIONAL"*

*(A Statement by the National Committee of the
Socialist Workers Party)*

This is the first issue, Volume I, No. 1, of *Fourth International,*
the new monthly theoretical organ of the Socialist Workers Party.
Fourth International will defend the program, ideas and traditions
which *The New International* can no longer represent. We owe our
readers an explanation for changing the name of our official magazine.

The New International was the official theoretical organ of the
Socialist Workers Party, American section of the Fourth International. The magazine had been in existence since 1934 and was
published regularly with the exception of the period when the
Fourth Internationalists of this country held membership in the
Socialist Party. At all times *The New International* was the property of our organization. It voiced in its columns the official
position of the Trotskyist movement, as a section of the International Communist League and later as a section of the Fourth
International.   The policies of the magazine were determined by
our National Committee. The editors and business staff of the
magazine were appointed by and subject to the decisions of the
party. *The New International* was financed by the nickels and
dimes and dollars of the worker members of the party and its
sympathizers. Its deficits were paid by the party. *The New International* was an integral part of the international Trotskyist
movement and its American section, the Socialist Workers Party.

By a breach of trust, morally and legally equivalent to a
misappropriation of funds by a financial officer of a workers'
organization, Burnham, Shachtman and Abern, who held posts
on *The New International* by party appointment, and who were
trustees for the party in The New International Publishing Company, have usurped the name of the magazine and attempted to
appropriate its mailing rights as their personal property.

These turncoats, defeated in the party convention after a
free and democratic discussion in the party, have sought to revenge
themselves on the proletarian majority of the party by stealing the
name and the mailing rights of the magazine entrusted to their
management, and attempting to cash in on its tradition. An issue of *The New International* has appeared under the auspices

*Published in *Fourth International* for May 1940.—*Ed.*

of these ex-Trotskyists. A casual reading of the forged copy is sufficient to convince any reader that it is not *The New International* they have known, but a miserable counterfeit.

The old *New International* defended the program of the Fourth International; it was the chief medium for the publication of the theoretical contributions of Comrade Trotsky, and was honored throughout the world as the theoretical protagonist of the Marxism of our time, i.e., "Trotskyism." The counterfeit *New International,* stolen in sneak-thief fashion from the party that owned it and paid for it, and published behind its back in the dark of night, has nothing in common with the traditions of its name and its past association.

Those who know the revolutionary traditions established by the magazine, those who appreciate its great work in the ideas of Marxism throughout the world cannot fail to be revolted by the publication of *The New International* under revisionist and anti-Trotskyist auspices. This feeling of revulsion must have been augmented by the appearance from the pen of Burnham under the heading "Archives of the Revolution," of a foul attack on the Marxist doctrine and method and on the author of most of the rich material in Marxist theory which in the past appeared under this heading.

There is no doubt that by every political and moral right *The New International* belongs to the Socialist Workers Party as represented by its convention majority. There is likewise no doubt, competent attorneys have assured us, that all legal rights to the magazine, its name, its subscription lists and its second class mailing rights belong entirely to the Socialist Workers Party, and that Burnham, Abern and Shachtman would stand in any litigation as betrayers of financial trust and common thieves. No class-conscious worker would censure us for taking legal action to protect our rights in this case. Obviously, we are dealing here, not with an ideological dispute but a case of petty larceny. Nevertheless, we have decided to forego any legal action. We are washing our hands of *The New International* and launching a new magazine, *Fourth International,* for the following reasons:

1. It is not worthwhile for us to spend time and effort in legal struggles over property rights which could only divert energies and resources from more serious and important activity.

2. We do not want our irreconcilable political struggle against the turncoats to be obscured or confused by squabbles over a magazine's name and property rights. Our aim is, in every respect, to

distinguish ourselves from the ex-Trotskyists, and to eliminate every possible point of *identification* with them.

3. The once glorious name of *The New International* has been irretrievably sullied by its appearance for one issue under the auspices of these betrayers of its tradition. The program of the Fourth International, the great theoretical contributions of Comrade Trotsky, the Marxist message of our party, cannot appear under its dirtied name. We want no deception, no confusion, no mixing of banners. We need a clean banner which will truly express what we stand for and at the same time sharply distinguish us from the prostituted *The New International*. They stole it. They have already identified its name with their own treachery. Let them keep it, and let the whole world know it is henceforth their magazine, not ours. Our magazine is *Fourth International*!

It alone is the theoretical organ of the Socialist Workers Party and of the Fourth International!

Fourth International will fill out all the unexpired subscriptions of *The New International*. The subscribers of *The New International* are entitled to get what they paid for—a theoretical organ of Bolshevism. We feel politically and morally responsible to give it to them by sending this magazine for the full time of the unexpired subscriptions.

We appeal to all readers who sympathize with the principles we stand for to help us maintain this magazine by subscriptions and contributions.

FOURTH INTERNATIONAL CONFERENCE RESOLUTION ON S.W.P. INTERNAL STRUGGLE

(The following is one of the resolutions adopted by the May 19-26 [1940] Emergency Conference of the Fourth International.*)

1. The recent split in the Socialist Workers Party, official section of the Fourth International in the United States, came as the result of an attempt by a petty-bourgeois minority to revise the fundamental program of the Fourth International on unconditional defense of the Soviet Union and the refusal of this minority to abide by the decisions of the majority in the convention called to decide the issues in dispute.

2. In attempting to revise our program calling for unconditional defense of the Soviet Union without at the same time relating the proposed revision to the question of the class character of the Soviet Union, which the Fourth International has exhaustively analyzed as a degenerated workers' state, the petty-bourgeois opposition was guilty of a fundamental revision of the methodology of Marxism. On the part of James Burnham, ideological leader of the group, this attempt at revisionism was extended to complete rejection of the basic principles of scientific socialism as first propounded by Marx and Engels and subsequently developed by Lenin and Trotsky.

3. The attempted revision of our fundamental principles was begun by the petty-bourgeois opposition immediately after the signing of the Hitler-Stalin pact and gained impetus with the outbreak of the Second World War, thus clearly indicating that the force pushing the petty-bourgeois elements of the party into opposition to the Fourth International was the war pressure of the democratic bourgeoisie.

4. Not only did the petty-bourgeois opposition attempt to revise the fundamental principles and political conclusions of the Fourth International, they attempted also to revise its Bolshevik organizational methods.

They participated in the April convention of the Socialist Workers Party, thus recognizing its authoritativeness and its validity. Nevertheless they rejected the majority decisions and in flagrant violation of democratic centralism launched an independent press in order to appeal to the public in its attack against the Fourth International.

---

*Published in the *Socialist Appeal*, July 6, 1940.—*Ed.*

In view of the previous discussion which was conducted with the fullest democracy in accordance with the best tradition of Bolshevism, and in view of the guarantees for the minority to continue its factional existence, to present its views to the party in an Internal Bulletin even after the convention adjourned, and to hold posts in all the leading bodies regardless of their views and without penalty for their previous infractions of party discipline, this rejection of the convention decisions and their subsequent desertion from the party can be interpreted in no other way than as additional evidence of the petty-bourgeois character of the opposition.

The Emergency Conference of the Fourth International endorses the action of the American section of the Fourth International in suspending all those who violated the decisions of its April convention. The Conference suggests to the N.C. of the S.W.P. that it set a definite time limit of one month after publication of Conference decisions within which the suspended members must signify their acceptance of the convention decisions under penalty of unconditional expulsion from the party.

5. The Emergency Conference of the Fourth International views the struggle of the proletarian majority in the Socialist Workers Party as a struggle in defense of the program of the Fourth International from the heights of its Marxist theory right down to its Bolshevik organizational principles. The Emergency Conference calls upon all the sections of the Fourth International to solidarize themselves with the Socialist Workers Party in this struggle.

THE EXPULSION OF THE SHACHTMAN-ABERN GROUP

(Resolution adopted by the Plenum Conference of the S.W.P. held in Chicago, September 27 to 29, 1940*)

By decision of the April 1940 convention of the party, the National Committee was instructed to take disciplinary action against the Burnham-Shachtman-Abern group if that group failed to abide by the decisions of the convention.

In accordance with those instructions, the National Committee on April 22 suspended those members of the Burnham-Shachtman-Abern group who, following the convention, refused to accept the decisions of the convention. The National Committee by suspending rather than expelling the undisciplined members of the petty-bourgeois opposition, gave them an opportunity to reconsider their refusal to abide by convention decisions and to return to the party. In the course of the ensuing months a number of the suspended comrades have reconsidered their refusal, have declared their adherence in action to convention decisions while remaining free to defend their political views in subsequent party discussions, and have on this basis been restored to full membership rights.

The Emergency Conference of the Fourth International, convened in May 1940, endorsed the decisions of the April convention of the S.W.P. It recommended to our party that only a limited period should remain in which suspended members would have time to reconsider their refusal. At the end of that period those still refusing to accept the convention decisions should be unconditionally expelled from the party.

The period recommended by the Emergency Conference has now elapsed. Meanwhile, since their suspension, the Burnham-Shachtman-Abern group has undergone a political evolution which has widened the chasm between them and the Fourth International. Burnham has drawn the final conclusion to the position he elaborated for his group, and has openly deserted to the class enemy. Shachtman and Abern lead a petty-bourgeois semi-pacifist sect. After the passage of nearly six months it is, therefore, time to draw a conclusion to this question and put an end to any possible ambiguity or confusion.

The plenary session of the National Committee declares that

---

*Published in the *Socialist Appeal* for October 5, 1940.—*Ed.*

those suspended members who have not up to this time signified their willingness to abide by the decisions of the April convention are hereby unconditionally expelled from the party.

APPENDIX: The War and Bureaucratic Conservatism

EDITOR'S NOTE:

This document was published in Internal Bulletin Vol. II, No. 26 of the Socialist Workers Party (January 1940) as the organizational platform of the petty-bourgeois opposition. It is reprinted here for the information of the reader who may wish to check the conceptions of the petty-bourgeois opposition against the Leninist principles defended by the majority as elucidated in this volume. Similarly, "Science and Style," the chief theoretical work of the petty-bourgeois opposition, was printed as an appendix to *In Defense of Marxism* by Leon Trotsky.

APPENDIX: The War and Bureaucratic Conservatism

1—THE ORIGIN OF THE PARTY CRISIS

It will not be disputed that the party is now in the midst of a serious political crisis. All the familiar signs of such a crisis are present: a factional division in the leading committees; the growing extension of factional lines into the membership; the use of the harshest language in designating opponents; the growing concentration of the energies of the party on the internal dispute to the grave detriment of constructive external activities; etc. The purpose of this document is to examine, analyze and explain the party crisis, and to indicate a solution of it.

*   *   *

Whatever the background of an internal crisis, however much it may be implicit in the general situation within a party, it very often comes first into the *open* in a leading committee. This is the case with the present crisis in our party, and the place and date of its breaking into the open can be precisely fixed. It occurred in the Resident Political Committee at a special meeting held on the evening of the day when the German army invaded Poland; that is, the first day of the Second World War. Between the end of the July convention and that day there had been no crisis and no "crisis atmosphere" in the Resident Committee. From that day there has been an uninterrupted and deepening crisis.

The crisis was precipitated by a statement and series of motions presented by Gould. Gould's statement condemned the sluggishness and inactivity of the Committee, and its failure to respond adequately to the war situation which had been signalled by the announcement of the German-Russian agreement and the subsequent mobilizations of the European powers. His motions, practical in character, called for a drastic re-orientation of the party's activities and attitude in order to meet the demands of the war: cancellation of all leaves; more frequent publication of the *Appeal,* and of pamphlets, leaflets and manifestos; the holding of public meetings and demonstrations; the immediate convocation of a full plenum of the National Committee. He proposed that the agenda of the plenum should include an analysis of the war, the preparation of the party's organization to meet the war, and the "Russian question" in the light of the new developments.

257

Neither Cannon nor Shachtman was present at this meeting. Abern, who also could not be present, had expressed substantial agreement with Gould's proposals earlier that day. The response to Gould's statement and motions already showed, however, the emergence of a sharp division in the Committee. On the one side, Burnham, McKinney, Carter, Bern agreed in substance with Gould. On the other, except for Lewit, the other P.C. members agreed with the proposal for an early plenum, and, after some questioning, virtually all of Gould's proposals were adopted. The question of the plenum date was held over to another meeting that Cannon would attend.

It is of the first importance to recall that the "Russian question" played a completely subordinate role at this meeting, as it had in all previous meetings, including those following the announcement of the German-Russian agreement. Gould did not motivate his demand for an immediate plenum only or mainly on the Russian issue. All of the Committee, without exception, recognized that discussion of the Russian question ought properly to be *part* of the business of the plenum. And the Committee at that meeting voted *unanimously* to appoint Burnham to make a verbal report on the Russian question to the next meeting, as preparation for the plenum.

At the next meeting, however, with Cannon present and under his pressure, there was a general reversal of position of all but the present minority members. Cannon, Lewit, Morrow, Gordon denounced Gould's contribution as "hysteria," "light-mindedness," "irresponsibility"; and contended that nothing in the situation called for "excitement" or drastic action.

A knowledge of its beginning is of the very greatest importance in understanding the real meaning of the present crisis in the party. Let us sum up what this brief review discloses:

A great event—the greatest since the beginning of the Fourth Internationalist movement, the start of the Second World War, occurred. *This great event precipitated a major crisis in our party,* in the first instance in the leadership. One part of the leadership held that this great event called for a drastic change in the organization and activity of the party, and a change in our policy toward Stalinism in the war along the lines already dealt with by Johnson, Shachtman and Carter, prior to the German-Soviet pact, at the July convention of the Party. Another section (the majority of the Committee) held that no change was necessary.

The view that the crisis broke out over the "Russian question" is entirely false, and is disproved by the record, the essential parts of which are cited in Shachtman's speech to the New York membership discussion meeting and *all* of which will be presented verbatim in the *Internal Bulletin.* The crisis broke out over *the war,* not over the Russian question. The Russian question entered and became acute, only as one phase of the more general question of the war.

The first stage of the crisis was completed at the plenum of the National Committee. The intervening actions in the Resident Committee have been reviewed in Shachtman's speech which, in written form, is before the membership, and we will not repeat the review here. We wish to emphasize only certain general features:

The minority kept pressing along three lines: 1) for concrete answers to the specific questions being raised by the war—in particular the Red Army's invasion of Poland, which was then the outstanding immediate issue; 2) for action on the reorganization of the party's structure and activities to meet the war; 3) for the opening of a discussion in the party, and the holding of a plenum.

The majority, on its side: 1) gave no answers whatever—neither right nor wrong—to the specific questions, merely repeating day after day that "nothing had changed," "we had predicted everything in advance," and, when it came down to committee motions, simply "reaffirming the fundamental position of the Fourth International"; 2) agreed in occasional words with the need of reorganization and did nothing whatever; 3) opposed for weeks the opening of a discussion, and delayed as long as possible the calling of a plenum.

The plenum, when finally held, revolved around the Russian question and the reorganization of the Political Committee. The first session, held nominally on "the party and the war," was hardly more than a formality, and has besides led to nothing. At the plenum there were presented for vote: (1) the resolution of Shachtman, which characterized the war in its present phase and the role of Russia in the war, and drew the conclusions from this characterization as to our attitude in such cases as that of the Polish invasion; and (2) a motion of Cannon re-affirming our basic position, but not in any way characterizing either the war or the role of Russia or the Polish invasion.

At approximately 2 a.m. on the Sunday of the plenum, the lengthy article of Trotsky, published subsequently in *The New International*, was made available to those Committee members who had not gone to bed. In spite of the fact that this document had not even been completely read by all Committee members during the course of that Sunday, that one of its pages was because of a technical slip missing, and that no one short of a super-man could have assimilated its meaning without serious and considerable study, it, together with Cannon's motion, was endorsed that afternoon by the plenum. The Political Committee was then reorganized, and provisions made for beginning a discussion in the party.

* * *

The present party crisis began under the impact of the war. Nevertheless, though this crisis is probably the most severe that has occurred during several years at least, many of its features are recognizably similar to lesser crises of the past—some of which, like the curious debate at the July convention over the "organizational secretary" were more or less carried to the party, others of which remained on the whole within leading committees. For one thing, there is roughly the same lineup of Committee members as in the lesser disputes of the past couple of years. Secondly, the same general sort of charges at once were made by both sides: the minority speaking of "routinism," "conservatism," "bureaucratism"; the majority of "irresponsibility," "light-mindedness," "petty-bourgeois instability," and so on.

It is necessary to emphasize—though not to over-emphasize—this similarity to past disputes in order to indicate that although the present crisis was provoked by the war and takes its special character from that circumstance, it nevertheless has its roots in a past before the war began.

2—THE WAR AND THE PARTY CRISIS

Too much cannot be made of the fact that the war was the occasion of the present crisis.

From one point of view, every comrade will naturally feel regret, disturbance and even dismay that when the war which we had so long been concerned with in preparation became a reality of the living present, our party did not meet it in a unified and positive manner but immediately plunged into a crisis.

Justified as such a feeling may be, an objective and scientific view must however conclude that what has happened is what was most likely to happen, even apart from the particular tendencies that were present in our own party. Indeed, in a certain sense, the occurrence of the crisis is understandable and might have been foretold: if the war had left things in the party just where they were, it would not necessarily have been a sign of health but perhaps of senility or death; even pain can be felt only by a living organism; it is a dead animal that makes no response whatever. Such a crisis affects the basically healthy and the basically unhealthy organism differently in that the latter is completely paralyzed by it while the former is able to emerge from the crisis without fatal consequences.

If a party is not completely monolithic and totalitarian (even such a case may not be an exception), the occurrence of a major historical event of world-shaking importance is bound to produce a crisis of one or another degree. Different members react differently to the event. Some think big changes are called for, others not, some want to re-orient, others to continue along the previous directions; some want to expand boldly, others think it is necessary to contract cautiously. Whichever of the opposing views is right under the given conditions, clashes are sure to result.

Wars and revolutions are the most decisive of all events in the lives of political parties. In 1914, the outbreak of the war had a shattering effect upon every working-class party in the world. In their bulk, the parties went over to their respective imperialists. But even within the left, ostensibly revolutionary wings, the Russian Bolsheviks not excluded, the outbreak of the war provoked the most profound crises. In spite of all that had been written and foretold, no one—neither Lenin nor anyone else—had anticipated the actual effect which the outbreak of the war would have. New groupments and re-groupments were to be found within every party, the Bolshevik Party included. Nor was a definitive solution to the various crises found in a day or a week. During the course of the entire war, even among those who stood committed to struggle against the war, a constant and changing debate went on as to just what struggle against the war meant concretely (Lenin, Liebknecht, Trotsky, Luxemburg, Debs . . .).

The same phenomenon was to be observed again, in 1917, with the outbreak of the Russian revolution. In Russia itself, inside and outside the Bolshevik Party, the response to this event was not at all uniform, and a crisis—or rather crises—occurred. It was necessary for Lenin himself to throw overboard some of his own most cherished doctrines, and to meet on common ground many, such as Trotsky, who had up to then been not merely organizational opponents but even members of different organizations.

The outbreak of the Second World War is not less but far more momentous in the history of mankind than the outbreak of the war of 1914. Indeed, in all probability the fate of mankind for centuries to come will be decided during this war and the period immediately following it. Small wonder, then, that in our own small group the war has a convulsive effect.

We are, in reality, facing the question of whether we are prepared to meet the challenge of the war; and, perhaps, we could not face that question fully and openly before the war itself began. The war challenges us every moment, without respite, *politically*: Can we answer concretely and rapidly (for the speed of events no longer gives us the luxury of delay) the political questions posed by the war? Can we explain our answers to others? Can we foresee, at least sufficiently, what is going to happen so that it will not take us by surprise? Can we give guidance and a program of action to ourselves and those others whom we can reach, every step of the way? And the war challenges us also, every moment, *organizationally*: Can we continue to exist as an organization, to act and to function? Can we find ways to make our program a reality in the minds of the workers, or at least of a significant section of the workers? Can we assimilate in our ranks the genuine and militant anti-war fighters, from whatever quarter, who are not now with us? Can we—have we the *will* to—develop the technical and structural means to continue to live and to be active through the war itself?

These questions are the background and foundation of the present dispute in the party, whatever form it may seem at a given moment to take. The Russian question became a center for a while not merely because of its own independent merits—and it is a very serious question indeed—but because in the first stage of the war the party leadership has shown itself incapable of meeting the political challenge of the war on the issues where that challenge first became acute—namely on the issues raised by Russia's actions. But the organizational problems could not be left out, even temporarily, because the leadership was simultaneously showing that it was not meeting the challenge of the war organizationally.

The issue, then, is the war.

3—WHAT THE PRESENT CRISIS EXPRESSES

In every serious political dispute, it is a necessary part of the duty of a responsible politician to define the *political* character of the various positions taken. If this is not done, we cannot understand the disputes politically, nor know what to do about them. We must decide whether a given position is "sectarian" or "centrist" or "reformist" or "syndicalist" or whatever the case may be.

It is not enough merely to say that your opponent is "wrong" —everyone always thinks that his opponent is wrong. We must know just why and how, *politically*, he is wrong. And it is not enough to give merely an impressionistic or psychological or moralistic analysis —to say that our opponent is "irresponsible" or "light-minded" or "unstable" or "wicked." Such psychological and ethical judgments might be true enough, but they would not aid us in a *political* definition of his position. The central question can never be whether he is light-minded or inefficient, but—into what kind of a *political* position has his light-mindedness or inefficiency led him.

It is the contention of the opposition that the position which the Cannon group has taken in the present dispute is the manifestation or expression of a type of politics which can be best described as *bureaucratic conservatism.* We hold that this bureaucratic conservative tendency has existed in the party for some time; that during the course of a number of years it gradually solidified, manifesting itself at first sporadically and then more and more continuously; and that the outbreak of the war crystallized this tendency and brought it to a head. The outstanding representative of this tendency in the party, we hold, is Comrade Cannon. The importance of Cannon, however, is not primarily as an individual but precisely as the embodiment of bureaucratic conservatism; and when we refer to him in what follows we do so in no personal sense but simply as the outstanding representative of a tendency.

The *crisis* in the party occurred fundamentally, it follows, because of the resistance by one section of the party, in the light of the war, to the solidification of the entire party on a bureaucratic conservative basis. The *resolution* of the crisis, therefore, must be sought in the definite ascendancy in the party as a whole of either bureaucratic conservatism or of the opposition which stands for party democracy and collective leadership.

* * *

How would it be possible to *prove* this political conclusion— namely, that the Cannon faction is bureaucratic-conservative in its political character? This can be done chiefly in two ways:

(1) First it is necessary to analyze carefully the immediate dispute, to determine whether "bureaucratic conservatism" is a correct description of the position and actions taken by the Cannon faction.

(2) Such an analysis would, however, be by itself inconclusive. It would leave the possibility that the present position of Cannon is an exception or an "accident." In order to show that Cannon represents a bureaucratic conservative *tendency*, it is further necessary to relate the position taken in the immediate dispute to *other* positions and actions of the Cannon group both during recent months and also in the past. If it is found that as a general rule in the past two-three years Cannon has shown himself to be not bureaucratic but democratic, not conservative but dynamic, especially as against other comrades, then the characterization of his present position becomes at least doubtful. If, on the other hand, we find numerous other examples showing Cannon to be bureaucratic and conservative, the characterization of his present position and of the tendency he represents is re-

inforced and established. We propose to make the analysis and to give some of the evidence. Many members of the party, however, are in a position to come to conclusions independently on the basis of their own experience.

It should be remarked that the N.C. majority is under exactly the same obligations as the minority. If it is to be taken seriously the majority must make up its mind—it has not done so up to the present —about how it characterizes the minority *politically*. It must then attempt to *prove* its characterization both by an analysis of the position taken by the minority in the present dispute and by relating this position to other actions of the minority both at the present time and in the past. In a later section of this article, we shall return to the unhappy troubles which the majority has had in trying to decide on a political characterization of the minority.

4—THE NATURE OF BUREAUCRATIC CONSERVATISM

It is a fact that from the outset in the present dispute there have been raised questions of "organization" and "regime." The majority has accused the minority of having been "responsible" for raising these questions, and in addition has made the mutually contradictory accusations that: (a) the minority has been using the question of "regime" as a cover for a false and revisionist position on the Russian question; and (b) the minority has been using the Russian question as a cover for an underhanded attack on the "regime."

In his letter of October 22 to Comrade Stanley (*Internal Bulletin*, II, 2, p. 14), Comrade Crux writes as follows:

... (4) You state in your letter that the main issue is not the Russian question but the "internal regime." I have heard this accusation often since almost the very beginning of the existence of our movement in the United States. The formulations varied a bit, the groupings too, but a number of comrades always remained in opposition to the "regime." They were, for example, against the entrance into the Socialist Party (not to go further into the past). However it immediately occurred that not the entrance was the "main issue" but the regime. Now the same formula is repeated in connection with the Russian question.

(5) I, for my part, believe that the passage through the Socialist Party was a salutary action for the whole development of our party and that the "regime" (or the leadership) which assured this passage was correct against the opposition which at that time represented the tendency of stagnation.

... (9) Thus in two most important issues of the last period comrades dissatisfied with the "regime" have had in my opinion a false political attitude. The regime must be an instrument for correct policy and not for false. When the incorrectness of their policy becomes clear, then its protagonists are often tempted to say that not this special issue is decisive but the general regime. During the development of the Left Opposition and the Fourth International we opposed such substitutions hundreds of times. When Vereecken or Sneevliet or even Molinier were beaten on all their points of difference, they declared that the genuine trouble with the Fourth International is not this or that decision but the bad regime.

A correct understanding of Cannon's bureaucratic conservatism will enable us to understand both how and why the question of "organization" and "regime" immediately entered, and also the falsity of the accusations made by the majority on the one side and by Crux on the other.

(1) The initiative in introducing the question of "regime" was taken not by the minority but by the Cannon faction. On September 5 Burnham submitted to the Political Committee a resolution on the character of the war (included in *Internal Bulletin*, II, 2). In sending copies of this resolution to members of the N.C., Cannon accompanied it with a letter signed by himself. This letter did not deal essentially with the *political* issues raised by Burnham, but made a sharp *organizational* attack, contending that the raising of the issues was irresponsible and scandalous and that the party could not afford the "luxury" of a discussion. This letter was only a pale written reflection of the "organizational" denunciations of the minority which were being made at Committee meetings. The unprincipled and bureaucratic manner of reorganizing the P.C. at the plenum, again on the majority's initiative, brought the "organization question" to the forefront. Goldman's article in *Internal Bulletin*, II, 1, contains a sharp organizational attack on the minority, on the usual personal-psychological plane. The first internal discussion meeting was held in Newark, a few days after the plenum; there, Weber, speaking for the majority, made a sharp organizational attack on the minority in his opening report. When Cannon subsequently accused Shachtman, at the New York membership meeting, of "dragging in" the organization question, he, was simply falsifying the facts that he was well acquainted with. On the basis of these facts, Comrade Crux is quite wrong in the impression and argument incorporated in his letter.

The record is unambiguous: the majority was the "aggressor" in pushing forward the organization question, the question of "regime" —as has repeatedly been the case in lesser incidents of the past. We do not make our decisions here, any more than in the case of war, on the basis of who is the aggressor party. The minority does not object to or condemn the majority for taking the initiative in raising questions of regime (though it does condemn misrepresentations about it). On the contrary, the minority believes that this flowed naturally from the real nature of the dispute.

(2) It is difficult to understand with what motivation Crux tries to draw an analogy between the present dispute and that over entrance into the Socialist Party. Leaving aside the fact that the latter dispute was some years in the past (1934-35), and without discussing here the issue involved, the composition of the present opposition does not in the least coincide with that of the opposition to entry. Indeed, the present opposition includes many of the most conspicuous leaders in the "pro-entry" group, including Shachtman and Carter and Burnham— who first posed the perspective of an S.P. orientation, as well as many comrades who were not even in the Fourth Internationalist movement in those years (among them the chief "pro-entryists" in the Socialist Party itself, Erber, Draper, etc.). On the other hand, prominent among the present Cannon group are Weber, for long the accepted theoretical

leader of the "anti-entryists," and the one who from any point of view did not play the least shabby role of all participants in the dispute of those years; and Goldman, whose role in the dispute over entry into the S.P. was not very politely characterized, in its time, by leaders of both the majority and the minority. The only objective meaning which reference to this past dispute can have today is to try to "smear" the present opposition, or at least some comrades of it, by arbitrary, sterile and irrelevant hints drawn from a quite different past.

The Cannon group has been concentrating, in "defense" of its political position, upon criticisms and even sharp polemical attacks made in the past by some members of the present minority against others, particularly against Comrade Abern. How much validity and merit are contained in the quotations from the past factional documents? How much clarity do they introduce into the present political dispute? With due regard for proportions, exactly as much as in the case of the "Old Bolsheviks" who condemned Lenin and Trotsky for uniting in the political disputes of 1917 by quotations from the violent polemical attacks the two leaders had directed at each other before the war and on the very eve of the March revolution; exactly as much as in the case of the "Triumvirate" who condemned the Moscow Opposition in 1923 with arguments drawn from the same quotations; exactly as much as in the case of the Stalinists who condemned the union of the Trotskyist and Zinovievist groups in 1926 on the basis of quotations from the polemical attacks the two groups had made on each other up to 1926.

(3) Crux' references to "Vereecken, Sneevliet and Molinier" are even more extraordinary. Quite apart from their proved loyalty to the Fourth International, all the members of the present opposition have consistently been in the forefront of the defense of the Fourth International against Vereecken, Sneevliet and Molinier. The listing of Molinier is particularly inappropriate, since for a considerable period it was Comrade Crux who in many respects *supported* Molinier against criticisms some of which were levelled by leaders of the present minority (Shachtman, Carter, Abern).

(4) Nor can we agree in general with the mechanical relationship which the majority constantly alleges to hold between "good regime" and "correct policy." The majority reasons as follows: good regime *automatically* follows from correct policy; if the policy is correct, then the regime which tries to carry through that policy is also correct. Though normally (not at all invariably) regime is or should be properly *subordinated* to policy, the automatic and necessary relationship between the two is a phantom of the imagination, and a dangerous phantom at that.

Assuming a correct policy, it is not merely possible, but it frequently happens, that this policy is carried through in a bad or false organizational manner: e.g., *bureaucratically*, by manipulation of the "apparatus," by arbitrary fiat, by removals from posts or expulsions, without education of the membership to the correctness of the policy, etc. When this occurs (and there are hundreds of examples in political history: the records of the Frey group in Austria and the Molinier group in France are but two instances in the history of the Left Opposition alone), a certain paradox arises within the given organization, especially acute for those who agree with the policy but object to the "methods." Ideally and in the abstract, this paradox can be solved by separating the two questions (policy and regime) carefully, and by supporting the policy but taking steps to alter the regime and methods. In practice the solution is not so simple, since the bureaucratic regime *exploits* its allegedly correct (or rather generally false) policy to uphold its regime and methods. Indeed, a bureaucratic regime, seeing its methods about to be attacked, often *provokes* a political dispute to turn aside the organizational attack. No absolute rule can be given in advance for meeting these problems in practice. At a particular time, the failure to alter the regime may have a more damaging long-term effect even than the adoption, temporarily, of a false or inadequate policy, especially in those cases where policy is only a secondary consideration in the mind of the regime.

We make these remarks not to suggest that the majority has in the present a correct policy—which it most certainly does not have, but to combat the loose and empty formalism of the conception that regime and policy are mechanically, necessarily and automatically united, and particularly against the conception that regime flows directly and harmoniously from policy.

(5) However, *bureaucratic conservatism* is unique among all political tendencies in precisely the relation that holds, in *its* case, between regime and policy. In *its* case, there *is* a necessary relation between regime and policy; and this relation is the *reverse* of the normal. In the case of bureaucratic conservatism, *policy is subordinated to regime*, not the other way around. Let us see what this means.

Bureaucratic conservatism is, put crudely and bluntly, *apparatus politics*. Its chief base, in any organization or movement, large or small, is the "apparatus." Objectively considered, the goal and purpose and aim of a bureaucratic conservative tendency is *to preserve itself*. To this aim all else is, in the last analysis, subordinated. To this aim, policy and political issues are subordinated.

It is for this reason that the policies adopted by the bureaucratic conservative tendency tend always toward being *conservative*. It is the defender of the *status quo*—until the point where its own preservation becomes incompatible with the preservation of the *status quo*. Normally a bold move, an abrupt change, a reorientation, the intrusion of something new, upset things as they are: that is, tend to undermine the established regime. That is why, to Cannon and his central core of supporters, those who propose bold and new steps, changes and reorientations, are almost invariably characterized *out of hand*, without even consideration or discussion, as "irresponsible," "light-minded," "yielding to pressure," etc.

This is the reason, moreover, why in a dispute with Cannon—especially of late years—the "organizational question" always makes its appearance almost at the start, from one side or the other. To imagine, as does Crux, that this is due to an "incurable habit" of the incorrigible comrades who opposed S.P. entry, is mistaken, for it is at variance with the facts. As a matter of fact, Abern, who with Weber led the fight against entry, has, during the past three years up to the outbreak of the present dispute, gone to the most extreme lengths to avoid all disputes and to quiet them when they arose; it was invariably others, and usually those who fought *for* entry, who have been concerned in the disputes of these years.

The fact is that most if not all of the leaders of the minority have proceeded in the past period from the standpoint that compared with risking the precipitation of a sharp struggle in the party, a conciliatory attitude and even silence on a whole series of questions in dispute among the leadership are the "lesser evil." Hence the refusal to take a number of disputed questions to the membership, a refusal that often involved keeping the membership uninformed about what they had a right to know. This is the fact, regardless of whether the leaders of the minority, singly or collectively, were right or wrong in their manner of dealing with past disagreements in the National Committee. It is this which, moreover, explains the obscure and perplexing character of the discussion at the last party convention over the question of the "organization department." If the discussion is now taking place in the ranks of the party in the form of a factional fight, the reason for it is not to be sought in the "incurable habits" of this or that comrade or group, but precisely in the fact of the outbreak of the war, the urgent and immensely important problems it raised, and the serious character of the disagreement over the answers that must be given to these problems. Only a disagreement over such vital questions—as contrasted with disagreements over relatively secondary matters in the past—could impel the comrades of the minority to present the questions, insoluble in the leadership itself, for fundamental decision by the membership.

To imagine, as Crux does, that oppositions revert to the "organization question" when "the incorrectness of their policy becomes clear" is likewise incorrect, at variance with the facts. In the first place, the organization question always enters before it is in the least "clear" whose policy is false (in the present dispute it is certainly not clear either to the minority of the N.C. or to the party membership that its position is false: the fact is that every day *more* of the party thinks it correct).

No, here as elsewhere we must seek a *political* explanation for the speedy appearance of the organization question in every dispute. And that explanation is found in the political character of the Cannon faction, in the fact that it is a *bureaucratic conservative* tendency, a tendency for which *every* serious political proposal with which it differs (and this includes virtually all proposals which involve something new) is interpreted as an attack on its regime. It replies always by raising, openly or implicitly, the question of "confidence." Its tone takes on the bitterness of the apparatus defending its control of the leadership.

Let us give two examples here to concretize the point we have been making:

(A) Comrade Goldman is a prominent supporter of Cannon. He himself has often declared that he supports the Cannon leadership and *regime*, independently of agreement or disagreement on policies. During the course of the present dispute, when the question of the invasion of Poland by the Red Army was before the P.C., Goldman made a motion supporting and *approving* the invasion. He alone voted for this motion. Nevertheless, during this entire period, Goldman supported Cannon in general, and acted as a chief spokesman for the majority. At the plenum, Goldman voted for both the Cannon political and the organizational motions, in spite of the fact that the political motions conflicted flatly with his own expressed opinion. He published an article in the *Internal Bulletin* (II, 1) among other things, to "explain" his change in politics. This explanation (dealt with by Shachtman in *Bulletin* II, 3) is so feeble as to deceive no one. The fact is that Goldman, caught in the trap of the bureaucratic conservative group, was compelled to subordinate his politics to his defense of the regime. Exactly the same procedure was followed later by Goldman on his slogan for the withdrawal of Soviet troops from Finland —suppressed by Goldman when the faction meeting voted it down.

(B) At the convention, a freely elected convention committee voted by a large majority to include a provision for an "organizational department" in the resolution on organization to be presented to the convention. In meetings of the ex-N.C. held during the convention, Cannon objected to this plan. His objections were based not in the least upon the merits of the proposal itself, but because he thought he saw in it some kind of "plot," a conspiracy to get a stranglehold on the "apparatus," to put a "commissar" in the National Office, etc. (This interpretation was, in passing, in the highest degree fantastic— and typical. The plan was presented quite spontaneously by several comrades in the convention committee, most particularly by Comrade Weiss, a Cannonite supporter, and in the light of their experience recommended itself at once to virtually all committee members.) To remove these absurd suspicions, Shachtman, Burnham, and others who favored the plan on its merits pledged themselves (as they did later on the convention floor) to vote for any nominee to the post of "organization secretary" who would be nominated by Cannon (expressing as their own opinion that Comrade "Smith" of Minneapolis, a well-known Cannon supporter, would be the best qualified man for the job). Cannon was not at all content. He turned this comparatively simple question—which could easily have been settled quietly on its merits, and about which a difference of opinion was certainly legitimate and to be expected—into what parliamentarians call a "question of confidence." To support the "org. dep." was—to attack the regime and the leadership. No one would get away with such an underhanded attack; he would go to bat on the convention floor if the plan were persisted in. And then, to underline the point that it was a "question of confidence," Cannon made the usual cheap announcement of a Chamberlain or a Norman Thomas or any bureaucrat under similar conditions: he told the N.C. that his term of office as National Secretary had expired at the convention and that he was not a candidate for re-election. In other words: play my way, or I quit. This bluster was enough to whip his faction into line, even those who (like Comrade Weiss) had, voting on the merits of the issue, supported the plan in the convention committee. Needless to say, nothing was heard subsequent to the convention about the resignation and withdrawal from further service as national secretary.

*   *   *

From the point of view of the minority, therefore, it is not in the ordinary sense that it raises the question of "regime." When we call the Cannon faction "bureaucratic conservative," we are giving a *political* characterization. But this particular political tendency manifests itself at one and the same time as *conservative* in its politics, and *bureaucratic* in its regime—these are the two sides of the same coin.

If we keep these conceptions clearly in mind, we shall find them a key to the understanding of the Cannon tendency, not merely in the case of the present dispute, but in its role in the movement generally.

5—BUREAUCRATIC CONSERVATISM IN ACTION

That the N.C. majority has manifested bureaucratic conservatism in the present dispute is so obvious that the merest recital of the facts suffices to prove it.

First, as to the conservatism of its policy: Conservatism in policy can be shown in either of two different ways—either by a failure to change a past policy when changes in events call for such a change, or by a failure to *apply concretely* a general position which itself may still be correct in its general form. The former type is more easily recognized than the latter. When, after the consolidation of power by Hitler, revolutionists refused to change the earlier policy of "working as a faction of the Comintern" to the policy of building a new party, they were displaying the first type of conservatism. The second type can be equally fatal for the progress of the movement. For example, a given situation might call imperiously for the application of a united front tactic toward some particular organization. This application might be opposed conservatively by those who would not at all call into question the "general policy" of the united front; indeed, these would probably be just the ones who would most solemnly "reaffirm" the "fundamental position" of the International on the united front.

What has been the position of the N.C. majority on the actual questions which have been before the party, the questions, namely, of the character of the war, the character of the role of the Red Army in the present stage of the war, the characterization of the Red Army's and Russia's intervention in Poland, the Baltics, Finland, etc.? As a matter of fact, no one can answer this question with any assurance—*for the simple reason that the majority has had no position at all!* Startling as this may seem, it is the undiluted truth. The majority has had no position on the most momentous events in the history of our movement and perhaps of mankind.

Does anyone doubt this? Then let him tell us what the position has been. The record of the committee speaks clearly for itself. The majority has some general and abstract remarks in its motions about "the class character of the Soviet state" and about "reaffirming our fundamental position on the defense of the Soviet Union." But *to this day* it has not answered the actual questions. To this day it has not characterized the Polish invasion, or the Baltic adventures or the moves toward Finland. To this day it has not characterized the present war, or the role of Russia in the war. To this day it has not even stated whether in the case of the invasion of Poland or similar threatened invasions we are for the "unconditional defense" of the Red Army. For the position it is obligated to state as a group, as the leadership (majority) of the party, it substitutes a number of *individual* positions, mutually exclusive and contradictory.*

It has not answered these questions. Much less has it given any concrete guidance for *the future*. It does not say what we should be telling the Finnish workers and soldiers, or the Red Army soldiers facing the invasion of Finland. For weeks it prevented even *mention* of India and the relation of Russia to India in the *Appeal;* and of course has had nothing to say about India itself. And while the minority was denounced for raising the "remote" question of India, it was peremptorily asked to state its position on the defense of Odessa from a British warship going through the Dardanelles and up the Black Sea, presumably on the grounds that this was indeed *the immediate* and not a "remote" question. Events finally *compelled* the majority to permit the minority to raise, in part, the Indian question—though this question is at least as burning as any other in connection with the present phase of the war. No, the majority has done nothing whatever—save to reaffirm "fundamentals."

Now the minority contends that the war which is going on is not entirely the war that we foresaw and that the role of Russia in it is not what we expected; and therefore that we must make *new* analyses related to the reality of today's events and give *new* answers, and that among other things we must also revise our slogan of "unconditional defense of the Soviet Union." The minority, concretely and clearly, has made the new analyses, given new answers, and proposed the revision of the slogan. This again is why we say that the policy of the majority has been conservative.

But let us assume, for a moment, that the minority is wrong, and that the old position and analysis are correct. Even with that assumption, the policy of the majority is revealed as starkly conservative—conservative in the second sense explained above. The majority was unable to *apply* the general position to the concrete events, and it is therefore reduced to the politics of mumbo-jumbo.

But it is no less clear that the majority has acted *bureaucratically* in the present dispute. This may be unambiguously shown in four ways:

---

*Although this was written before the actual invasion of Finland, the charge is not invalidated but substantially confirmed by the actions of the majority. As is shown in more detail in our document on the Russian question, the Cannon group, characteristically, evaded taking a clear-cut position on the invasion by the device of taking *several* positions, containing mutually contradictory lines of policy, and each succeeding position being adopted with a renunciation of those it succeeded. Under pressure of the minority and the membership as a whole, the Cannon group felt compelled to do in the case of Finland what it denounced as superfluous in the case of Poland, that is, to formulate a specific position on the concrete situation. In actuality, however, it remained true to itself. On Poland it said nothing and therefore its "position" could be and was all things to all men. On Finland, it says several *different* things in several different documents (all written within a week or ten days!) so that its "position" can again be and is all things to all men.

(a) At the time of the Hitler-Stalin pact and the beginning of the war crisis, it was *unanimously* recognized by the committee that at the very least a "reexamination" of our position was called for in the light of the new events. Nevertheless, for weeks, the majority bitterly opposed any party discussion, and delayed as long as possible the calling even of an N.C. plenum—in spite of the fact that the need for a discussion and the wish of the membership for it became daily more apparent. This attitude meant nothing else than an attempt to solve the political difficulties within the "apparatus," to solve them bureaucratically. (After the discussion was finally forced by the minority, Cannon, of course, changed his tune, and said that a "discussion was imperatively required in order to clarify the membership"—but, he added, "fruitful" discussion could only be "on the character of the Russian state.")

(b) During the entire first period of the dispute, the majority (in public and private, in committee and out) hurled charges of "irresponsibility," "light-mindedness," "instability" at the opposition, and condemned it for "throwing the party into a crisis on the eve of war," *while at the same time making no reply whatever to the opposition on the political points it raised.* We have here the classic response of the bureaucrat to political criticism: no answer to the criticism, charges of irresponsibility and disruption against the critic (for further analysis of this attitude, see Trotsky's article on the P.S.O.P. in the October 1939 *New International*).

In the few weeks elapsing since the opening of the discussion, with the contending groups having scarcely had the opportunity to state their positions fully before the membership—in other words, with the discussion really in its first stages—the Cannon faction has enormously sharpened the atmosphere with the most violent attacks ever known in our eleven years of existence. Bureaucratic disloyalty and misrepresentation of an opponent is developing in exact proportion to the majority's inability to give a political defense of its political position. Every day now sees increasing attempts by the majority to displace the axis of the discussion from the political and organizational dispute (the organizational questions involved are in this case also political questions), to questions of personalities and the type of abuse known to us up to now only from the records of the Stalinist campaign against the Russian Opposition. It is not so much the "Russian question" and the "question of the party regime" that is discussed by Cannon now— the ground under his feet is too weak for that—but Abern's personal record, Burnham's personal record, and the like. It is not a political characterization that the Cannon group gives of the opposition; it substitutes for that such characterizations as "traitors," "scabs and strike-breakers," "Finland's Foreign Legion," "enemies of the Soviet Union," "agents of imperialism." The tone and style fit the regime, and while it is unprecedented in our movement, it has its precedent in the Stalinist party.

(c) When the specific problem of characterizing the Red Army's invasion of Poland came before the P.C., the majority passed Cannon's motion which gave no answer to the specific problem but merely "reaffirmed the fundamental position." It then instructed Cannon to prepare an article for the *Appeal* on the invasion. But it had already been shown that on the alleged basis of the "fundamental position," three entirely *different* positions on the Polish invasion had been held: approval of the invasion, disapproval, and "explanation" without either approval or disapproval. This fact proves that the action of the majority here was *bureaucratic.* It did not have the committee (or even itself) take a position. Instead, it turned a blank check over to Cannon, and said in effect—whatever you write is the position. Such a procedure, if there is any serious issue in dispute, is *always* bureaucratic. The democratic procedure must always be to have the proper party body make the decision, and then assign someone to *carry out*—not to make —the decision.

(d) The reorganization of the P.C. at the plenum was bureaucratic. Cannon has denied this charge, claiming that the reorganization was entirely proper. He argues as follows: There was a political dispute; we had a majority, and therefore we had to construct a P.C. majority to carry out our politics. He further argues: Our majority was 16 to 9 in the N.C.; in the new P.C. our majority, when the youth representative is included, is 8 to 4, a close and reasonable approximation of the N.C. majority.

The minority does not at all deny the right of those who have a political majority to elect committees in accordance with the majority, nor does it deny that Cannon had an N.C. majority. It nevertheless maintains the charge that Cannon's reorganization of the P.C. was bureaucratic. Let us examine the facts.

On what *political basis* does Cannon establish his majority? Does he establish it on the basis of those at the plenum who voted *against* the Shachtman resolution? If so, the vote was 14 to 11, not 16 to 9.

Or does he (as would seem more plausible) establish his majority on the basis of those who voted *for* his motion of "reaffirming the fundamental position." This would get him his 16 to 9 majority. But in this case, what happened to Erber, McKinney and Abern (who voted for his motion) when the problem of constructing the new P.C. was decided? The P.C. slate was drawn up by a faction meeting; neither Erber, McKinney nor Abern was present at that meeting; none of them had any voice in selecting the new P.C. Why not? Will Cannon answer: Because by their vote *also* for the Shachtman motion, they showed "instability," that they could not carry out the line "firmly." (On what basis, in passing, is Cannon the only judge of "stability" and the proper way of interpreting the fundamental position? On what basis is Goldman, who participated in the caucus, even though his views on the disputed question were rejected unanimously, more "stable" and "firm" on the issue in dispute then, say, Abern?) But if so, Cannon cannot have it both ways. He cannot count his majority on one basis, and select the personnel of his P.C. on another. To be consistent, he would either have had to propose at the least a bloc with Erber, Abern and McKinney in selecting the new P.C.; or he would have had to organize the P.C. on a different basis, namely, on the vote on the Shachtman resolution. This he could not do without reducing his alleged majority to 14-11. But he could not have done it even then for the simple reason that Cannon had no motion of his own in real opposition to Shachtman's motion—which would have had to be a motion including a specific characterization of the Polish invasion.

All this would have had to follow *if* Cannon had proceeded on a democratic and principled basis. In reality he proceeded on a *clique* basis, calling his caucus meeting and constructing his P.C. not on any political foundation, but solely on the basis of assured membership in his bureaucratic conservative clique. For this reason, naturally, Erber, Abern and McKinney were excluded—even though, in the political rationalizations which were cooked up later, their votes were counted as part of the "justification" for the lineup of the new P.C.*

* * *

Was this series of incidents an accident, something extraordinary and unusual? Not in the least: it is normal and typical. But before citing other examples of the mode of operation of the Cannon clique, we wish to clear up an apparent—but only apparent—difficulty in our argument.

---

*Let us dispose in passing of the Cannonite contention that the minority is an "unprincipled bloc." This contention stands or falls on the claim that Abern and others voted for Cannon's plenum motion on the Russian question but did not join with Cannon against the minority; and further that these comrades voted for the Cannon motion in favor of "unconditional defense" and also for the Shachtman resolution in favor of revising that slogan. The facts are these: Abern did vote for the Cannon motion, but added a statement making clear the meaning of his vote. A *loyal* reading and interpretation of this statement shows that Abern voted for that motion only in the sense of a reaffirmation of the official party position that the Soviet Union is a "degenerated workers' state, whose basic structure must be defended by the Russian and international proletariat against world imperialism and against the anti-Soviet bureaucracy of Stalinism." His vote was not, however, an endorsement of the—at best—ambiguous conception of the slogan of "unconditional defense" which is interpreted by the majority in several mutually contradictory ways, and which, at the plenum, was used by the majority as a *substitute* for a position on the concrete events facing us. Abern's statement added: "With this basic evaluation I find no contradiction in the resolution of Shachtman which I accept in its essentials as an interpretation or analysis of specific current issues therein cited, not invalidating the basic party position. I am ready to leave to the next period the enfoldment or otherwise of the interpretations or implications asserted by some comrades here as to the 'bridge' character of the Shachtman resolution, or whether it stands episodically by itself; and to make my judgment accordingly on the merits of any issue." No wonder the Cannonites have carefully avoided quoting this statement! It should be added, finally, that the "next period" referred to in the Abern statement has showed more clearly that more than an "episodic" difference was involved; that our old formula does require revision, as the Shachtman plenum resolution proposed, if only because the Cannon faction employed and interpreted it in defense of an indefensible line (or variety of lines) which is essentially a political capitulation to Stalinism. Erber and McKinney, in voting for the Cannon motion, also subscribed to the Abern statement.

6—WHAT HIDES THE ROLE OF THE CANNON CLIQUE

If our contention is true—namely that the Cannon faction represents a bureaucratic conservative tendency in the party, and operates as a clique—it would seem, offhand, that this ought to be obvious to nearly every member of the party. If this is indeed the case, and if it has been going on to one or another degree for some years, why doesn't everyone know about it? Now many comrades, including not a few who are members of the Cannon faction, do know about it; and, especially when speaking "off the record," show that they have no illusions. But it is still true that there are sections of the party to whom our charges will come as a surprise, and will even seem to be unfounded.

There are three chief factors which have obscured the role of the Cannon faction:

(1) The first is that Cannon, upon all occasions without exception, accepts the *politics* of Trotsky, accepts them immediately and without question. Since Trotsky's politics are, as a rule, correct and progressive, this tends often to make Cannon's politics *appear* correct and progressive—that is, the opposite of conservative.

If this is the case (and no one will seriously dispute it) it might seem to refute, in itself, our contention that the Cannon tendency is *conservative*, unless we are saying that Trotsky's politics in general are also conservative.

Everyone knows that comrade Trotsky is the outstanding theoretical leader of the Fourth International. It is entirely proper that every revolutionist should give the maximum weight to his opinions: other things being equal, more weight than to those of any other individual. Nine times out of ten, perhaps ninety-nine times out of a hundred, we find ourselves on the right course when we take the course mapped out by Trotsky. It would be superfluous to elaborate upon the irreplaceable contributions he has made to the international Bolshevik-Leninist movement for more than fifteen years, and for a long time before then. Even if less known, his contributions to the solution of theoretical, immediately political and internal problems of the American movement have been none the less solid. We reject with the contempt it deserves that philistine protestation of "independence from Trotsky" which is calculated to promote "independence" from the Fourth International and the principles of revolutionary Marxism. At the same time, we can have nothing in common with the theoretical and political slothfulness which, under cover of hypocritical humility, seeks to *counterpose* and therefore *replace* serious political reflection and discussion of the membership and leadership with references to Trotsky's position and demagogical invocations of his rightfully enjoyed authority. The Fourth International has not the slightest ground for "apologizing" for its outstanding leader, who, alone among the older generation of the world movement, has consistently defended the principles of revolutionary internationalism. Nevertheless, there are ways and ways of seeking and accepting advice.

For a genuine revolutionary politician, the thought of another cannot be a *substitute* for his own thoughts; the politics of another a *substitute* for politics of his own—regardless of who that other may be. The ideas of another can be correctly accepted only intelligently, only *critically*. Otherwise, what we have is not a policy really understood and capable of being utilized as a guide to action, but merely the ceremonial repetition of phrases.

For the Cannon faction, Trotsky's politics function precisely as a *substitute* for politics of their own. As a bureaucratic conservative group, they merely utilize Trotsky's politics, as they utilize politics in general, as an instrument of their regime. Thus, a policy, which as advocated by Trotsky has a progressive character, takes on a sterile and conservative coloration in their hands.

This is not at all a psychological comment, but a political judgment; and it can be demonstrated by the evidence.

Consider the way (already described) in which the majority at the plenum "endorsed" the long article on the "Russian question." Some of them had not even read it in its entirety; none of them could possibly have studied and assimilated it, and the complete document was not even on hand. What had happened? They had arrived at the plenum with their faction, their clique, but *without a policy*. A policy dropped into their laps (fortunate for them that it was not a day or two late) and they snatched it at once as a *substitute* for their own inability to develop a policy, as a "political justification" for the clique which they *already* had, though without any political basis.

But, it might be argued, whatever the lacks of the past, they finally got a "correct" policy. This does not in the least follow, *even if Trotsky's policy is considered correct*. Their endorsement of Trotsky's policy, here as usual during the past couple of years at least is essentially formal, verbal, *ritualistic*. (For in reality, let us repeat again, the policy is the instrument of the regime, not vice versa.) Being adopted as a substitute, without intelligent examination, without critical thought, the Cannon faction does not in reality understand it—their own avowed policy from then on—nor know how to apply it in the concrete.

The ideas and theories of Trotsky, like the theories of revolutionary Marxism in general, are not a dogma or a ritual but a guide to action. Their formal acceptance, however correct by itself, does not eliminate the need of applying them to concrete situations and problems. To repeat a thousand times that we stand by the fundamentals of Marxism is no answer to urgent questions posed by specific instances of the class struggle; indeed, very often it is a way of evading an answer. To repeat a thousand times that we are followers of Trotsky is no answer to the question of what course the leadership proposes that the party shall follow in a given case, or what the party proposes that the workers shall follow.

Nothing could be clearer than this during the present dispute. Granted their policy (that is, Trotsky's policy) in the abstract, in general, they are unable to use it for anything but the purposes of internal polemic. Neither in committee nor in their public writings and speeches have they made a single illuminating analysis of a single concrete event; they have made no predictions, suggested no guidance whatever. They merely repeat, parrot-like, in their own phrasing and rhetoric, the ideas already presented by Trotsky.

Here, too, there is nothing exceptional. The same situation *exactly* obtained in the case of the "Transition Program" adopted at the N.C. plenum held in the spring of 1938. Though many of the N.C. members, as usual, had not even read the entire document; though it was in many parts very difficult to understand; Cannon insisted on an immediate vote of endorsement with the threat to "ride roughshod" (as he put it) over anyone who hesitated. But, again, the Program was, and remained, for Cannon not a policy but a substitute for a policy. Endorsement meant not understanding, not the effort to apply the policy in the concrete life of the movement, but simply the ritualistic nod of agreement with its *words*. Shachtman, Burnham and others, including Goldman at that time, insisted that it meant nothing merely to "accept" the transition program; that in incorporating it into the life of our own party, distinction would have to be made between those parts of it which were directly applicable to the United States, and those parts which were not, between those slogans which were of a general propagandistic and educational character and those suitable for immediate agitational uses; and they insisted further that the *concrete* meaning of many of the general concepts of the program had to be sought in terms of living developments in this country. For Cannon, the test of the true believer was whether he made the sign of the cross with proper piety. "All or none!"—100 per cent *verbal* acceptance of the program just as it stood, *and nothing more*. Cannon went even to the preposterous extreme of putting through a *motion* in the P.C. that there is no difference between propaganda slogans and agitation slogans (comparable to a motion that two plus two does not equal four). It took nearly a year to force through the conception that the movement and slogans arising in the labor movement for "Thirty hours, thirty dollars," "Thirty hours' work at forty hours' pay," etc., were concretizations of the general transition slogan for "A sliding scale of wages and hours"! It took a year before it was possible to treat the slogan for a workers' guard as suitable for anything but the most vague and general educational propaganda. As a consequence of this thoroughly sterile approach, the transition program has as a whole not to this day become a significant living factor in our movement.

The Cannon faction covers the conservatism of its own politics and seeks prestige and control through appearing as "the unyielding representative" of Trotsky's views. In the light of the foregoing analysis, we deny categorically that the Cannon group has the slightest right to be regarded as the representative of Trotsky's views in a genuinely political sense.

But even if it were true that the Cannon group were a responsible representative of Trotsky's politics and were able to apply those politics, the result would remain wholly unsatisfactory.

To begin with, Trotsky is not only capable of being wrong but has a number of times been wrong. The *habit* of automatic, uncritical acceptance of Trotsky's views eliminates the basis for fruitful discussion, in whole or in part, and the possibility of mutual influence and correction.

Secondly, it is impossible for Trotsky to present a line of daily policy for the development of the American section, that is, to substitute for the party leadership, its problems and its tasks; nor does he seek or desire to do so. So far as the American section goes, he can give guidance only on the more general, the international, the basic questions, and occasionally on specific national problems which arise. If this guidance were invariably right, it would still be only a part of what has to be done. There remain a thousand-and-one political problems of the American movement and the American revolution. These can be answered only by an independently and critically thinking leadership and membership of the American section itself. This is, as we understand it, the attitude that Trotsky has always had to this problem, and it is the only one admissible in our movement. There is not the slightest element of provincialism or nationalism in such a view. It is common horse sense. And unless such a leadership and membership is not developed—and it cannot be under the regime of bureaucratic conservatism—the Fourth International in this country is foredoomed to sterility.

The Cannon group, we have said, accepts automatically, in words at least, the *politics* of Trotsky. But this does not mean that it accepts *all* the views of Trotsky. We have defined the Cannon group as bureaucratic conservative, and have pointed out that for a bureaucratic conservative group, politics is *subordinate* to regime. The *independence* of the Cannon group, what keeps it alive and makes it possible for it to be a group, is *not* its political policies—which, in the last analysis, are wholly secondary for it—but its central object of the maintenance of itself. On questions of regime, or "organizational methods," Cannon is not in the least the "follower of Trotsky," but, on the contrary, though willing to listen to Trotsky's opinion, pursues an assured and independent course. Political or theoretical questions can be left to others—to Trotsky, or even, on "normal" occasions, to Burnham or Shachtman. But Cannon will keep a firm and guiding hand on "organization." This difference in attitude is infinitely revealing the true nature of bureaucratic conservatism. Politics, programs, are more or less routine matters for others to take care of; the business of the "real Bolshevik" is—to cinch up the majority and retain party control. Yes: Trotsky or Burnham or Shachtman writes the "political resolutions" for plenums and conventions; but the organization resolutions come from the firm Bolshevik hand of Cannon. From the end of the Chicago convention in November 1937 to June 1939 *not one word* of Cannon's appears in the public political press of the party; but his articles on "organization" feature the pre-convention discussion.

The articles themselves are characteristic, too. In the pre-convention discussion in the P.C., comrades of the present opposition pointed out, objectively and self-critically, the justified discontentment of the membership with the sluggishness and apathy of the leadership, with its failure to elaborate or carry out a program of action, in particular the failure to make a living reality out of the Transition Program; point out, further, that the preparations for the convention are routinist to the core, providing for no critical examination of the past or program for the future. The articles by Cannon, many of the ideas in which were a collective product even though they were printed as a personal contribution, were written essentially for the purpose of *warding off* the necessary criticism of the party leadership's stewardship between the two conventions. No clearer proof of this assertion is required than the fact that following the convention nothing more was heard of the "program of action" contained in the articles. They were a defense mechanism for preserving the regime from criticism, nothing more.

(2) The second chief factor which hides the true role of the Cannon group is Cannon's undoubted organization skill—as it has sometimes been called, his "organization flexibility." This, well known to those who have been associated with him for a period of years at the center, is difficult to describe briefly and explain. No politician is more careful of "the record" than Cannon. He waits as long as possible to commit himself to writing and specific motions. And much, perhaps the most part, is done quietly in action, without motions at all, or motions only to record or sanction what has already taken place.

A trip by Cannon to Minneapolis seems advisable. Why? The comrades would like some "consultation." A few weeks after the trip is over, it turns out that a very important decision about the work of comrade "Smith" has been made. Naturally, the P.C. approves the decision.

A few weeks ago, Cannon evinced, for the first time in three years, a sudden interest in the Youth. Frightful conditions had come to his attention—by a coincidence, just as a severe factional struggle was getting under way. Comrade Tanner of the YPSL N.C. (up to yesterday, as proved by the record and by letters, well satisfied with the YPSL leadership) had, by a happy chance, felt compelled to tell Cannon, in an interview and then by letter, how bad things are. And a couple of days later—again by happy chance—comrade Art Preis, who a few months ago publicly found the YPSL to be the only salt in his Ohio earth, wrote in to the national office a denunciation of the YPSL that must have exhausted his supply of adjectives.

The membership, approaching the July 1939 convention, feels that all is not well with the functioning of the party. Cannon's excellent literary style, long slumbering, springs to life. What we need is ten thousand dollars, a three-a-week *Appeal*, and thirty new organizers. To try to talk soberly and critically about the past and what to learn from it—that is to sabotage the chance of a "constructive convention." The convention ends, but the new "program of action" does not get off the paper it was written on.

The New York organization has been slipping away from the Cannon influence? Luckily, just before a local convention, Cochran turns up in New York; and, though the P.C. has not known about it, it happens that his work in auto (three months before defined as the main concentration point) has come to an end. The articulate Cannon supporters in New York are not so many and not doing so well as in the old days? Murry Weiss, fortunately, is no longer needed so urgently in California and is specially assigned to New York; while auto has so thoroughly quieted down that George Clarke also is no longer required in the Detroit area.

The Organization Committee, discussing the severe financial crisis in the party, unanimously recommends a retrenchment policy to the P.C., which just as unanimously endorses it. To save the *Appeal*, it is imperative, under the conditions, to return to weekly publication, and to cut down the staffs of the national office, and the press. There is to be only one full-time editorial worker and one full-time business manager. After the defeat of the Cannon faction at the New York city convention of the party, the financial crisis disappears over night. Goldman is added to the national office staff; Clarke, who has never had the slightest experience in this field, is added to the *Appeal* staff as general manager of the press, without the P.C. majority deigning to give the slightest argument, good or bad, either for increasing the staff or for the candidate's qualifications. Other departments of the work, however, not less important than these, but manned by oppositionists cannot be maintained for "financial" reasons.

And none of this is done with mirrors.

(3) The third chief factor which has obscured the role of Cannon is the cover which has been provided for him by other N.C. members, in particular by members of the present opposition. This has had, for many party members, one of two effects, both of which serve to cover Cannon: it has led some party members, who decided for themselves that the party leadership was conservative and bureaucratic, to place responsibility on the leadership as a whole; whereas others, who did not believe that this, that or the other members of the N.C. was conservative and bureaucratic, felt that the failure of such members to separate themselves from Cannon proved Cannon himself to be neither bureaucratic nor conservative. (It may be noted that some N.C. members even now supporting Cannon—such as Goldman—still serve as covers.)

It is true that, with the exception of a partial and inadequate discussion at the convention, we have not spoken out and have therefore undoubtedly served as a cover for Cannon's bureaucratic conservatism. Why not? The party must understand the reasons for this silence, in order not to be misled by such suggestions as the one to the effect that we speak now in order to divert attention from an allegedly false policy.

(i) In the first place, the present N.C. minority, while opposing Cannon's organizational conceptions and actions as bureaucratic, does not in the least counterpose to them an anarchist conception of organization. We believe in centralism as well as democracy for the party; and we believe it leads to nothing but chaos when every dispute in a leadership is at once "taken to the ranks." We believe that there is a certain order in the party structure, and that this is as it should be. When disputes arise in the leadership, we believe that, in most cases, the possibilities of solving these disputes *in* the leadership should be explored and exhausted before they are taken to the ranks; and at the very least that they should not be taken to the membership until the differences—if there continue to be differences—are clarified and crystallized. A party pays a heavy cost for membership disputes, in terms of the lessening of positive external activity, the loss of members through discouragement and disgust, the waste of energies and funds, etc.; and such disputes are therefore not to be initiated lightly.

It is not in any degree true that the minority has suddenly "discovered" organizational and other differences with Cannon subsequent to the emergence of a political difference on the Russian question. During the past several years, one or another member of the present minority has time and again posed the questions herein discussed within the leading committees in the attempt to work out some solution. This was done, for example, at the time of the special enlarged P.C. meeting during the "auto crisis." Prior to the July convention, there were attempts to discuss them in a number of meetings. Burnham presented to the committee a long written document as a basis for discussion. The document did not pretend to solve all problems, or to deal with all of them; nor could it. It was meant to initiate an orderly discussion among the leadership so that, by a frank and general discussion, some solution of the questions raised might at least be approached. Apart from McKinney, who spoke briefly on the document, only Abern took the floor to discuss it. He dealt at length and in detail with the criticisms directed at him. Cannon however whose regime was the main burden of the document, did not deign to utter a single word of comment, either in defense or rebuttal. On a later occasion, he made it clear that he had no intention of even trying to resolve the problem by discussion in the formally constituted leadership of the party, or for that matter, in the national convention of the membership. Such problems are to be dealt with and disposed of only by the clique. In other words, the Cannon regime and it alone may judge the Cannon regime.

At the N.C. meetings immediately preceding the convention, Shachtman proposed to raise these questions at the convention, through placing on the agenda of the convention a report on the leadership's record since the last convention. This proposal was rejected by the N.C., on the ground that "such questions could not be decided by a convention." By whom, then, by the way? It was made clear that any attempt to raise any question however limited, specific and partial, relating to "the regime" would provoke a crisis in the party. The majority operated under an American version of the famous slogan: "These cadres can be removed only by civil war." When nevertheless these questions forced their way to the surface in the convention, they did so in the distorted and confusing form of the debate over the "org. sec."

(ii) The problem of Cannon's conservatism in politics has also often been before the committees. We have cited one important instance in connection with the interpretation of the transition program. Comrades of the present opposition at this time debated whether to submit an independent resolution to the party in the discussion and referendum, and did submit a draft resolution to the committee. But here, as has a number of times happened, the following factor operated to keep the dispute from the membership: Virtually all committee members were in general, at least formal, agreement in supporting the transition program and the new Labor party position. Separate documents to the party would have been hard to understand, and would have interfered with the education of the party to acceptance of the new program, and to successful opposition to the opponents of the change in position on the Labor party. It seemed impossible to accomplish everything at once, and the main task seemed to be the general political one. Political scruples, justified or unjustified, blocked the road to the membership. This we believe has often happened with honest party members, who have closed their eyes to the meaning of the Cannon tendency because of conjunctural agreement on a question temporarily in political dispute. Cannon need not be troubled by such considerations, since his policy is the instrument of his regime, and since often the political dispute is for him simply the means of stifling the impending attack on his regime.

(iii) We have already pointed out that the Cannon group is in a state of development. Its bureaucratic conservatism is not the product of a day or a year. It has become crystallized, become a *system*, only gradually, over a long period. It is our conviction that the outbreak of the war is what precipitated it clearly and crassly. It was difficult to attack before the party as a whole what was primarily a threat, a tendency, an embryo. Nor would this have been justified. By taking things as they came, a point at a time, the tendency might be corrected in time; at least we might "muddle through."

(iv) Nor is a real understanding of the Cannon group arrived at overnight. Not all members of the present opposition reached their present views simultaneously. The intimate experience of years was necessary; and the war itself was required to make matters fully clear.

(v) These four are, we think, legitimate reasons for having hesitated to bring the dispute for open discussion and decision by the full party membership. We do not wish to pretend that only legitimate reasons motivated all members of the opposition. Other reasons, not so worthy, also influenced their action: a certain inertia; even cynicism at times with regard to what often seemed an incurable evil in the party; unwillingness to take responsibility for a serious struggle —all of which boiled down to a shrinking from the kind of fight which a bureaucratic conservative regime is compelled to make against its opponents. . . . Certain members of the present opposition, in particular Burnham and Shachtman, do not pretend to be free from having shared responsibility in several of Cannon's bureaucratic actions, and from having themselves acted bureaucratically.

7—THE CLIQUE AND ITS LEADER

The leading members of the Cannon faction are well known as such. They are not new recruits, either to the party or to the faction. They include such comrades as Lewit, Gordon, Dunne, Skoglund, Weber, Turner, Clarke, Cochran, Morrow, Wright, Weiss, etc. We have called this faction a *clique*. We do so not for the sake of employing an epithet with unpleasant associations against our opponents, but, as always, in the effort to give an exact and scientific political description.

The Cannon faction is a clique because it is a grouping that exists, that has a continuous existence, without any principled political foundation so different from the policies of others as to warrant a separate (and secret) formation.

Cannon has stated, in the present party discussion, that for two years there was no "Cannon faction," but that now there is; and there is one now because a serious political dispute arose (over the

Russian question) and a faction representing an identical point of view took shape on the foundation of that political view. This claim is put forward only to pull wool over the eyes of the innocent. It is quite true that, in the present dispute, many supporters and members of the present (temporary) "Cannon faction," are *not* members of the (permanent) Cannon clique. But the *clique* itself has a lasting life.

Is this doubted? It can be confirmed by a single incident. At the July convention, Shachtman presented a slate for the new N.C. He gave a political motivation for his slate: relating it to the difficulties and problems revealed in the party's activities, to the need for shaking off routinism and conservatism, and to the approach of the war; he advocated a committee which would: retain the core of the old leadership, in order to assure political stability and experience, and add a large draft of "new blood," especially of "youth" members.

After Shachtman finished, comrade Dunne presented a slate. *He offered no motivation for it whatever.* He simply presented it for the delegates to take and like. An adjournment was proposed by Cochran, and voted. As at a signal 30 or 35 delegates then proceeded like a man to the back of the hall, where they held a caucus meeting. What *political* visa granted admission to that caucus meeting? There was none, and could have been none. It met as a clique, the Cannon clique.

Two other points were of interest in connection with this revealing incident. Cannon did not go to the back of the hall—nor does he usually on such occasions. Why not? Isn't the selection of a slate a sufficiently crucial problem to occupy the talents of the best leaders of the party—above all a slate, presumably, for war-time? Or is Cannon so purely interested in "political ideas" that he doesn't dip his hands into the business of selecting slates? Questions to trouble the innocent. The explanation is this: Cannon is very much indeed interested in slates and N.C.s; but he is interested only in having an N.C. whose majority will *vote* the right way when necessary. Consequently, he can safely leave to his faction associates—and does—the specific personnel.

And second: Cochran asked the adjournment because of the surprise and puzzlement at the slate which Dunne read off. But doesn't this disprove the existence of the clique, or at least Cochran's membership in it? Again, a question to bother the innocent. The explanation is the following: The inner circle of the clique's leadership has a contempt for the clique's own members, and especially for its outer circle of less informed supporters. Consequently, the inner circle didn't even bother to inform the rest of the members what the slate was; it merely declared, through Dunne: Here is what you vote for. A shock, and a pitiful little "rebellion" resulted. Then it was quickly, and peacefully, straightened out by the clique gathering during the intermission. The P.C. members are all well acquainted with these little rebellions from committee meetings: they usually last just up to the time that a vote is taken.

* * *

The Cannon faction is a bureaucratic conservative clique, not a group built on a commonly accepted political platform. But what, then, holds it together, if not a political platform? It, like all such groupings, if it is to endure, has only one resort: to group itself around an *in-*

dividual, a *leader*. The "platform" of the grouping becomes—the leader. It could not be otherwise.

It is natural, in politics, that individuals who have shown talent and ability should come to occupy somewhat special places in the minds of their associates, and that some or many persons will put considerable confidence in what the talented individuals do and say. It is natural that these leading individuals should carry weight as *persons* and not merely as embodiments of political ideas. There need be nothing wrong with this, though it contains undoubted dangers in the best of circumstances. But the relation of the followers of a clique to its "leader" is something very different; and the "cult of the leader" is not at all the same thing as confidence in an outstanding, tried, and talented comrade. It is in this latter sense that we say that Cannon is regarded as a leader by his followers. He is the *substitute* for a political platform.

Is this charge groundless? It is proved over and over again, often in the very eyes of the party. Let us take an example or two:

At the July convention, Weiss (as already referred to in another connection) was a member of the convention committee which sponsored the proposal for an organizational secretary. Weiss in the convention committee, favored the plan and voted for it. But Weiss is also a supporter of the Cannon clique. In his ten minute speech on the convention floor, when the point came up on the agenda, Weiss disclosed that he had "changed his mind" (not on the merit of the issue, he admitted, but because he had had pointed out to him "what was behind it"). But the greater part of his speech, as convention delegates and visitors will remember, was a song of adulation to his leader. He had observed Cannon, he told us, for many years. On organizational questions, he declared, he had found Cannon right 999 times out of 1000 (our reference is literal); *maybe* Cannon had been wrong in the final 1 out of the 1000, but if so, he, Weiss, did not know it. Weiss, in spite of his honest opinion on the issue, was another victim caught in the bureaucratic conservative trap.

A more revolting occurrence took place at one of the N.C. meetings which preceded the convention. The question under debate was the Shachtman proposal to have on the agenda the report of the secretary on the record of the party leadership. Morrow took the floor, in opposition to the proposal. And why did Morrow oppose it? Because it was a scheme to attack Cannon, and Cannon was the one and the only one leader of the party. What was the evidence for this judgment? When the little movie of the workings of the *Appeal* staff was shown to the members in New York, Cannon's picture on the screen was the only committee member's picture, except for McKinney's, to be greeted with applause. (Is it trivial gossip to recall such an incident? Alas, no: we know the school where such incidents are bred.) Morrow, by the way, was once explaining in a less formal meeting why Cannon "showed so much contempt for committee members" (these were Morrow's words). "It is because," we again quote literally, "Cannon towers above his fellow committee members as far as Lenin towered above his." Unfortunate for Lenin that he cannot defend himself from the praise of his self-avowed disciples!

Or a year ago, when the question of who should be the party representative in France was being discussed, and Clarke ended up a speech in favor of Cannon by demanding in a loud and belligerent voice: "Does any one here dare to deny that Cannon is the one outstanding leader of this party?"

Or more recently, and still more revealing: At the P.C. meeting of November 9th, the question of the attitude of the party toward Browder's arrest was discussed. Two motions were proposed, one by Burnham and the other by Shachtman. Whether the difference between the motions was great or slight, there was nevertheless a difference that had to be decided. Burnham's motion carried by a considerable majority, with Cannon and all of his group supporting it, and only Abern and Shachtman voting for a motion of their own. At the next meeting (November 16th), the point came up again. Cannon spoke for a minute or two: he had, he said, been thinking it over, and he wanted to change the record of his vote; he found after thought that he favored Shachtman's motion. He had spoken in a mild tone, and given no serious motivation for a change. Then Cochran spoke, and said he saw no reason for changing. After him, Weber: Weber not only saw no reason for a change to Shachtman's motion, but declared that in his mind the Burnham motion did not go far enough in the direction away from Shachtman's motion. While Weber was speaking, Weiss (at times an uneasy captive in the bureaucratic trap) triumphantly passed a note to Shachtman. You see, the note said, how wrong you are about the "Cannon hand-raisers"! Shachtman shrugged his shoulders, remarking to Burnham that on so minor a matter Cannon did not have to make it a "vote of confidence." But, lo, Cannon took the floor for a brief summary. He turned the heat on, became most fervent in defense of Shachtman's motion, since—he amazingly discovered—Burnham's motion implied his position on the "class nature of the Soviet State." The vote was taken, and Burnham found himself in a minority of one. Solid with Cannon were the votes of Cochran and Weber. But perhaps Cannon had "persuaded" them, in his summary, of the incorrectness of their position. Not so: an hour later, after the adjournment of the meeting, Weber repeated exactly the argument against Shachtman's motion that he had stated in the committee. But, caught in the bureaucratic conservative trap, he had voted in line with the demand of his leader.

(We do not mean to say that the Cannon followers *never* vote against Cannon. If you search the record carefully, you will find that on this or that occasion, some—not all by any means—have differed. But, as in a parliament, they never vote against him when the question is posed as a "vote of confidence," and it is Cannon, like Chamberlain or Daladier, who decides what constitutes a vote of confidence. A certain leeway for "self-expression" is tacitly assumed and allowable. But the leeway has been narrowing steadily.)

A clique with a leader-cult has its own laws of development, and the Cannon faction cannot escape the operation of these laws. In order to keep the leader in his niche, all other leading comrades must be toppled. Consequently, a systematic undercover campaign to poison the minds of party members is conducted, in terms often of the most fan-

tastic slanders. An "anti-New York" propaganda is spread, which is
at bottom a catering to prejudices that are not always healthy. This
campaign was especially whipped up by Cannon at the last convention
of the party in the most artificial manner and to such an extreme
point that it was carried over to the public mass meeting celebrating
the convention. It served the interests of the clique to do so at the
national convention. But, at the New York city convention a few
months later, when it served the clique's interests to laud to the skies
everything Cochran, the city organizer, had done and to deny violently
that anything was wrong or deficient in his administration, the New
York organization was suddenly presented as an all but perfect section
of the party—at least that section of it which supported the Cannon
group.

Above all, an "anti-intellectual" and "anti-intellectuals" attitude
is drummed into the minds of party members. The faction associates
are taught, quite literally, to despise and scorn "intellectuals" and
"intellectualism." A loud laugh is guaranteed for a joke or story about
an intellectual. Such symptoms, though they have been rare in the
"Trotskyist" movement, are familiar enough. Some of us will remember
a prominent appearance of them in the American movement some six
years ago: Within the A.W.P., the struggle against fusion with the
C.L.A. was conducted by Hardman under the banner of "anti-New
York," "anti-intellectual" (not unlike many of the present campaigners,
the banner-carrier was himself a New York intellectual). The self-
avowed "trade-union" faction of Foster and Co. in the old Communist
Party fights distinguished itself in the same way, although in those
days Cannon combatted Fosterite demagogy with all his strength.

Rudeness and harshness, of a personal rather than a political kind,
more and more make their appearance. At the very beginning of the
present dispute, before positions and lines were even clearly drawn,
Cannon and his associates were referring to the opposition constantly
as "traitors," "snivelling" this and "stinking" that. Not on the floor
of the plenum, but during its sessions Dunne described the minority as
"snivelling strike-breakers" (our quotations are, as always, literal).
The opposition has since become "agents of imperialism," "scabs" and
"strike-breakers." Vocabulary, too, is caught in the bureaucratic conservative trap.

* * *

Cannon has argued: How can I be blamed for the ills of the party?
Do not the members of the minority occupy many of the most prominent posts? Was I not a minority of one in the P.C. that existed from
the Chicago convention to the recent July convention? (In passing:
We do not blame Cannon for all the ills of the party. We blame also
the harshness of the times, and ourselves. But, in order to cure, it is
necessary to diagnose the main danger and the root disease.)

It is true that the members of the minority occupy many posts,
that they do their good share of the work of the party. Why not? Cannon has not the least objection to everyone in the party doing as much
work, even in prominent posts, as he is capable of handling. Even
Abern, who is now the target of Cannon's most venomous attacks on
the ground of irresponsibility and incompetence, may be assigned to

the most responsible or confidential work, often on Cannon's initiative. But on one condition: that the comrade in question carry out his task without exercising his right to criticize or differ with the regime and its line. As soon as he seeks to exercise this right in any important question, the qualifications of yesterday are instantly converted into disqualifications, and every conceivable means is employed to discredit and blacken him in the ranks of the party.

As for the P.C.: It is true that at the beginning of last summer, Cannon found himself in a minority of one in the P.C. Indeed, not once but a dozen times, he repeated: "I do not take responsibility for a *single* member of the committee." A damaging excuse, surely, when it is remembered that Cannon at the Chicago convention expressed himself as well satisfied with both the N.C. and the P.C. there chosen. A curious leader who in a year and a half has succeeded in driving every one of those who should be his closest colleagues into opposition!

But the full truth is more complex. The P.C. is in reality a fiction, or at best a semi-fiction. Its authority is strictly limited: here it may act, but into this territory it may not venture. Over the P.C. looms the N.C. (which, formally, is as it should be); and over the N.C. looms the final authority—the Cannon clique.

Often during the past eight months Cannon has been stressing the —formally quite correct—point that the P.C. has no independent status, that it is merely a sub-committee of the N.C. Why has this obvious truth become so prominent? For an important reason. Cannon is unable to construct a plausible and convincing and proper-sized P.C. on which his clique has a firm majority (the new post-plenum P.C., which is neither plausible nor convincing nor proper-sized, is no exception). But it always keeps a "safe" majority on the N.C.

But even the N.C. is largely fictitious. It is called to act only rarely, and then its deliberations have an air of unreality. The clique itself is the court of last appeal, on all "crucial" questions—i.e., questions "of regime."

We will illustrate these observations with three decisive examples:

On New Year's Eve of last year, comrades Dunne and "Smith" of Minneapolis suddenly appeared in New York. When they were asked how they happened to be around, they replied facetiously that they wanted to attend the New Year's Eve party. On New Year's morning a number of invited comrades appeared at Cannon's apartment. These included: Cannon, Shachtman, Burnham, Smith (with status as P.C. members); and Dunne, Clarke, Cochran, Morrow from the N.C. No one else had been invited. At this meeting there were taken up and *decided* plans for an "auto campaign"—including personnel and finances; plans for a projected more extensive campaign in the Michigan area; and the setting up of a special "field committee" with vaguely defined directorial powers; and, lastly, plans for the "harmless" presentation of this program to the P.C., for nominal approval. By what authority did this body sit as a *deciding* body, usurping the functions of both P.C. and N.C.? The full meaning of this meeting can only be grasped when we recall that Cannon was about to leave for Europe: this meeting was designed to sterilize the P.C. during his absence. (Here, by the way, is the source of the famous "auto crisis." Burnham and Shachtman have no defense to make for their attendance at this meeting, even though it was clear to them at that time that their invitation to the meeting was calculated to give a somewhat more acceptable status to its decisions—which had in reality already been made by the Cannon group. It is not today, however, that they realized their error: last spring, in writings and in speeches, they stated and analyzed it.) Cannon, it may finally be added, has never commented upon this meeting, never repudiated it or what it symbolized.

Second: In accordance with a mandate of the Chicago convention, a trade union department was set up, and Widick named trade union secretary. Presumably, Widick was to *head* the party's trade union work. There is no point in arguing whether Widick was or was not the most qualified comrade for the job; it was up to the N.C. to place in the job the most competent man available, and then to give him support and confidence. But this department and post remained also a *fiction* or at best a semi-fiction. The department was never even half-properly financed. Widick was compelled to spend much time keeping himself going. Wherever possible, he tried to carry out his assignment: in such places as Lynn, Newark and Akron his influence was felt, and trade union work in these localities advanced notably during this period. But never, at any point, was Widick permitted to "interfere" in Minneapolis, maritime or auto. These fields were within the special province of the Cannon group. Nor was the P.C. in any different relation to them. Indeed, questions that arose in these three fields were, more often than not, brought to the attention of the P.C. only *after* actions had been taken. Of the comrades at the center, Cannon, and Cannon alone, and Cannon not as a representative of the P.C. but as an individual, was in reality consulted. In this light it will not appear so strange that the trade union secretary was excluded from the New Year's meeting which made such far-reaching decisions precisely in trade union matters. But why, then, was Widick given the job? Because no one of sufficient stature in the Cannon group would take the trade union job at the center. And because though Widick with his post was a fiction he was yet a useful fiction: like other useful fictions, he helped to *hide* the reality.

Third: Prior to and during the convention, comrades of the present minority proposed that comrade "Smith" of Minneapolis should come to the center as organization and trade union secretary. For this proposal they were denounced by the Cannon faction in N.C. meetings as light-minded petty-bourgeois who never did or would grasp the meaning and importance of trade union work. Three weeks following the convention, a motion submitted in writing by Cannon, Dunne and "Smith" made exactly the same proposal, which was hailed as a triumph of statesmanship. What had changed? Not the N.C., not the P.C., not the conditions and prospects of "Smith's" trade union work. What had changed was—for reasons that have never been explained—the clique decision.

8—CANNON'S "THEORY OF CRISES"

We have explained to the party, consistently and openly, our *political analysis* of the party crisis. It is our duty to do so. It is no less Cannon's duty to give *his* theory, *his* political analysis. It is not without significance that since the beginning of the present crisis, he has shifted back and forth among no less than four different theories of the party crisis; and only one of these four, the one to which he has devoted least attention, is a political analysis.

(1) Cannon's first theory was that the leaders of the opposition are "irresponsible," "light-minded," "subjective," and using their own inner doubts to "throw the party into a crisis." This, it may be observed, is what Cannon has said at the outset of every even minor conflict in the party during the past several years. Let us note:

(a) Even if this were true, it would be of very minor significance politically. Granted that we are irresponsible and light-minded (a rather cavalier charge against comrades few of whom are either new or untried in the movement), this is at most a *psychological* comment. The *political* analysis must show into what kind of false political position our "irresponsibility" throws us.

(b) But it is more important to see that this theory is an expression of a typically and time-dishonored bureaucratic approach. "Whoever disagrees with me—is irresponsible." This is the reply of the bureaucrat to his critics, the *substitute* for a political reply.

(2) The second theory of Cannon was that the position of the minority is an expression of "the pressure of democratic imperialism": that is, that the minority's position on the question immediately under dispute is *social-patriotic*. This is Cannon's sole attempt at a *political* analysis. But apparently he senses the weakness of this analysis, for he mentions it only occasionally and in passing. He never, so far, has dwelt on it, never attempted to *prove* it.

To prove it convincingly, it will not be enough for him to give an abstract analysis of the minority's position on "the Russian question." He must bolster his proof with evidence from *other* actions—motions, speeches, writings—of the leaders of the minority during this period and before it, must show that these too reveal the *tendency* toward democratic imperialist patriotism. But everyone knows that he cannot do this. Everyone knows that the leaders of the minority have consistently and day by day upheld the internationalist, anti-patriotic position of the party, above all on the question of war, where it means most. Everyone knows that they have been not the last but the first in the party in this all-important task.

Our party, true enough, is subject to the pressure of democratic patriotism, and we must guard against it. Fortunately, this pressure has not yet had serious and crystallized results in our ranks. Where it has been manifested concretely—when Cochran in Cleveland jumped head over heels into the Keep America Out of War Committee, when the comrades in Toledo slipped reformist versions of our transition slogans into the unemployment pamphlet they sponsored, when a couple of months ago our Minneapolis comrades supported a resolution at the Minnesota State A. F. of L. convention hailing William Green as a fighter against war—in these concrete cases we find that it was never members of the present minority who were primarily involved, or involved at all.

(3) The third theory of Cannon, advanced at a New York membership meeting, is that the present minority constitutes a "stinking office bureaucracy" (the adjective was very much insisted upon). As proof of this he offered flat falsifications of three incidents in party history. We shall not here counter these with the truth, though if the falsifications are persisted in or committed to paper we shall take occasion to do so, and do so conclusively. But we wish now only to observe, as in theory 1, how this reply is typically bureaucratic. "You call me a bureaucrat? You are yourselves not only bureaucrats, but stinking bureaucrats." Again: a *substitute* for a political answer.

(4) The fourth theory of Cannon is as follows: The present dispute in the party is the expression of a conflict between the petty-bourgeois, middle-class elements (the minority) and the proletarian elements (the majority). A luscious and satisfying theory indeed! What we—the majority says to itself, licking its chops—have in the party is: the class struggle. Thus the majority can get compensation by participation in "its own" class struggle for the party's inadequacies in the real struggle which is proceeding in its own way in the outside world.

This theory also is not *political*, but *sociological*. If it were true—and significant—it would *still* be necessary to characterize the *position* reached by the "petty-bourgeois current" *politically*. It is not enough just to call it "petty-bourgeois."

Now, in the first place, this theory—even if it were significant and relevant as it is not—is not true even as a description of the facts, quite apart from their interpretation. We do not miss "petty-bourgeois elements" prominently in the Cannon faction in many localities from Boston to the Pacific Coast to, above all, the national center. If we really think it worth while to speak of social status, we must remember that it is not altered by learning to speak out of the side of one's mouth, to smoke large cigars, or to sprinkle one's speeches with resounding cuss words.

We are the first to admit that the social composition of our party, above all its lack of genuine proletarians, is a tragic weakness, and that all justifiable means must be used to overcome this weakness. We find, however, that this has been a weakness of the entire Fourth Internationalist movement, and in fact of wide sections of the revolutionary movement from its inception. We do not expect, therefore, to solve it in a day or by an easy formula. "Pursue a correct Marxian policy, translate our views into terms understandable by the masses, participate directly in the mass movement along this line"—that is the only "formula" we know and it is not an easy one.

The revolutionary *program* is *not* the spontaneous or automatic product of the proletarians themselves; the "natural" proletarian policy is reformist or syndicalist. Indeed, from at least one most important point of view, the most radical influence in our party is the youth, the disinherited generation who above all have "nothing to lose but their chains" and their hopeless social situation. And the youth is in its overwhelming bulk *against* Cannon and his policies and his regime.

Cannon's "class struggle" theory of the party crisis is a very dangerous fraud. Its *concrete* meaning is to encourage the trade union comrades to free themselves—not from "petty-bourgeois elements"—but from *political control by the party*. The talk about "petty-bourgeois elements" serves them as a rationalization to excuse rejection of political control by the party when that control seems to (and sometimes, necessarily, does) interfere with local or temporary advantages in trade union work. In this fundamental respect it is identical with the "theory" and agitation of the Foster faction in the C.P. years ago, often condemned by our movement in the past and meriting the same condemnation today.

9—THE STERILITY OF BUREAUCRATIC CONSERVATISM

A political party cannot continue as a living organism in a period of crisis, above all of war crisis, merely with a policy of "reaffirming our past position."

More and more we find that the Cannon faction *resists* every new idea, every experiment. Let us grant that half at least of the new ideas and proposed experiments are wrong. Still: we can better afford to make mistakes than to do nothing. What is revealing is that the Cannon associates always have as their *first* response to a new idea—"hysteria," "romanticism," "light-mindedness." In small things as in great: Whether it is the attempt actually to *do* something about building a "workers' guard" or even to hold, in New York, an out-of-door May Day meeting (which Goldman and Cannon opposed as not feasible and sure to flop—though, as usual with experiments we try, it far more than justified itself when carried out). We must not "rush into" taking concrete positions on concrete questions of the day—the embargo or the invasion of Poland or municipal ownership of New York subways or what is going on in India—because, forsooth, we "might be mistaken" or "might violate our fundamental position" or "involve ourselves in speculation."

Bureaucratic conservatism, by its very nature, is *sterile*. Its self-preserving objective allows it to be skillful in organizational maneuvers, but blocks the outward road; if it tries the outward road, it is only because its inner difficulties have compelled it to seek external solution; and its expansion is also therefore conservative and bureaucratic.

The growing sterility of the Cannon faction is shown most clearly of all by its attitude toward the youth, and by its inability to assimilate the best of the youth. It has never even noticed the youth except to smash down on its leaders for an alleged "anti-party" attitude and, characteristically, for their alleged "ultra-leftism" and "adventurism," —which is in reality only the resistance of the youth to the Cannon clique's bureaucratic conservatism and to its leader-cult. It is not yet a decided question in our party that failure to adulate Cannon as infallible leader constitutes an anti-party attitude.

Entirely prepared for the easy bureaucratic charge of "flattering the youth" and well recognizing the distinct weaknesses in our youth organization, we say without hesitation that our youth—the YPSL organization itself and those comrades recently come from the YPSL to the party—are in every essential respect the *most progressive force in the movement, and 90% of its hope for the future.* The approach of war only makes this truth the more weighty. The youth carry the burden of the work of the party as well as of the YPSL; in responsible organization they put the party to shame; in receptivity to new and experimental ideas they are a standing lesson; they supply the party with most of its new members; and it is they alone who have actually done something to put themselves in readiness for work under war conditions. And it is this force, the potential force of the revolution, which Cannon, instead of educating and assimilating, brutally dismisses as "irresponsible petty-bourgeois triflers," "Lovestoneites" and *"traitors to the party"*!

What, we ask, *is* the perspective of the Cannon group? We know very well what are its intentions with regard to the coming special convention. It has become increasingly plain that the Cannon regime is *preparing a split.* The party must not be taken in for a moment by solemn "unity resolutions" which Cannon presents and has adopted for the sake of the record. Despite the "unity resolution" the line and the conduct of the Cannon group have already made it abundantly clear that if they are in the majority at the convention, they will wipe out the opposition (that is, one form of a split); and if they are in the minority, they have no intention of abiding by the discipline of the party (that is, another form of a split). Whichever variant materializes, that is, no matter how the annoying opponents and critics are disposed of, the Cannon group will still have before it the question: What is its perspective? To continue forever "re-affirming our old position" in answer to the political questions of the day, and to reply to all proposals for new organizational steps by denouncing them as "hysteria"?

The truth is that the Cannon group has no perspective beyond that proper to it as a bureaucratic conservative grouping: self-maintenance; hanging on.

This is the truth: If bureaucratic conservatism completes its crystallization and engulfs the party as a whole, then the party cannot survive the war. It will not, as a whole, *capitulate* to the war. But it will simply be lost, swamped by great events that leave it helpless, to which it cannot respond. That is the destiny of bureaucratic conservatism in the crises of war and revolution.

10—THE ALTERNATIVE

This document has been very long. We know that some comrades who will read it, some of those who agree with it altogether or in part, will draw from it cynical or discouraged or defeatist conclusions. This cannot be helped. It is necessary now to tell the truth and the whole truth. If we cannot face the truth, how can we hope to face the revolution? Nor are we in the slightest degree affected by the demagogic charge that we "have broken the harmony of the party on the very eve of war." It is precisely because it is the eve of war that we realized we had to speak out bluntly.

There is in our presentation a certain possibility of distortion, hard to avoid in a polemical document. Just as we reject a "Messiah theory" of how to make the party succeed, so we equally reject any

"Devil theory" of what is wrong with the party. We do not for a moment contend that Cannon has been engaged in any deliberate "plot," that he, as an individual, has consciously conspired to impose upon the party a bureaucratic conservative stranglehold, with himself as leader. Not at all. Of all the victims, it is Cannon who is himself most painfully caught in the bureaucratic conservative trap. We know Cannon's virtues and services and abilities—better, with a juster appreciation, we imagine, than many of his own most slavish idolaters. And it is his greatest virtue of all—his complete identification of himself with the movement—that, by a not uncommon irony, has played a great part in leading him to his present impasse, and that blocks a road out for him. And we know and estimate at their true value the qualities of the best of his associates; some of them are very great indeed.

What has led to the spreading growth of this evil of bureaucratic conservatism that now threatens the very life of the party? The general causes are clear: It is a consequence of long years of isolation, defeat, uphill struggle, fighting always against the stream; of the weariness, discouragement, even cynicism and despair that these engender in the hearts of men. Bureaucratic conservatism, creeping stealthily up, seems a last desperate means of somehow "hanging on," and refuge against a better day.

So far as *individuals* are responsible for this growth, we exempt no one, least of all ourselves. When Cannon replies to us by saying: "You are also responsible for these same crimes," we answer: "We will take upon ourselves our rightful share of the responsibility." Furthest from our minds is any desire to embellish the minority, as individuals or as a group. It would be absurd for us to pretend a freedom from political mistakes, bureaucratic practices and even personal derelictions. Beyond doubt, however, most reprehensible in our conduct was our failure to present the problem under discussion to the calm and responsible and *timely* consideration of the party as a whole. Although we have not organized or functioned as an opposition until recently, we are prepared to submit our individual records for the examination and criticism of the entire party. But important as this may be, important as the examination of other individuals may be, they do not compare in urgency and decisiveness with the central problem treated by the present document—the regime of bureaucratic conservatism and how to eliminate it.

The minority presents this chief claim as against the majority: Whatever the past may have been, we recognize the disease in the party, we diagnose it, we propose to cure it—and the first, most important step in the cure is the diagnosis. The majority, so far, refuses to recognize the existence of the disease; nay, more, proclaims that the disease is a vital and healthy plant. By this attitude they make their own even those evils which, in their origin, were not theirs alone. And by this attitude they prevent a cure.

We shall, in an independent document, present to the party a specific program of action, the initial steps in the cure. What is needed is, in its general outline, clear enough: In place of conservative politics, we must put bold, flexible, critical and experimental politics—in a word scientific politics. In place of bureaucracy in the regime, not an abandonment of centralism naturally, but democracy also, democracy to the utmost permissible limit. Wherever there is a doubt, resolve the doubt on the democratic side. Only a truly democratic inner life can develop the initiative, intelligence and self-confidence without which the party will never lead the masses. All the *formal* democracy enjoyed by the party today—and it is abundant—is worse than meaningless, it is a mockery, if the real policies and the leadership and the regime of the party are continuously determined only by a clique which has no distinctive political foundation. The removal of party control from the hands of this clique is a pre-condition to the establishment of *genuine* party democracy and progressive policy. In place of a leader- cult, not another leader (we propose none and want none) but a *collective leadership*, genuinely collective, coordinating and integrating by a real exchange of opinion and an efficient division of labor the best talents of the party. If there is one in the party who is outstanding from all others in his abilities and devotion and political insight, he will be known and recognized; but let him be *primus intra pares*—first among *equals*. In place of "reaffirming old positions," let us like free and intelligent men use our mighty programmatic concepts to meet the living problems of history, to foresee and to guide in action. A maximum of branch and local initiative! Comradely education, not brutal and disloyal attacks, for those in error. A *warm*, if critical, welcome for every new idea, even a doubtful idea, not a denunciation for "irresponsibility." *Comradely* criticism, encouragement, help, praise for the youth—even when the youth errs on the side of exaggeration or over-zealousness. And let us be less terrified of mistakes! Only the dead make no mistakes.

The future is hard, true, but not black. *Already,* on a world scale, the revolt against the war is rising. Tomorrow a storm will break in whose light our difficulties will be no more than the passing dream of an infant. It is for us to decide what role we shall then play.

December 13, 1939

(P.C. *Minority*)
ABERN
BERN
BURNHAM
SHACHTMAN

INDEX

Abern, 3-4, 8, 11-2, 16-8, 33-49, 52, 54-5, 59-61, 63-4, 67, 75, 89, 100-1, 105-6, 108-12, 115, 118, 121, 141-2, 160, 174, 192, 206, 226n, 233, 241, 248-9, 253, 258, 265-6, 271-3, 280, 284-5, 293; unprincipled combinationist, 4, 11-2, 16-8, 33-49, 108; defensist, 33; turns defeatist, 34; an "American Stalin," 38; splitter, 35-6, 40, 42-5, 49, 111-2, 174, 226n; alliance with Stalinist agents, 43-44; splits frustrated, 43-5; continues intrigues, 45-9; investigated by control commission, 48; irresponsibility, 142. *See also* Abern clique, Abernism.

Abern clique, 8, 11-2, 17-8, 35-49, 59-60, 75, 108-9, 115, 233; petty-bourgeois, 8, 12, 59-60; intrigues, 12, 45-9; unprincipled combinations, 12, 36-49; gossip-mongers, 12, 35, 38-9, 41, 45-8; history, 36-49; recruiting methods, 41; politics, 42, 46-7, 49, 59-60; conservatism, 59-60. *See also* Abern, Abernism.

Abernism, 35-49. *See also* Abern, Abern clique.

Abernites. *See* Abern clique.

Abern-Muste group, 11, 44-5.

Abern-Shachtman coalition, 11, 42.

Abern-Weber faction, 42-3, 45, 112.

A.F.L., 216, 288.

Akron, 159, 287.

Allentown, 44.

"all-inclusive party," 14, 188-91, 230, 234.

Altman, Jack, 48, 56, 117.

American Communist Party. *See* Communist Party of U.S.

American Labor Party (A.L.P.), 56.

American Workers Party (A.W.P.), 75, 285.

Anarchists, 212.

Andrews, Chris, 97, 203.

Appeal. See Socialist Appeal.

"Appeal to Members and Followers of the Socialist Workers Party, An," 73.

"Archives of the Revolution," 249.

Argentine section Fourth International, 195, 199, 245.

Austin (Texas), 97.

Australian section Fourth International, 200, 245.

Austria, 265.

"auto crisis," 56, 66-8, 70, 77-8, 202, 280, 286.

"Back to the Party" (Leon Trotsky), 184.

Bakunin, 11.

Baltics, 269-70.

Barcelona, 220.

Bay Area, 155-6.

Bay Area Committee, 155.

Bay Section, 151.

162

9278 4